Integral Human Development

Integral Human Development

Challenges to Sustainability and Democracy

EDITED BY JACQUINEAU AZÉTSOP, SJ

☙PICKWICK *Publications* • Eugene, Oregon

INTEGRAL HUMAN DEVELOPMENT
Challenges to Sustainability and Democracy

Copyright © 2019 Jacquineau Azétsop, SJ. All rights reserved. Except for brief quotations in critical publications or reviews, no part of this book may be reproduced in any manner without prior written permission from the publisher. Write: Permissions, Wipf and Stock Publishers, 199 W. 8th Ave., Suite 3, Eugene, OR 97401.

Pickwick Publications
An Imprint of Wipf and Stock Publishers
199 W. 8th Ave., Suite 3
Eugene, OR 97401

www.wipfandstock.com

PAPERBACK ISBN: 978-1-5326-9165-2
HARDCOVER ISBN: 978-1-5326-9166-9
EBOOK ISBN: 978-1-5326-9167-6

Cataloguing-in-Publication data:

Names: Azétsop, Jacquineau, editor.

Title: Integral human development: challenges to sustainability and democracy / edited by Jacquineau Azétsop, SJ.

Description: Eugene, OR: Pickwick Publications, 2019. | Includes bibliographical references.

Identifiers: ISBN 978-1-5326-9165-2 (paperback). | ISBN 978-1-5326-9166-9 (hardcover). | ISBN 978-1-5326-9167-6 (ebook).

Subjects: LCSH: Church and social problems—Catholic Church. | Christian sociology—Catholic Church | Catholic Church—Doctrines. | Economic development— Social aspects. | Political development—Social aspects. | Social systems.

Classification: BX1753 I57 2019 (print). | BX1753 (ebook).

Manufactured in the U.S.A. 12/05/19

Contents

Contributors   vii

Abbreviations   ix

Introduction   xi
   Broadening the Anthropological Bases of Social Progress and Adopting a Comprehensive Approach to Development Challenges
   JACQUINEAU AZÉTSOP, SJ

1 The Service of Integral Human Development   1
   Theoretical Approaches, Philosophy and Challenges
   CARDINAL PETER K. A. TURKSON

2 The Ideal of Development in the Thinking of the International Community   9
   Evolution, Changes, and Challenges
   SIMONA BERETTA

3 The Anthropological Bases of Integral Human Development   32
   From Integral Human Development to Integral Ecology; Some Responses to the Challenges of Governance and Sustainability; Considerations on the Encyclical Laudato Si' of Pope Francis
   FAUSTO GIANFREDA, SJ

4 Challenges to Solidarity   50
   Governance and Democracy in a Sustainable European Union
   SILVANA SCIARRA

5 Promoting Sustainable Integral Human Development and Rural Poverty Reduction in Developing Countries through Bottom-Up Approaches and Grassroots Institutional Building   66
   MONICA ROMANO

6 Structural Challenges to the Realization of the Sustainable Development Goals   88
   JEFFREY SACHS

7 Good Governance, Leadership and Social Justice in Africa   95
   LUDOVIC LADO, SJ

8 The Ethical Challenge of Convergent Technologies   109
  STEFANO ZAMAGNI

9 Cultural Diversity and Political Culture in India   136
  ANTHONY DIAS, SJ

10 Weaving Voices for Our Common House   156
   Closing Ceremony
   DAVID FERNANDEZ, SJ

11 Sustainability   170
   Agreement and Opposition: Possible Cultural Change
   JOSIP JELENIĆ, SJ

12 Concluding Remarks towards Integral Development   197
   FERNANDO DE LA IGLESIA VIGUIRISTI, SJ

Contributors

JACQUINEAU AZÉTSOP, SJ, is the Dean of the Faculty of Social Sciences at the Pontifical Gregorian University. He has authored or coauthored a number of academic articles, and his books include *Structural Violence, Population Health and Health Equity* (2010) and *HIV and AIDS in Africa* (2016).

SIMONA BERETTA is Professor of International Macroeconomics at the Sacred Heart University of Milan. She is author of *Contro la Fame* (2015).

ANTHONY DIAS, SJ, heads the Xavier Institute of Social Research (XISR) in India. He is the author of *Development and Its Human Cost* (2012).

DAVID FERNANDEZ, SJ, is the Rector of the Universidad Iberoamericana Ciudad de México. He is the author of *Malabareando* (1995).

FAUSTO GIANFREDA, SJ, is Professor of Ignatian Aesthetics of Creation at Pontifical Gregorian University. He is author of *Parzival* (2014).

JOSIP JELENIĆ, SJ, is Professor Emeritus of Catholic Social Doctrine at the Pontifical Gregorian University. He is the author of *Društvo i Crkva* [*Society and the Church*] (1999).

LUDOVIC LADO, SJ, is Professor at the General Manager Centre d'Etudes et de Formation pour le Développement (CEFOD) in Ndjamena, Chad. He is the author *of État, Religions et genre en Afrique Occidentale et Centrale* (2019).

MONICA ROMANO works for the program called Povertà, sviluppo rurale e interventi strutturali at the Pontifical Gregorian University. She is author of *Integrated Homestead Food Production* (2015).

JEFFREY SACHS is a University Professor and Director of the Center for Sustainable Development at Columbia University. His many books include *The Age of Sustainable Development* (2015) and *A New Foreign Policy* (2018).

SILVANA SCIARRA is a judge of the Constitutional Court of Italy. She is also the author of *Solidarity and Conflict* (2018).

CARDINAL PETER K. A. TURKSON is the Prefect of the Dicastery for Promoting Integral Human Development. He is the author of *Corrosione* (2017).

FERNANDO DE LA IGLESIA VIGUIRISTI, SJ, is Professor of International Economy at the Pontifical Gregorian University. He is the author of *"La globalización" en Preguntas éticas en cuestiones disputadas hoy* (2005).

STEFANO ZAMAGNI is Professor of Ethics and Markets at the University of Bologna. He is the author of *Civil Economy* (2016).

Abbreviations

CA	*Centesimus annus* (The Hundredth Year), encyclical of Pope John Paul II, 1 May 1991
CIV	*Caritas in veritate* (Charity in Truth), encyclical of Pope Bendict XVI, 29 June 2009
EG	*Evangelii gaudium* (The Joy of the Gospel), encyclical of Pope Francis, 24 November 2013
GDP	Gross Domestic Product
GS	*Gaudium et spes*, (Joy and Hope), one the four constitutions coming out of the Second Vatican Council and promulgated by Pope Paul VI on 7 December 1965
LS	*Laudato si'* (Praise Be to You), encyclical of Pope Francis 24 May 2015
MDG	Millennium Development Goals
PP	*Populorum progressio* (The Development of Peoples), encyclical of Pope Paul VI, 26 March 1967
RN	*Rerum Novarum* (Of the New Things), encyclical of Pope Pius Leo XIII, 15 May 1891
SDGs	Sustainable Development Goals
SP	*Summi Pontificatus* (Supreme Pontificate), encyclical of Pope Pius XII, 20 October 1939
SRS	*Sollicitudo rei sociales* (The Social Concern), encyclical of Pope John Paul II, 30 December 1987

Introduction

Broadening the Anthropological Bases of Social Progress and Adopting a Comprehensive Approach to Development Challenges

Jacquineau Azétsop, SJ

The development of "every man and all men" (*PP*, 14), this important notion of social teaching of the Catholic Church, that of integral development gave its name to a new Dicastery created by Pope Francis with an apostolic letter of 17 August 2016, in the form of a *Motu Proprio Humanam Progressionem*. The reflections contained in this volume aim to honor both the fiftieth anniversary of the publication of the encyclical *Populorum Progressio* and the creation of a new Dicastery devoted to integral human development by Pope Francis. Pope Paul VI was the first to mention the concept of "integral development," using the formula of development "of every man" and "of all men" and arguing that "The development we speak of here cannot be restricted to economic growth alone. To be authentic, it must be well rounded; it must foster the development of each man and of the whole man." To support his claim, Paul VI cited the French Dominican Louis-Joseph Lebret, who greatly influenced and inspired him saying: "We cannot allow economics to be separated from human realities, nor development from the civilization in which it takes place. What counts for us is man—each individual man, each human group, and humanity as a whole" (PP, 14).

This development is not just about having more assets available, which would be reduced to the search for material well-being and economic fulfilment. Hence,

> Authentic human development concerns the whole of the person in every single dimension. Without the perspective of eternal life, human progress in this world is denied breathing-space. Enclosed within history, it runs the risk of being reduced

> to the mere accumulation of wealth; humanity thus loses the courage to be at the service of higher goods, at the service of the great and disinterested initiatives called forth by universal charity. Man does not develop through his own powers, nor can development simply be handed to him. (CIV, 11)

The integration of body and soul into this concept avoids an approach based on a fragmented anthropology that would value one aspect of development to the detriment of another or some of the human needs to the detriment of others. As a result, we may affirm that development is not just about economic growth. To integrate body and soul means, therefore, that no work of development can truly achieve its goal if it does not respect the place in which God is present for us and speaks to our heart. In the same line, John Paul II clearly stated the goals of integral development: "Finally, development must not be understood solely in economic terms, but in a way that is fully human. It is not only a question of raising all peoples to the level currently enjoyed by the richest countries, but rather of building up a more decent life through united labour, of concretely enhancing every individual's dignity and creativity, as well as his capacity to respond to his personal vocation, and thus to God's call. The apex of development is the exercise of the right and duty to seek God, to know him and to live in accordance with that knowledge" (CA, 29). Hence,

> Such development requires a transcendent vision of the person, it needs God: without him, development is either denied, or entrusted exclusively to man, who falls into the trap of thinking he can bring about his own salvation, and ends up promoting a dehumanized form of development. Only through an encounter with God are we able to see in the other something more than just another creature, to recognize the divine image in the other, thus truly coming to discover him or her and to mature in a love that "becomes concern and care for the other. (CIV, 11)

The anthropological unit of measurement is not the individual but the human person. Whoever speaks of the person refers not to individualism but rather to the inclusion of the individual in a relational network in which the human being realizes his or her essence of being-with, being-with-others. Such an anthropological perspective cannot fail to question the prevailing individualism and the pursuit of gain that favour economic exclusion and hegemonic use of power in society. The individual is very often opposed to the community. The latter is then perceives as a fragmented whole, incapable of serving as a spring for the growth of the person. In the contrary, the human family is an organic whole, a place where the person does not compete with the community. Development is communal as well as personal. Our personal development takes place within the context of the development of our communities. We help each other to grow and develop for the good of us all. A just society is inclusive. Church's institutions ought to promote integral human development for every person, every community, and all peoples. Pope Benedict XVI stresses the importance of being a community saying: "Only if we are aware of our calling, as individuals and as a community, to be part of God's family as his sons and daughters, will we be able to generate a new vision and muster new energy in the service of a truly integral humanism" (CIV, 78).

The perspective of an organic approach to human society is part of the theology of creation and redemption of the human race. The God who creates human beings in his image and likeness is the same who sends his Son to save the human race. Through his redemptive love, Jesus Christ makes human beings brothers or sisters, persons who are the beneficiaries of the divine graces. Through his presence as messiah-servant sent by the Father, the praxis of Jesus is affirmed as the norm and the foundation of Christian action. In other words, Jesus's way of being and proceeding becomes the mode of being and service that the Church ought to embody in order to become Christ-like in the world. As an institution whose way of being is the *imitatio Christi*, the Church ought to serve as Christ served, working for the liberation of the afflicted of all kinds of evils. The foundations of such an anthropology clearly reveal that the development of which Paul VI, Jean Paul and then Pope Francis speak about echoes a call to be faithful to the transcendent, a fidelity which is not only theological but always already anthropological.

A unitary and integral anthropology cannot help but be the basis for integrating into the concept of development and into development practices all the elements that could contribute to it, such as economics, finance, work, culture, family life, and religion. None of these social institutions can be an absolute, nor can any of them be excluded from integral human development, for human existence is an organic whole. In addition to uniting all aspects of social life, integral development requires reconciliation between the social and the individual in a world where individualism is gaining more and more ground, thus opposing ideologies and forces that have reified human dignity either through political oppression or through economic exploitation.

Following John XXIII's leadership, which was already tingling with the question of the political, economic, cultural and technological changes of the world after the Second World War, Paul VI orients the Catholic Social

Thought on the labour to a more global thinking on development in the broad sense. Far from dwelling on a specific social issue, he proposes a more comprehensive approach to societal issues:

> It is not just a question of eliminating hunger and reducing poverty. It is not just a question of fighting wretched conditions, though this is an urgent and necessary task. It involves building a human community where men can live truly human lives, free from discrimination on account of race, religion or nationality, free from servitude to other men or to natural forces which they cannot yet control satisfactorily. It involves building a human community where liberty is not an idle word, where the needy Lazarus can sit down with the rich man at the same banquet table. (PP, 47)

Thus, the Encyclical *Populorum Progressio* lays the foundation for a properly religious conception of development which, supplemented by the writings of its successors, will gradually diverge from the modern project of economic and technological prosperity of nations. Twenty years later, John Paul II, in *Sollicitudo Rei Socialis*, deepens the thought of Paul VI criticizing a development solely based on the economy.

> Modern underdevelopment is not only economic but also cultural, political and simply human, as was indicated twenty years ago by the Encyclical *Populorum Progressio*. Hence at this point we have to ask ourselves if the sad reality of today might not be, at least in part, the result of a too narrow idea of development, that is, a mainly economic one. (SRS, no. 15)

The papal doctrine of development is in favour of economic growth, technological innovation and the implementation of social programmes. As integral human development, however, it emphasises the religious goal of reconciling humanity and God through the creation of a human family over these more material social and economic issues. In this sense, it cannot be equated to secular development theory,[1] because "Development must include not just material growth but also spiritual growth" (CIV, 76). Development is closely related to the way we understand human soul, because, ultimately, it is the liberation of every single human beings of the chains of evil. Hence, « progress of a merely economic and technological kind is insufficient. Development needs above all to be true and integral » (CIV, 23). So, the human person is more than *homo economicus* or *homo politicus*, these reductionist understandings of the person which have guided profit-based,

---

1. Bertina, "The Catholic Doctrine."

materialistic-oriented and power-focused approaches to human progress and development have shown their limits. Pope Francis opposes an ungodly approach to development stressing that:

> The necessary realism proper to politics and economy cannot be reduced to mere technical know-how bereft of ideals and unconcerned with the transcendent dimension of man. When this openness to God is lacking, every human activity is impoverished and persons are reduced to objects that can be exploited. Only when politics and the economy are open to moving within the wide space ensured by the One who loves each man and each woman, will they ... become effective instruments of integral human development and peace.[2]

Pope Francis' strong assertion about the disrupting nature and consequences of politics and economy without God echoes and highlights meaning given to integral human development by Pope Benedict XVI in *Caritas in Veritate*. Pope Benedict affirms vehemently that

> the decisive issue is the overall moral tenor of society. If there is a lack of respect for the right to life and to a natural death, if human conception, gestation and birth are made artificial, if human embryos are sacrificed to research, the conscience of society ends up losing the concept of human ecology and, along with it, that of environmental ecology. It is contradictory to insist that future generations respect the natural environment when our educational systems and laws do not help them to respect themselves. The book of nature is one and indivisible: it takes in not only the environment but also life, sexuality, marriage, the family, social relations: in a word, integral human development. (CIV, 51)

Economic development alone is not enough to create a just society. Even though people and communities have justifiable material needs, human flourishing and well-being have spiritual, social, cultural and political components. The multidimensional nature of human flourishing and constitution stands as part of the founding ground for an option to a holistic or integral approach to development. Rather than economy and material goods or even the individual, this approach places people at the centre of development. It is about development for people, by people and to people according the God's creative and redemptive intention. Development is rooted in God's creative and redemptive purpose on humanity. Human

2. Pope Francis, *World Day of Peace Message*.

beings are created out of love and call to love by serving their follow human beings. The task to bring God's creation to his fulfilment requires that everyone grows as a person and develop his or her God-given talents. Positive response to God's self-disclosure is the fundamental attitude for those who are willing to fight for justice:

> Openness to God makes us open towards our brothers and sisters and towards an understanding of life as a joyful task to be accomplished in a spirit of solidarity. On the other hand, ideological rejection of God and an atheism of indifference, oblivious to the Creator and at risk of becoming equally oblivious to human values, constitute some of the chief obstacles to development today. . . Awareness of God's undying love sustains us in our laborious and stimulating work for justice and the development of peoples, amid successes and failures, in the ceaseless pursuit of a just ordering of human affairs. (CIV, 78)

Society is then important for allowing each one to flourish so as to become an agent of social grace within God's creation. Such views of human flourishing raises the question of social justice in relation to how society can be the right place of human flourishing. A just society is the one that favours social and economic inclusion so as to address the dimensions of well-being needed for human flourishing. Here, inclusion is another name for social justice. It means recognizing the irreducible connections that exist between the socioeconomic and political, and even the emotional wellbeing of communities, families and individuals. Once again, this view of inclusion calls for multi-dimensional interventions rather than mere actions oriented towards alleviating material poverty alone.

This book is made up of three main sections. The first section provides much needed anthropological foundations for an integral human development taking into account socioeconomic challenges, global governance and democratic sustainability. The second section addresses issues of democracy and governance as related to integral development and outlines structural changes needed to materialize such a broader approach to development. The third section addresses socio-political ills and cultural resistances to sustainability.

In his keynote speech, Cardinal Peter Turkson laid out the foundations of integral development relying on the *Laudato Si'* framework. The Dicastery for Promoting Integral Human Development of which he is a leader places the human person and God's redemptive love at the centre of any initiative that aims at caring for our common home Cardinal Turkson argued that the caring for the development of the person and of society, therefore, cannot be disconnected from the caring for the Earth. The vision of integral development, present in the embryonic form in the *Populorum Progressio*, has been developed in the Magisterium of the Church over the past 50 years, in particular in the social encyclicals of the Popes, and has culminated in the creation of the new Vatican Dicastery at the Service of promoting Integral Human Development. Social and ecological issues go hand in hand; the cry of the earth and the cry of the poor are interrelated, and we should listen to both (cf. LS, 49, 50) in order to promote integral development, in order to integrate social and ecological justice. But integral ecology is more than the mere connection between the social and the environmental dimensions of our existence. It includes the need to foster personal, social and ecological harmony, for which we need personal, social and ecological conversion, both individual and social conversion. In fact, as Pope Francis points out, isolated individual conversion is absolutely necessary, but not enough. "Social problems," therefore, "must be addressed by community networks" and "community conversion," and not simply by the sum of individual good deeds" (LS, 219).

Fausto Gianfredo argues that Pope Francis's Encyclical *Laudato Si'* is in continuity with the social teaching of the Church in the Encyclical *Populorum Progressio* of St. Paul VI, particularly in the way it treats the ideas of sustainable development and governance within ecological discourse. By means of a Trinitarian theological anthropology, Francis carries out a critical reading of these realities, removing them from the purely economic realm. The theological anthropology that sustains the entire discourse shows another hidden source which is Ignatian spirituality. These spiritual and theological foundations of sustainable development and *governance* give rise to an aesthetic of creation based on a mystical foundation of ecology beyond the cure for environmental disasters.

Following the same line of thought, Professor Simona Beretta from the Catholic University of Milan provides a sketchy evolution of mainstream thinking and ensuing policy practices, highlighting innovations and discussing their implications. Comparing convergence and divergence paradigms, in particular, offers the possibility to reappraise the role of ethical considerations in development policymaking. She argues that Catholic social teaching offers a valuable contribution to set development challenges in a realistic and viable framework. Three challenges are specifically discussed: the risk of technocratic drifts in development theories and practice, how to make sense of an integral development perspective, and how to reorganize the joint action of international, national and local institutions. According to Professor Beretta, even if the world in which we live in is a complex and plural world, we have some global commons which are not only material goods. Some of these commons are non-material goods that are co-essential to sustainable development: interpersonal and international relations to be healed and promoted, on the basis of recognizing each other's humanity as the common precious gift we all received. Human dignity is related to the awareness that human beings, each and all of them, are of incomparable value. Every new day offers new opportunities for the international community to take the path of "caring for our common home," abandoning bargaining in favour of humble dialogue, open to encountering the humanity of others, reinforcing the international community's awareness of being one family.

Within the same ethical framework, Professor Stefano Zamagni throws light on some consequences of an ethical nature associated with the current rapid diffusion of convergent technologies. If those who praise the Fourth Industrial Revolution are wrong, those who disparage it are not right either. In fact, I regard the present techno-scientific trajectory as something positive in itself, and, even, unstoppable. However, it is something that has to be governed with wisdom and not only with competence. Having forgotten the fact that it is unsustainable to have a human society in which the sense of fraternity is extinguished and in which everything is reduced, on the one hand, to improving transactions based on the exchange of equivalents, and, on the other hand, to increasing the transfers effected by organisations of the welfare state; this explains why, despite the quality of the intellectual powers in play, a solution to that trade-off has not yet been reached. The society in which the principle of fraternity is dissolved has no future; that is, the society in which there exists only "giving to have" or "giving through duty" is not able to advance. That is why, neither the liberal-individualist vision of the world in which everything is exchange nor the statist vision of society in which everything is compulsory are safe guides to bring us out of the shallows in which the Fourth Industrial Revolution is putting our model of civilisation to a harsh test—as the most recent Social Doctrine of the Church does not cease to emphasise

The second section of this book shows for how democracy and governance is lived and experienced in different parts of the world. In her contribution to this volume, Professor Sciara highlights two systems of representation which should be vehicles of solidarity within EU states. On the one hand there is space for groups rooted in civil society, holders of collective interests, responsible for the enforcement of standards. They must qualify as representative groups, in order to prevent inequalities and enhance fairness and justice. On the other hand states and supranational institutions should translate solidarity into binding norms, establish the right priorities, select the relevant measures to be adopted and provide support to the ones most in need. Within the EU states are responsible for the enforcement of European law. At an international level they must respect international standards and be accountable for the protection of human rights.

Professor David Fernandez, a Jesuit from Mexico, argues that the postmodern collapse of the great stories of meaning has left a society with no clarity on the horizon towards which it directs its steps. Society, however, continues to move forward. As a conclusion to this extraordinary colloquium, it is clear that this world in crisis, looking for its way, needs at least the following elements; the hermeneutic element aimed at construing history from the reverse direction, that is, of the victims of history, the poor and the excluded. The ethical element places, above any other social understanding, compassion as the key value that shape human relations. Finally, the utopian element is a project of a world transformed in favor of those who suffer.

Professor Jeffrey Sachs introduces us to the structural challenges and obstacles to the realization of the Sustainable Development Goals (SDGs) relying on the theoretical lens offered by the Pope Francis Encyclical Laudato Si' in which Pope Francis called rightly for a common plan for our common home. Soon afterwards, governments adopted the Sustainable Development Goals (SDGs). Now they need to follow through on their promises. Professor Sachs argues that the world is blessed with profound technical knowledge, vast wealth, and shared goals. The SDGs are indeed within reach. Our greatest challenge is a moral one: to choose our purposes and use our resources justly and wisely, in accordance with the virtue of phronesis or practical wisdom, in Aristotle's terms. Laudato Si', and indeed all of the Church's great social teachings, are vital guideposts and deep inspirations for our generation's journey to a sustainable development and to the world we seek for our children and for generations to come.

The third section highlights the Consensus around this concept, strengths that it brings about and possible cultural changes required by its implementation. Professor Josip Jelenić, SJ, contends that integral sustainable development requires a cultural change. Alongside the multiplication of the obstacles and opposition which are usually caused by the hardness of the human heart, there is a need to find more agreements on the future destiny of humanity. Moreover, every reflection on every question, including that on sustainable development, is carried out on at least two levels, higher and lower. The first is that of ideal-real theoretical concepts where problems are resolved easily by a clear and convincing logic. However, as soon as one comes back down to reality, the previous clarity vanishes in the face of the complexity of the desires and actions of people in real life. The authenticity of any theoretical conception can be proven here. Concrete steps towards the realisation of the project of sustainable development, and that in the sense of a continual planning which aims, step by step, to involve all the participants on the common path. Furthermore, there is a need for a necessary change of lifestyle, a cultural change which, in the vocabulary of ethics and morals, signifies conversion of heart: conversion from evil and from indifference to the good in its totality. This is a never-ending process, that is, it requires from each one of us a permanent effort: responsible involvement that is personal and communitarian.

Professor Antony Dias from India highlights the composite culture of India, which, with its diversity has held the country together and fostered human development, despite limitations and imperfections. Today this diversity is threatened. Economic growth, production of wealth, a narrow and flawed understanding of culture and nationalism are privileged over sustainable and holistic human development and a celebration of diversity. The GDP, and not sustainable development with its intra- and inter-generational equity, is the focus. The human person is no longer at the center of development. This has already harmed nature and the minorities and other vulnerable groups in many ways, affecting their full human development. In India, there are also threats from a culture of politics that has deteriorated from what it used to be. This is a threat not only to cultural diversity but also to sustainability, both of which are needed for integral human development. These dangers can be overcome by having more and better democracy in which there is full people's participation. At the same time institutions of democracy will have to be strengthened for which active engagement of civil society, the Judiciary, the media and other actors are needed. More democracy should be in the form of more political participation of the people in non-party political movements led by self-less men and women who will empower the people even as they keep interrogating the state and its agencies.

From Cameroon, central Africa, the Jesuit priest Ludovic Lado emphasizes that the question of governance in Africa is less a problem of the existence of appropriate institutions than that of the political leadership's lack in ethical concern, namely, its inability to put the service of the common good above the pursuit of its own interests. After independence, the first African rulers were faced with the management of the ethnic and political pluralism within their young nations. They claimed that this political pluralism was prejudicial to the task of national building. In the name of national unity or national integration, they gradually suppressed political pluralism in favour of monolithism and authoritarianism. Since the 1990s, Africa has again taken up the multiparty system, but still aspires to political regimes that are truly democratic. As statistics have shown, the level of good governance in Africa remains very average even if there are signs of hope. It is within this matrix of imitation of the West that the questions of governance and leadership in Africa are included. Today, after all these experiences, there is good reason to think that everything that is good or has worked for the West is not necessarily good for Africa. However, at the end of the day, everything depends on the Africans themselves. It is a question of responsibility and dignity.

From a global standpoint, Monica Romano strongly affirms that building sustainable institutions and bringing about community-driven social and institutional change require long time and may entail a sensitive and complex process. It is about working with poor, sometimes marginalized communities and groups of people, socially and economically disadvantaged, and living in institutionally weak environments. Intense support, capacity building, and mentoring, combined with holistic approaches, are required to nurture and accompany these groups so that they can become institutionally robust and self-sustaining entities with a strong and inclusive membership base that is able to lead its pathway out of poverty, towards sustainable and integral human development.

As a way to conclude the reflections contained in this book, Fernando de la Iglesia, SJ, issues a historical and theoretical significance of the concept of integral development based on the move from *Populorum Progressio* to *Lauda Si'*.

BIBLIOGRAPHY

Bertina, Ludovic. "The Catholic Doctrine of 'Integral Human Development' and Its Influence on the International Development Community (abstract)." *International Development Policy | Revue internationale de politique de développement*, 115–27, April 2013. http://journals.openedition.org/poldev/1402; DOI: 10.4000/poldev.1402.

Francis, Pope. *World Day of Peace Message*, 1 January 2014, 10.

1

The Service of Integral Human Development

Theoretical Approaches, Philosophy and Challenges

CARDINAL PETER K. A. TURKSON

This year we celebrate the fiftieth anniversary of Blessed Paul VI's landmark encyclical *Populorum Progressio (On the Development of Peoples)*, which profoundly marked the life of the Church in the contemporary world. It is a providential coincidence that precisely in the Golden Jubilee Year of *Populorum Progressio*, Pope Francis created the new Dicastery for Promoting Integral Human Development, which I have the honour to preside.

What is integral human development? Not everybody understands the concept, some do not take into account its deep anthropological basis, and many neither acknowledge nor face the many challenges that the service of integral human development entails. I am sure that the International Conference "Integral Human Development: Challenges to Sustainability and Democracy" that we begin this morning will be able to shed much light on this important theme. From my part, I would like to propose a few simple reflections on "The service of integral human development: theoretical approaches, philosophy and challenges," the title proposed by the organizers for my keynote address. I shall begin with an examination of the evolution of the concept of integral human development. I will then reflect on the philosophical underpinnings of the concept of integral human development as articulated in the idea of integral ecology proposed in *Laudato si'*. Thirdly, I will enumerate some of the important challenges that await us on our journey to work for and guarantee integral human development for all. I will conclude with a brief reflection on the ministry of "service" that my Dicastery is called to render in this regard.

EVOLUTION OF THE CONCEPT OF INTEGRAL HUMAN DEVELOPMENT

"Development" has different conceptualizations that, in turn, lead to very different socio-economic and political paths. The core problem with the concept of development is that it remained "under-developed" for a very long time. For too long, the conventional idea of development was almost entirely reduced to economic growth, strongly based upon the acceleration and increase of the production processes. The overarching belief that guided modern economic system was that the physical objects are merely resources to be utilized for human consumption. It is a perception that continues to condition contemporary social values and thinking, as nations and societies come to be valued in terms of GNP, and development is seen in terms of capacity to exploit and utilize the resources of the Earth. The ravaging of the planet in modern economy does not spare even the human beings and their bodies, seen like the rest of the natural world, as only resources for utility and profit. Despite its benefits on health, infrastructure, mobilization, and communications, among others, this model of development has also led in its way to an increasing level of inequality and serious environmental damage.

For these reasons, alternative models of development appeared around the 1970s. Some of them were inspired by anti-capitalist, human rights, green, or cultural movements. The Church also drew the basis for an alternative development model based on its social tradition. In his Encyclical Letter *Populorum Progressio*, Blessed Pope Paul VI explained that development cannot be restricted to economic growth alone. To be authentic, development must be well rounded; it must foster the development of each person and of the whole person, of each human group, and of the humanity as a whole (PP, 14). For this concept, integral human development is about "*being*" or "becoming," rather than about "having." Development, therefore, must be promoted and measured according to all the dimensions of human existence: economic and political, cultural and ecological, historical and spiritual, etc.

This idea of development resonated with other alternative development models of that time, such as that pioneered by David Goulet[1] and later developed by Amartya Sen and by the United Nations Development

---

1. Goulet, *The Cruel Choice*.

Programmes. Goulet proposed that, when promoting development, we must consider at least three basic components to complement material growth: (i) life sustenance: concerned with the provision of basic needs such as housing, clothing, food, or minimal education; (ii) self-esteem: concerned with the feelings of self-respect and independence; and (iii) freedom: concerned with the ability of people to determine their own destiny.

These alternative and more holistic models of development still need, of course, an economic system that, whilst promoting economic growth, it is still amenable to actual human progress. Although it is not the task of the Church to ideate such a system, it is her responsibility to participate in the public arena so as to help correcting systems that hinder integral human progress, and to help promoting systems that can truly serve humanity (*Octogesima-Adveniens*, 4; *Caritas in Veritate*, 30–31). This participation is a crucial dimension of the Church's prophetic mission in terms of development and justice. It is in this line of thought that the new Dicastery for promoting Integral Human Development has been created.

The current development economic model, as Pope Francis explains it, raises numerous questions about its *integrality* (wholeness?) and authenticity. In fact, because it foments exclusion and inequality[2], it corrupts the social nature of our existence. Also, being underpinned by the myth of individual autonomy, it belittles interpersonal bonds and the necessary communitarian dimension of humans to flourish (EG, 67). The model is also inauthentic because it does not acknowledge the reality of the limits of prosperity (EG, 54). Following uncritically the idols of mammon (i.e. money) and the market, which, as false gods, rule rather than serve humanity (EG, 57), the current economic model is complicit in distorting the idea of the person created in the image and likeness of God. For these idols and their models, individuals are defined more according to their consumption power (consumers) and to what they 'have', rather than according to what they really 'are'. Worse, often 'human beings are themselves considered consumer goods to be used and then discarded', being the 'left-overs' or victims of a 'throw-away culture' where 'the priority is given to the outward, the immediate, the visible, the quick, the superficial and the provisional' (EG, 53.62). This criticism, as I explained in numerous other occasions to economists and business people, is not against the economy in itself, but against a particular model based on a partial or distorted idea of human development.

But how to create a holistic model of development that can guarantee the integral flourishing of the human person and of all human beings? How can we arrive at a paradigm of development capable of integrating

2. *Evangelii Gaudium*, 53.

economic, environmental, political and social dimensions of our human existence as communitarian beings in our common planetary home? It is here that the concept of integral ecology proposed by Pope Francis in *Laudato si'* appears to be promising. It is to the examination of integral ecology that we turn our attention now.

INTEGRAL ECOLOGY: MOVING FROM A REDUCTIVE TO A HOLISTIC PERSPECTIVE ON HUMAN DEVELOPMENT

In the encyclical *Laudato si'*, after having examined the alarming state of our common home in the very first chapter and the theological vision of the natural world in the second chapter, Pope Francis moves on to two important questions: the "human roots of the crisis" in the third chapter and the proposal of "integral ecology" in the fourth chapter. These chapters respectively offer a diagnosis of the precarious state of our common home and a way out of it. At a deeper level, these two chapters also make explicit the philosophical underpinnings of the false notion of development that has been in vogue during the last centuries and of the new paradigm of integral development that we need to usher in.

In the third chapter of *Laudato si'*, Pope Francis notes how the "dominant technocratic paradigm." (*Laudato si'*, 101) tends to dominate various spheres of human life: social, economic, ethical, etc. He points out that "that technological products are not neutral, for they create a framework which ends up conditioning lifestyles and shaping social possibilities along the lines dictated by the interests of certain powerful groups." (*Laudato si'*, 107) The technocratic paradigm extends its tentacles to the economic spheres as well. "The economy accepts every advance in technology with a view to profit, without concern for its potentially negative impact on human beings. Finance overwhelms the real economy." (*Laudato si'*, 109) Accordingly, "we have 'a sort of "super-development" of a wasteful and consumerist kind which forms an unacceptable contrast with the ongoing situations of dehumanizing deprivation,'[3] while we are all too slow in developing economic institutions and social initiatives which can give the poor regular access to basic resources." (*Laudato si'*, 109)

Pope Francis goes a step further and searches for the deeper conceptual roots behind the very technocratic paradigm. As he notes, "the basic problem goes even deeper: it is the way that humanity has taken up technology

---

3. Benedict XVI, *Caritas in Veritate*, 657.

and its development *according to an undifferentiated and one-dimensional paradigm.*" (106) The problem ultimately has to do with a reductive perception of human development wherein the human person is reduced to a mere consumer, the natural world is reduced to a mere object for human use and consumption, and consequently, a conflictual relationship between humanity and the rest natural world. As Pope Francis writes: "Human beings and material objects no longer extend a friendly hand to one another; the relationship has become confrontational." (*Laudato si'*, 106)

In response to the above reductive philosophical vision that underlies the false notions of human existence and development, Pope Francis goes on to elaborate the concept of "integral ecology" in the fourth chapter of *Laudato si'*. The opening paragraph of this chapter is programmatic and provides the essential constituents of the concept of integral ecology offered in the encyclical.

> Since everything is closely interrelated, and today's problems call for a vision capable of taking into account every aspect of the global crisis, I suggest that we now consider some elements of an *integral ecology*, one which clearly respects its human and social dimensions. (137)

What is the underlying philosophy or metaphysics of the "integral ecology" of Pope Francis in *Laudato Si'*? It is the ontology of the interrelatedness of the whole of reality and the interdependence of all created entities. Pope Francis points out that human beings, and all beings for that matter, can exist only within a web or relationships. *Laudato Si'* (nn. 137–142) introduces integral ecology as a paradigm able to articulate the fundamental relationships of the person: with 'God', with 'oneself', with 'other human beings', and *also* with 'creation'. The caring for the development of the person and of society, therefore, cannot be disconnected from the caring for the Earth. Social and ecological issues go hand in hand; the cry of the earth and the cry of the poor are interrelated, and we should listen to both of them (cf. LS, 49, 50) in order to promote integral development, in order to integrate social and ecological justice.

But integral ecology is more than the mere connection between the social and the environmental dimensions of our existence. It includes the need to foster personal, social and ecological harmony, for which we need personal, social and ecological conversion, both individual and social conversion. In fact, as Pope Francis points out, isolated individual conversion is absolutely necessary, but not enough. "Social problems," therefore, "must be addressed by community networks" and "community conversion," and not simply by the sum of individual good deeds" (LS, 219). This entails the need to change what Saint John Paul II called *structures of sin*[4] (*Sollicitudo Rei Socialis*, 36), these are, the structures that generate poverty, inequality, forced migration, and ecological damage.

We should remind ourselves that, if we aim at changing structures, we would face numerous challenges. An important contribution of academics is to study and delve deep into these challenges so as to propose to economists and policy-makers concrete solutions with which to face the current socio-ecological crisis. Without aiming at listing an exhaustive list of challenges, please allow me to mention just a few.

CHALLENGES

The first one is about *dialogue and global governance*. An integral model of development, enlightened by an integral ecological view, cannot be imposed, but just proposed. Therefore, as *Laudato Si'* points out, we need the participation of all agents at all levels of the political realm, but especially the participation of those most affected by economic and ecological issues.

I cannot emphasise enough the importance of dialogue for integral human development. First, because a dialogical approach is the one that can counter the attitude of dominion that is causing violence. Secondly, because an inclusive dialogue can counter the social exclusion that foments conflicts. Thirdly, because when we dialogue, we are forced to go beyond our self-interests, encountering the other and discovering the richness of what we have in common. In a dialogue, the other is not an enemy, but a partner, a neighbour.

Dialogue is difficult, yes, especially when it is not limited to superficial negotiations, and when it addresses the structural causes of conflicts. But it is precisely this dialogue through which we best deploy the idea of integral human development, which includes but transcends nations. A concrete way of supporting the dialogue on this issue is to intervene and support the dialogue at the international level of the Agenda 2030, and to ensure that the weakest voices are not silenced. But we also need to create different dialogical frameworks that can respond to different circumstances. Many places in the world do not have even formal structures for public dialogue, and to promote proper public dialogue in democratic countries is becoming more difficult than ever. Social sciences, alongside experiences of good dialogue between religions, could be of great help in this regard.

The second challenge is about *the relation between economics and ecology*. It is too easy to say they need to come together, but when they collide, we experience tells us that economics prevails over ecology. When leaders have

---

4. *Sollicitudo Rei Socialis*, 36.

to take decisions, they are pressured by economic interests and economic needs that are difficult to ignore. For example, at the national level, how are politicians going to fulfil the national commitments of the Agenda 2030 and the Paris Agreement? If they want to do so, they will have to encourage the reduction of the fossil fuels industry, which will create unemployment. Can they afford this? We are witnessing how, in so many countries, leaders are giving up to the development of the fracking industry or coal industry, despite their serious environmental consequences. Moreover, who and how will finance the technology required to transfer the energy industry from fossil fuels to renewables? And what about the tension between work and the advancement of robotics and artificial intelligence? Furthermore, how are local communities located at ecological reservoirs going to defend their territories and cultures, if the country is urged to generate income from natural resources located in their land? We can continue mentioning many situations where economics and ecology are in tension. Studying seriously how to deal with these tensions is another massive contribution academics can provide.

A third challenge is related to the *way we address "time."* As *Laudato Si'* explains it, one of the roots of the problem of the current development model is 'rapidification', this means, a path of development that prevents us from being attentive to the relationships that enable us to flourish as human beings, a speed of living and working that prevents us from being fully attentive to the cry of the earth and the cry of the poor. This is also connected to the prevailing short-term mentality, particularly dominant in business and politics; to the increasing patterns of consumption, which foment a 'throwaway culture' that hinders relationships and hurts the earth; and to the difficulty to integrate a spirituality of care into our lifestyle and ways of working. How to "decelerate" in business, in hour consumption habits? How to work for the long term in all our dimensions of existence? This is another topic I hope academics can shed light on.

CONCLUSION: THE MINISTRY OF "SERVICE"

On 7th December 1965, while closing the Second Vatican Council Blessed Pope Paul VI spoke of the Church as the *servant of humanity* and declared that the Church is entirely *on the side of man and in his service*[5]. It is a service for the development of the entire human person and of all human beings; as he went on to say in 1967 in his social encyclical *Populorum progressio* (cf. n. 14) which opened with the following words:

5. Pope Paul VI, Address of Pope Paul VI during the last General Meeting of the Second Vatican Council, 7th of December 1965.

> The development of peoples has the Church's close attention, particularly the development of those peoples who are striving to escape from hunger, misery, endemic diseases and ignorance; of those who are looking for a wider share in the benefits of civilization and a more active improvement of their human qualities; of those who are aiming purposefully at their complete fulfilment. (*Populorum Progressio*, 1)

The vision of integral development, present in the embryonal form in the *Populorum Progressio*, has been developed in the Magisterium of the Church over the past 50 years, in particular in the social encyclicals of the Popes, and has culminated in the creation of the new Vatican Dicastery at the Service of promoting Integral Human Development. We are grateful to the Lord for this gift. *Laudato si'*, may the Lord be praised! I am also grateful to all of you, participants of this International Conference, who have come from far and near, to discuss, from an academic perspective, issues and challenges around integral human development. The new Dicastery I preside has the mission to promote integral human development, and therefore to find ways of addressing its challenges. But we cannot do it on our own. We can only do it in partnership with people like you, experts in different fields, so as to take the current socio-ecological crisis as a big opportunity for serving humankind and for reforming the structures that hinders human development. This is a good way of collaborating with the mission of making the Kingdom of God present in the world. Thank you and God bless.

BILBIOGRAPHY

Benedict XVI, *Caritas in Veritate*, 2009, 22: AAS 101. http://w2.vatican.va/content/benedict-xvi/it/encyclicals/documents/hf_ben-xvi_enc_20090629_caritas-in-veritate.html.

Francis, *Evangelii Gaudium*, 2013. http://w2.vatican.va/content/francesco/en/apost_exhortations/documents/papa-francesco_esortazione-ap_20131124_evangelii-gaudium.html

Goulet, Denis. *The Cruel Choice: A new Concept on the Theory of Development*. New York: Atheneum. 1971.

Ioannes Paulus PP. II , *Sollicitudo Rei Socialis*, 1987. http://w2.vatican.va/content/john-paul-ii/en/encyclicals/documents/hf_jp-ii_enc_30121987_sollicitudo-rei-socialis.html

2

The Ideal of Development in the Thinking of the International Community

Evolution, Changes, and Challenges

SIMONA BERETTA

ABSTRACT

Development ideals have constantly informed the works of post–World War II international institutions, often in close dialogue with the international academic community. The paper provides a sketchy evolution of mainstream thinking and ensuing policy practices, highlighting innovations and discussing their implications. Comparing convergence and divergence paradigms, in particular, offers the possibility to reappraise the role of ethical considerations in development policymaking.

Catholic social teaching offers a valuable contribution to set development challenges in a realistic and viable framework. Three challenges are specifically discussed: the risk of technocratic drifts in development theories and practice, how to make sense of an integral development perspective, and how to reorganize the joint action of international, national and local institutions around so that the poor can be active protagonist of their own development.

1. THE UN DEVELOPMENT DECADES: FROM A GROWTH-DRIVEN MODEL FOR DEVELOPMENT TO AID FATIGUE

The post-1945 world witnessed a tremendous effort to imagine and realize a "better world," amid profound contradictions and huge challenges: the pacification process and the cold war, decolonization and development. Peace and development ideals also permeated the academic environment of the time; many scholars, including some that would receive Nobel prizes in subsequent years,[1] contributed to keep the attention of the international community high on the issue of development (that remained scientifically controversial).[2]

The most urgent developmental concern of the time was reducing hunger, through the coordinated work of specific new institutions.[3] The widespread agreement that defeating hunger was part of the much wider issue of promoting durable economic growth and development provided the consensus for launching a broader initiative aimed at sustaining economic growth: the first Development Decades, inaugurated in 1961 by J. F. Kennedy who, during his inaugural address as US President, had indeed expressed his purpose in international affairs in these terms: "To those peoples in the huts and villages of half the globe struggling to break the bonds of mass misery, we pledge our best efforts to help them help themselves."[4]

---

1. William Arthur Lewis and Theodore William Schultz, in particular, contributed to the 1951 seminal UN Report on *"Measures for the Economic Development of Underdeveloped countries."* Other scholars involved included Jan Tinbergen, Hans Singer, Nicholas Kaldor, Paul Rosenstein-Rodan, Michael Kalecki. See Jolly, *United Nations Intellectual History Project.*

2. International institutions supported development efforts by providing specific frameworks for transferring financial flows to low-income countries: the UN, with a Special Fund for Development created in 1958, and the World Bank, with its International Development Association (IDA) branch in 1960. Development became a central theme for United Nations action over the 1960s, when 17 newly independent countries became members, significantly changing the composition of UN membership. At that time, the international community's sentiments were quite optimistic about the possibility to extend development beyond the boundaries of industrialized nations, and to reduce poverty.

3. The "Freedom from Hunger" Campaign was launched on 1 July 1960 by the Food and Agriculture Organization of the United Nations (FAO). On 19 December 1961, the World Food Program (WFP) was established.

4. UNICEF, *The 1960s*. Poor countries' higher incomes would support their own better access to goods and services—a statement that today may suggests ambivalent interpretations, but at the time was very likely to express international solidarity.

The First Development Decade was based on coordinated international action: developing countries were to produce an action plan for "growth plus change," where growth represented the precondition to other dimensions of "change,"[5] combining national economic planning and international technologic and financial support. Under-development—as it was significantly labeled at the time, as if low-income countries were simply lagging behind in term of production and consumption outcomes—was predominantly viewed as ensuing from lack of technologies, infrastructures and financial capital. Poor countries were to plan domestic action so to reach growth targets at a minimum annual rate of 5 per cent of aggregate national income, expanding investment in productive capital by accessing external financing given the chronically insufficient levels of domestic savings. International financial transfers—both private and public—were targeted to reach the remarkable level of 1 per cent of industrial countries' GDP.[6]

This operational synthesis actually represented a drastic simplification with respect to the vision offered in the seminal 1951 UN Report *"Measures for the Economic Development of Under-developed countries,"* which was much more articulated. However, the operational synthesis summarized above permeated the mainstream view on development for decades: industrialization and attraction of foreign investments became *de facto* synonymous to development,[7] key to modernization and to poverty reduction (through different "trickle down" effects). The ideals of international solidarity expressed during the First Decade were followed by practical actions, by both UN agencies and domestic authorities: the national plans to promote economic growth were supported by many newly created institutions within the international community.[8]

5. The six areas of change included

> systematic surveys of physical and human resources to make possible the maximum mobilization of domestic resources; the formulation of development plans for social as well as economic development; the improvement of administrative machinery and incentives for effective implementation; a redirection of science and technology to focus on national problems; an increase of export earnings through the increase of manufactured and semi-manufactured goods; and an increase and more assured flow of capital to developing countries.

Jolly, *United Nations Intellectual History*, 3.

6. This level was reduced to 0.7 percent during the Second Development Decade; it was actually never met on average. For details on financial development flows, see http://www.oecd.org/dac/financing-sustainable-development/development-finance-data/.

7. Baldwin, "Trade and Industrialisation after Globalisation's Second Unbundling."

8. In the First Decade, the UN established in 1964 the United Nations Conference on Trade and Development (UNCTAD), especially meant to develop market opportunities for exports commodities originating in the new independent countries' (mostly

As a matter of facts, the First Development Decade produced important results in terms of growth: the average growth rate of domestic product of 60 developing countries exceeded 5 percent, with an average growth of 5.6 percent[9]. At the same time, improvements of living standards for the poor were far from satisfactory: higher per-capita incomes co-existed with significant malnutrition, poor health, and socio-economic marginalization. The International Labor Conference, Forty-fourth Session, held in Geneva in 1970, was in fact marked by Director-General's Report *"Poverty and Minimum Living Standards: The Role of the ILO,"* which stated that "policies for minimum living standards and for the distribution of income should be given as much importance as policies for economic growth."[10] Subsequent specific country-studies, coordinated by ILO, led to launching the Basic Needs approach in the mid-Seventies. This innovative idea supported "micro" direct interventions in favor of the poor along with "macro" structural interventions, with the priority of ensuring that the poorest group in each country should achieve a minimum standard of living within a defined time horizon. Thus, the Basic Needs approach required each country to make plans on how to provide for satisfying minimum requirement for families' private consumption (food, shelter, clothing), to ensure essential services for the community at large (clean water and sanitation, public transport, health, education), and to foster participatory institutions and human rights promotion. The Basic Needs approach, while producing negligible policy impact at the time it was launched, remerged as a karst river in subsequent approaches,[11] including contemporary ones; one important common feature is the special attention paid to institutional conditions for access to resources, beyond mere availability, as key for inclusive development.

The First Development Decade showed that achieving positive—even excellent—rates of material growth was not always conducive to improving the standards of living of the poorest population; in the Seventies and Eighties, per-capita income growth was overall very unsatisfactory and the socio-economic situation of the poor in low-middle income countries actually deteriorated. During the Second and Third Development Decades,

---

composed of primary products). The United Nations Development Program (UNDP) was established in 1965, and the United Nations Industrial Development Organization (UNIDO) in 1966. The United Nations Children's Fund (UNICEF, formerly United Nations International Children's Emergency Fund), created in 1946 as a humanitarian program, changed into a development agency with the Development Decade.

9. Jolly, *United Nations Intellectual History*, 7.

10. ILO, *Poverty and Minimum Living Standards*.

11. In a sense, the MDGs and SDGs expand and update a perspective similar to the Basic Needs approach.

two connected waves of shock hit low-income countries, well beyond any possibility of control on their side, and made the Eighties the "lost decade" in development: the oil shocks of the Seventies (1973, 1979), and the international debt crisis of highly indebted countries (from 1982 onwards), with their macro and microeconomic repercussions. The worsening of the global growth outlook in the post 1973 and post 1982 world is undeniable: over the twenty years from 1980 to 2000, per capita income fell on average in Sub-Saharan Africa, and rose by a miserable 9 percent in Latin America—reversing the positive growth rates observed in the period 1960 to 1980 in the same areas, respectively 36 percent and 80 percent.[12]

In the meanwhile, the international geo-economic landscape had significantly transformed, with new regions emerging both economically and politically, which reclaimed institutional reforms and the redefinition of the global relative power balance. The UN approved in 1974 a document on the Establishment of a New International Economic Order (NIEO), which reflected the new geopolitical structure of the international community, with Non-Aligned Countries becoming more powerful; however, the NIEO project fell into non-application in the subsequent years, for a complex set of reasons.[13] Aid fatigue[14] became prevalent in international cooperation; bilateral aid, in particular, ended up being increasingly driven by geopolitical considerations, and multilateral aid to focusing on emergency situations.

2. INTERNATIONAL IDEALS AND POLICYMAKING IN THE SEVENTIES AND EIGHTIES

The events that took place in 1973 and 1982 were game-changers in global politics. The same international community found itself in charge of a rapidly changing global political situation, trying to preserve the system of international economic and political relations while facing unprecedented

---

12. This poor performance strongly contrasts with observed "growth miracles," especially in South East Asia, where countries followed unconventional, un-orthodox policies.

13. United Nations, "A prehistory of the Millennium Development Goals." It is interesting to note, however, that an ambitious and encompassing approach to development may be easily frustrated by facts; and that there is a deep difference between encompassing and "integral" perspectives.

14. The "aid fatigue" that plagued high income countries consistently reduced the levels of official aid and its incidence on resource flows to low-income countries, to the point that, at present, workers' remittances to their home country are much bigger that all official aid. Moreover, we systematically observe the so called "reversal" of capital flows, flowing from poor to rich countries.

political and economic challenges. The world had become a very different place, with respect to when the UN system and its development agencies had been created. First, new sovereign actors had come into play; old national powers were waning, while new were emerging. In addition to new States, new non-state actors begun to strongly influence the overall functioning of the international community, in particular private (and public) enterprises and financial institutions, with different geopolitical horizons (national, international, transnational). Non-Governmental Organizations (NGO), including some that had been called into play during the Development Decades as key partners in pursuing development, also took on a bigger role in shaping both national policymaking and the global landscape. No way of playing "good guys, bad guys" games: inclusive and extractive attitudes, both domestically and internationally, were observed both across sovereign actors and across geo-political divides, across companies and NGOs.

One common interpretation of the dismal performance of official development policies in the seventies and especially the eighties identifies as a culprit the shift in international economic governance that occurred over those decades: the leading role the UN played during the First Decade waned, while the Washington institutions (IMF and WB) ended up taking the front line in the subsequent Decades, setting their policies and interventions along technocratic lines, later epitomized by the so-called Washington Consensus. This "easy" interpretations remains however on the surface of facts. It is undeniable that international economic governance had changed, but why was that change observed to start with? The question is serious, since the above mentioned institutions (both the "good guys" and the "bad guys") were the actual expression of the same international community of the time; and they were (and remain) eminently intergovernmental organizations in nature, in structure and in functioning. Thus, the same set of ultimate decision makers (nation states) were involved in managing global affairs both before and after the change in international development governance; and they evidently choose to play differently at different tables. Any country, in fact, is likely to behave differently when contributing to writing declarations for unanimous approval, which bear little operational consequences (as it is the case for many UN documents), with respect to when costly national actions are expected to ensue international decisions (as it is the case in IMF decisions, which normally imply budget implications at the national level).

Facing situation that were extraordinary in nature and in complexity, pre-existing international institutions had to cope with terms of trade shocks, increased international debt, exchange rate instability, domestic macroeconomic instability, and unresolved situations of poverty and social deprivation that often led to violent conflict. The Washington institutions found themselves on the front line, with the task of tackling global problems for which the set of policy instruments they had previously developed was often inapplicable; thus, they were suddenly projected into taking a more public, "political" role which extended well beyond their traditional role of applying the technical solutions identified by intergovernmental political consensus among few key industrialized nations. The institutional experience of the seventies and the eighties was a reality check on development thinking and practices: it put an end to the mainstream dichotomy between the "technical" dimension of international cooperation, aimed at pursuing growth and efficiency on the one side, and the "political" pursuit of fairness and more equitable distribution on the other side. Across the variety of international actors present on the scene—from supposedly "technical" international agencies to non-state actors—the challenge became that of integrating sensitivity to economic growth and development, fairness and peaceful living-together, a challenge that is at the same time ideal and practical.

3. BEYOND ECONOMIC GROWTH: THE HUMAN DEVELOPMENT PERSPECTIVE

The ideals stated in the preamble of the UN Charter: *"faith in fundamental human rights, in the dignity and worth of the human person, in the equal rights of men and women and of nations large and small,"* despite difficulties, were never completely abandoned by the international community, although their practical translation into policy action, their importance in shaping international relations and the functioning of international institutions *"waxed and waned"*[15] over time. In spite of its immediate success within in the international community, the people-centered approach to development launched by ILO in 1976 (Basic Needs) ended up being shelved in the early eighties, when political priorities dramatically changed.[16] However, the recessions faced during the eighties by many countries, where poverty and inequality were on the rise, led to a serious reappraisal of the ideal of human development, beyond mere economic growth.

In 1990, the United Nations Development Program published its first annual Human Development Report (HDR), successfully bringing the ideal of human development to the world's attention.[17] Building on Amartya Sen's

---

15. Jolly et al, *The UN and Human Development*.

16. For an interesting account of the rising and fading of the basic needs approach to development, see Jolly et al., *UN Contributions*, 111–37.

17. The HDI project proved successful because it was both philosophically (Amartya Sen) and empirically grounded (Mahbub ul Haq).

seminal scientific work on poverty and inequality, war and famines, and especially trying to empirically implement his notions of "functioning" and "capabilities,"[18] the HDR project builds on the idea that expanding income and wealth are but means to the real end of human well-being. Human development is there formally defined as "a process of enlarging people's choices. The most critical of these wide-ranging choices are to live a long and healthy life, to be educated and to have access to resources needed for a decent standard of living. Additional choices include political freedom, guaranteed human rights and personal self-respect."[19] Thus, the human development approach supported the creation of fair opportunities and choices for all people, so to improve the actual lives people lead, rather than assuming that economic growth would automatically lead to greater opportunities for all.

The yearly UNDP Reports made systematically available to the international community two main contributions: thoroughly collected statistics on micro, local data relative to human living conditions in different areas of low-income countries, with the possibility of comparing the Human Development Index[20] (HDI) over time, within and across countries; and a yearly special focus on a theme, chosen for its relevance to human development. Both the Report and HDI proved influential in creating consensus about the need of new well-being measures "beyond" GDP,[21] also considering income distribution and inequalities, health and education levels, social cohesion, propensity to innovate, environmental quality; last but not least, gender disparity issues. Most current efforts of measuring well-being "beyond GDP," also in high income countries, build upon the UNDP experience with HDI and analogous composite indices.[22]

18. Sen, *Commodities and Capabilities*.

19. UNDP, *Human Development Report*.

20. A composite index is built as a weighted average of a plurality of indicators. For details, see United Nations Development Programme, *Human Development Index (HDI)*.

21. GDP growth measures still play the most visible role in synthetically assessing national economic performance, in low income and high income countries alike. In fact, the utmost value of non-GDP indicators lies in their providing details and nuances, while synthetic indices provide summaries easy to rank but hard to interpret.

22. *Cave!* In providing synthetic indicators of well-being and progress, the risks of ideological drifts are significant, especially if indicators are meant to drive and/or monitor policy interventions. What is well-being (or happiness), how to measure it, how to respectively weight objective and subjective indicators, how to provide comparable indicators across national district and across nations have nowadays become over time important topics of debate also within high income countries. The recent Great Recession brought about lower rates of growth (even actual declines) and increasing poverty and inequality also within "old" industrial countries; this made it clear that

4. THE CONVERGENCE PARADIGM, AND ITS ETHICAL IMPLICATIONS

The early endeavor of the international community to promote development via national investment planning and international cooperation relied on simplified (often simplistic) economic models, which however were analytically powerful and characterized by a robust inner logic. Variations of these models, currently classified as relative to the "convergence paradigm," still represent the core explanation of long-term national income dynamics.[23] Quite optimistically,[24] the convergence paradigm maintains that per-capita incomes of poorer economies tend to grow at faster rates with respect to richer economies, eventually leading to per-capita income convergence. The rationale of convergence dynamics is the following: by investing in productive capital and adopting the production methods and technologies of developed countries, developing countries will grow at faster rates per year than the latter, because investment initiatives exhibit diminishing returns.[25] That is: newcomers benefit more in terms of production growth from investment activities, with respect to capital-rich countries, as the latter face stronger diminishing returns because of their high level of capital stocks (cumulated investments). Contemporary theoretical and empirical studies still consider the convergence approach as their point of departure for explaining growth performances of different countries, and for identifying other variables, such as investment in human capital and the role of

---

GDP indicators alone could not capture the core of societal well-being. The focus on non-strictly economic dimensions of development has deepened over the years, along with the focus on development sustainability: Two broad dimensions become prominent : the social dimension, and the environmental dimension, suggesting some continuity between the human development approach of the nineties, and the more recent MDGs and SDGs approach to development.

23. Convergence is the basic implication of the early growth models, such as the Harrod—Domar (HD) model, based on independent research by the two authors over the period 1939 and 1946. The HD model, Keynesian in inspiration, assumes savings to be a constant proportion (s) of income, and the existence of a fixed proportion (v) between capital stock and production, and between capital and labor. Under these assumptions, the equilibrium rate of growth (g) that equates savings to investment is g=(s/v). The Solow model, developed in 1956, provides the foundation for the massive subsequent work aimed at testing convergence, or measuring and explaining deviations from convergence. Burda et al., *A European Text*, chapters 3 e 4 are respectively devoted to "convergence" and "conditional convergence."

24. Burda, et al., *Macroeconomics*, 83.

25. Diminishing returns occur when, given the amount of other production factors (say, labor), increasing the stock of capital does make production grow, but with a slower pace as investment continues.

institutions, that explain growth differentials in addition to different levels of investment in productive capital.

The optimism of convergence undoubtedly played an important role in gathering early support for the "big push" of the early Development Decades, centered on investment planning and international flows of capital and technology, with ex-post redistribution interventions targeting those that for different reasons had remained excluded from the automatic "trickle down" effects of production growth. This two-stages vision deserves discussion: it is true that, in a trivial sense, we need a "cake" (growth) in order to be able to "feed the poor" (development); however, if taken too seriously, that truism implies a fundamental dichotomy between the spheres of production and distribution, or between economic "means" and "ends."

This dichotomy is very dangerous, both in theory and in practice. From a theoretical point of view, the separation between production and distribution processes holds only within extreme theoretical simplifying assumptions: the existence of a complete set of perfectly functioning, perfectly competitive, anonymous markets where time and uncertainty do not interfere with economic decisions (a *de facto* non-existing world). In other words, the dichotomy view is theoretically irrelevant in "real" economic systems where time and uncertainty, personalized interactions and power relationships are the normal *milieu* where economic activities occur.[26] From the practical point of view, assuming the dichotomy vision leads to disconnecting two spheres of policymaking, production and distribution, as if they were independent: first, material growth is preliminary pursued as a "technical" issue, which brings with it negligible ethical implications; subsequently, when policymakers come to facing redistributive issues, ethics finally enter the scene. But, as different ethical visions exist, redistribution is perceived as an optional, controversial "political" issue: in fact, the *a priori* separation between efficiency and fairness dimensions make them appear in constant trade off with each other.[27] However, in the real world where time and uncertainty matter, along with power relationship, efficiency and fairness dimensions, deeply intertwined, enter all economic and policy decisions, and may very well be positively related to each other.

The convergence paradigm, at the end of the day, tends to be associated to a technocratic perspective, with ethical considerations confined

---

26. Beretta, "Wealth Creation."

27. Ex post redistribution aimed at pursuing fairness is costly as it reduces available product: besides administrative costs, it induces inefficient changes in individuals' behaviour (such as reducing work efforts with higher taxation rates). This negative trade off, however, does not necessarily occur: for example, equitable working conditions enhance personal motivations and efficiency.

within the (contentious) realm of distributional issues. In real economic systems, however, the ethical qualities of the economic and social system (how a community faces uncertainty about the future and allocates powers) matter for explaining the levels of actual production, and also how and why those products are produced. The "how" and the "why" are no details, for economic growth to be conducive to human and social development: respecting the dignity human labor, promoting social participation, collaboration and solidarity are policies that matter for the success of all economic activities, including effective production and equitable distribution.

5. AN ALTERNATIVE VIEW OF DEVELOPMENT: CUMULATIVE CAUSATION AND SELF-REINFORCING DIVERGENT DYNAMICS

Socioeconomic paradigms challenging the convergence consensus existed even at the time when the First Development Decade was launched. Non-mainstream contributions, including Nobel laureate Gunnar Myrdal's, were highly intellectually respected at the time, but exerted little impact on the prevailing views and on the shaping of development policies. The different strands of heterodox perspectives developed in the early period of the global development endeavor, however, keep offering even today important insights for understanding contemporary world dynamics, and for development policy design.

The earlier contributions (A. Young, R. Nurkse, G. Myrdal[28]) explored and explained the possibility that different countries, despite exhibiting similar levels of initial key parameters—including rates of population growth and saving rates—could move along diverging growth paths. Myrdal, in particular, coined the term *cumulative causation* to explain why poverty creates poverty.[29] Other non-conventional strands of development studies focused on structural change (H. Chenery, M. Syrquin, L.L. Pasinetti[30]): as differ-

---

28. Young, "Increasing Returns and Economic Progress." Nurkse, *Problems of Capital Formation in Developing Countries*"; Myrdal, *Asian Drama*; Myrdal, *The Political Element in the Development of Economic Theory*; Myrdal, *Economic Theory and Underdeveloped Regions*.

29. Myrdal, *An American Dilemma*. Myrdal explained how the prejudice of the white populations and the low living standards of the black populations could reinforce each other in a downward spiral.
See also Encyclopedia, *Cumulative Causation*. As to Myrdal' cumulative causation vision of development, see Myrdal, *Asian Drama*.

30. Hollis et al., *Patterns of Development*; Pasinetti, *Structural Change and Economic Growth*; Luigi L. Pasinetti, *Dinamica economica strutturale*.

ent productive sectors tend to expand at different rates, economic growth reshapes the composition of a country's production and deeply transforms its social and political environment. Conjugating economic and political perspectives, other contributions focused on explaining why the economic development of some countries could directly cause other countries' underdevelopment; this was the case when commodity exporting countries faced declining terms of trade for their exports, as in the *dependencia* paradigm proposed by R. Prebish, H. Singer[31] with reference to Latin America. Other similar approaches were developed to explain the underdevelopment of different countries and macro-regions, along the lines of Marxist analysis on "unequal exchange."[32]

All of the above strands challenged the traditional academic boundaries separating economics from other among social sciences, providing an interdisciplinary perspective on development. Myrdal's notion of cumulative causation is a remarkable example of how economic analysis benefits from expanding the social analysis horizon, questioning the reassuring mainstream economic assumption that there exists a self-stabilizing equilibrium to which systems tend to converge. Indeed, cumulative causation and divergence make full economic sense in the real world: the initial advantage of firms, regions or nations is preserved and expanded as they keep attracting migration, capital, and trade flows, to the detriment of development elsewhere. Power structures also matter: circular causation mechanisms describe how political processes produce institutional settings that reinforce the existing power structures.

Everything is indeed connected:[33] efficiency and fairness, economics and politics. The cumulative, self-reinforcing nature of the economic and political transformations we observe today, due to economic growth and international integration, explains many of the divides we observe in our world: increasing inequality, both international and internal, and marginalization of regions and social groups that end up being "discarded."[34] Culturally, divergence approaches imply that the economic and the socio-political dimensions of development cannot be dealt with in sequence, as if dichotomous. Growth issues (efficiency) cannot be disconnected from redistribution and social policies (fairness), simply because poverty, inequality, marginalization are no accident to be dealt with specific remedial policies:

31. Prebisch, *The Economic Development of Latin America*; Singer, "The Distribution of Gains,"

32. Frank, "The Development of Underdevelopment"; Amin, *L'accumulation à l'échelle mondiale*; Amin, *Le développement inégal*; Emmanuel, "Unequal Exchange."

33. Francis, *Laudato si'*, §16, 42, 56, 92, 111, 117, 138.

34. Francis, *Laudato si'*, §22, 43, 123

they are inscribed within the growth process itself. Cumulative causation and structural asymmetries endogenously reinforce the strengths of strong actors (individuals, sectors, regions), and marginalize and impoverish weak actors; thus, poverty and inequality are systemic in nature, and cannot be effectively solved with *ex-post* remedial policies.

6. THE TYPICAL FEATURES OF THE "MODERN" ECONOMY (PAUL VI) PRODUCE DIVERGENCE

After 50 years, *Populorum progressio* (PP) remains a milestone in conjugating development ideals with pragmatism in development policies. Many aspects of Paul VI's encyclical letter written in 1967 continue to impress today, for their prophecy and realism.[35] PP was indisputably ahead of times in facing developmental issues that entered the international community debate only in later decades. A non-exhaustive list of such issues includes the ambivalence of economic growth, of international trade for developing countries, of economic competition and even of labor itself;[36] the scandal of inequalities[37] development sustainability, including the environmental dimension;[38] the necessary yet ambivalent role of public authorities;[39] the possible contradiction between development assistance and other international policies promoted by advanced countries,[40] the (highly contentious) issue of demographic growth;[41] last but not least, the non-material dimensions of development that are key to "integral," "well rounded" development:[42] "*To be authentic, it must be well rounded; it must foster the development of each man and of the whole man.*"[43]

Paul VI, in PP, clearly takes side for non-mainstream visions of economic growth. When speaking of the "modern" economy, the encyclical implicitly embraces the analytical perspective of divergence: "*Unless the existing machinery is modified, the disparity between rich and poor nations will increase rather than diminish.*"[44] That is: replicating the modern economic

35. Beretta, "Cinquant'anni di politiche per lo sviluppo."
36. PP 19, 27, 33, 61.
37. PP 9, 76.
38. PP 22.
39. PP 33, 34.
40. PP 44, 52, 61.
41. PP 37.
42. Beretta, "Freedom and Agency."
43. PP 14.
44. PP 8.

machinery in under-developed areas—a mainstream policy which would make sense in the convergence paradigm—is likely to worsen, rather than to improve, cross-country disparities. While development policies based on the convergence paradigm suggest to correct the disadvantage of under-developed countries by alleviating capital scarcity and technology backwardness, the actual outcome of such actions would be highly unsatisfactory in a modern economy where economies of scale, learning by doing and other similar mechanisms exist. Where divergence dynamics prevail, those who enter the modern system at a later time will keep being late, especially if they play the same game of the first-comers.

Asymmetries, inequality and exclusion are structural features of an economic, social and political system where the power of incumbents shape divergent development paths. PP outspokenly highlights "the flagrant inequalities not merely in the enjoyment of possessions, but even more in the exercise of power,"[45] as economic and institutional dynamics are indeed intertwined. The famous 2012 book by Acemoglu and Robinson[46] illustrates with many historical examples that cumulative causation and other divergence-creating structures tend to concentrate economic power and to consolidate it in the political sphere, making it more likely for actual policy-making to serve the interest of powerful groups. However, likelihood is no necessity: here lies the huge responsibility of powerful agents, in breaking the power circuits and promoting inclusive institutions, both in the economic and in the political arenas.

7. DEVELOPMENT IDEALS AND PRACTICES: FROM MDGS TO SDGS

The new millennium signed a renewed effort of the international community for global development. This renewal was prepared during the Nineties through enhanced inter-institutional cooperation at the international level, especially in managing the process of debt rescheduling and debt cancellation associated to the Jubilee year, and was expressed in the solemn Declaration of the Millennium Development Goals (MDGs) for the period 2000–2015. By launching the new Sustainable Development Goals (SDGs) in 2015, the global community reaffirmed its ideals of global development and approved specific lines of action towards 2030—significantly expanding the list of goals and targets with respect to MDGs: while the 2000–2015 MDG process included 8 goals and 22 targets, the new SDG process

45. PP 9.
46. Acemoglu and Robinson, *Why Nations Fail*.

includes 17 goals and 169 targets related to human, economic, social and environmental sustainability.

The MDGs and SDGs signal that ideals of development and human dignity are still powerful drivers of global community activity; however, ideals are to be rendered into tangible realities to keep being credible and attracting participation. Thus, what can we learn about which tangible results ensued the MDG process, in terms of economic and human development? One important lesson, at the conclusion of the 2000–2015 MDG process, actually replicates what we learnt from the First Development Decades, namely that achieving economic growth is much easier that improving the lives of the poor. MDG1, for example, was about halving poverty (in terms of per capita income) and halving hunger; while the first target was met in 2015, the secondo was not.[47] That is: reaching food insecure people in distressed situations, especially in peripheral areas, proved much harder than increasing average incomes. We also learnt that hunger reduction over the MDG years was jeopardized by external events, untouched by food policies: higher (and volatile) food prices due to the financialization of commodities markets, macroeconomic recessions and increasing unemployment, extreme weather events and natural disasters; last but not least, local political instability and civil strife. That is: eradicating hunger requires actions beyond sound technocratic management of food availability.

How much of the lessons learnt from the MDGs experience can be traced, in the post-2015 process design? Not so much, I dare say. For example, MDG1 evolved into three SDGs, with SDG2 focusing on food security: "End hunger, achieve food security and improved nutrition and promote sustainable agriculture." According to the official summary description of how to reach SDG2, "this will require sustainable food production systems and resilient agricultural practices, equal access to land, technology and markets and international cooperation on investments in infrastructure and technology to boost agricultural productivity."[48] The strategy seem to rely once again on practices, technology, investment, productivity, pursuing enhanced food availability—which is a necessary, but definitely not sufficient, condition for hunger eradication.[49] Pursuing ideals is surely about defining

---

47. Balestri, Beretta, *Poverty Eradication*.
48. United Nations, *Sustainable Development Goal 2*.
49. See Economic and Social Council, *Progress towards the Sustainable Development Goals*. The UN Secretary General, in 2016, provided a much broader picture:
> Many countries that failed to reach the target set as part of the Millennium Development Goals, of halving the proportion of people who suffer from hunger, have faced natural and human-induced disasters or political instability, resulting in protracted crises, with increased vulnerability and food

deserving goals and targets; but most relevantly it is about identifying appropriate methods and implementing sensible practices. In sum, pursuing ideals implies facing interconnected challenges, where the ethical dimensions inevitably impact on political and technical choices.

8. THREE CHALLENGES FOR DEVELOPMENT POLICIES AND PRACTICES

a. Rethinking development (and beware of technocracy!)

The question that signed the official beginning of modern economics as a science is still with us. What are the "Nature and Causes of the Wealth of Nations?," asked Adam Smith (1776). Adam Smith's answers remain surprisingly fresh even today: human labor creates the wealth of nations; more specifically, division of labor and extension of markets. Both these conditions require some "social friendship," which make it possible to reasonably expect generalized stable, pacific relations across society. Key non-material conditions are the driving forces of material development: personal motivations, beliefs, and expectations of reciprocal trust sustain development; on the contrary, distrust breeds decline.

If we do not address these non-material conditions at the global level, "extensive" strategies for coping with complex development issues risks failure. Pursuing desirable goals and targets only by applying specific technocratic solutions cannot lead to sustainable improvements. Technocratic interventions may produce immediate results in their specific field of application, but they offer no overarching perspective for prioritizing those actions that are needed for results to be sustainable within the broader, dynamic picture.[50] In addition, far from being neutral, technocratic perspectives embody and express existing structures of power, and can be easily captured by particular interests (of a firm, of a social group, of a political elite, of a geopolitical entity). That is, particular interests can be prioritized thanks to a narrative of "objective" evidence, which relies on presenting scientific results that are favorable to pursuing those interests, without mentioning their limitations. More generally, particular policy perspectives can be offered as the best (or the only) "technical" solution.

---

insecurity affecting large parts of the population. The persistence of hunger is no longer simply a matter of food availability.

50. "The specialization which belongs to technology makes it difficult to see the larger picture. The fragmentation of knowledge proves helpful for concrete applications, and yet it often leads to a loss of appreciation for the whole, for the relationships between things, and for the broader horizon" (Francis, LS, 110).

Beware of technocracy,[51] if you are convinced that development needs to be "integral" in order to be sustainable. Non-material dimensions matter for finding the path of action that integrate and conjugate all dimensions of true sustainable development: economic development, equity and fairness, respect for human dignity, care for the environment, peaceful living-together. This integrating perspective is more likely to be familiar to grass-root people "expert in humanity," that walk the path of development in real space and real time, than to development specialists with specific technical competences that tend to suggest "one size fits all" policy suggestions.

Paul VI, in *Populorum progressio,* denounced the risks of entrusting sustainable development to technocrats, separating the pursuit of efficiency on the one side, and fairness on the other side:

> It is not enough to increase the general fund of wealth and then distribute it more fairly. It is not enough to develop technology so that the earth may become a more suitable living place for human beings. The mistakes of those who led the way should help those now on the road to development to avoid certain dangers. The reign of technology—technocracy, as it is called—can cause as much harm to the world of tomorrow as liberalism did to the world of yesteryear.[52]

Today, the relevance of these prophetic words is amplified by technology advances that are both promising and dangerous.[53]

---

51. See *Caritas in veritate* teaching on technology/technocracy, as they apply to development policies and programs, communication, even peace (CV 70, 77). In the chapter "the globalization of the technocratic paradigm" of *Laudato si'*, Pope Francis writes (LS 106):

> The basic problem goes even deeper: it is the way that humanity has taken up technology and its development according to an undifferentiated and one-dimensional paradigm. This paradigm exalts the concept of a subject who, using logical and rational procedures, progressively approaches and gains control over an external object. This subject makes every effort to establish the scientific and experimental method, which in itself is already a technique of possession, mastery and transformation. It is as if the subject were to find itself in the presence of something formless, completely open to manipulation.

52. PP, 34.

53. See the final chapter of *Caritas in veritate*, "The Development of Peoples and Technology" (par. 68–77), and Pope Francis' *Laudato si'* (2015): "There is a tendency to believe that every increase in power means an increase of 'progress' itself . . . as if reality, goodness and truth automatically flow from technological and economic power as such . . . we stand naked and exposed in the face of our ever-increasing power" (LS 105).

b. Making practical sense of "integral" development

If technocratic programs are insufficient for integral, truly sustainable development that encompasses material and non-material conditions, how can we imagine a way to translate development ideals into practical action? Integral development, in fact, is not simply an end-target (or worse, a long list of specific targets) that we set as for the future; it is a dynamic experience that is built along the way. If integrality is not sensed and at least initially experienced "here and now," it is unlikely to magically appear tomorrow. So, where and how we can experience a method for recognizing and practically implementing development actions that are integral and truly sustainable?

Hard questions need simple answers that can be practiced and tested. The subtitle of *Laudato si'* offers such an answer, by identifying with simple words a practical method for experiencing sustainable development "here and now": namely, taking "care for our common home." Home is how we name the place where we belong (notice: not our ownership, but the place of our belonging!); home is both a physical space, and a space for relations and communication, where overtime we learn what it is to be human. At home, the material, relational and symbolic dimensions are so integrated with each other that its practical organization (*oikos nomos*, economics) depends on criteria that necessarily go beyond technocratic routines. In fact, we human beings need "things" to survive, but also recognition, love and truth, beauty, peace and justice. In a word, being cared in our full humanity makes home the place where we can flourish.

Far from being sentimental, the word "care" suggests a well-defined method for approaching integral sustainable development, a method which challenges both the ordinary way of thinking about development (the "intelligence" of the situation), and the ensuing practice of deciding and acting (policies and practices). Technocratic approaches that aspire to integrality need to become ever more comprehensive, and dealing with an increasing number of theoretical and practical challenges as new dimensions of sustainable development arise. By adding additional elements as they are recognized as necessary to a comprehensive approach, development policy-making becomes increasingly demanding, and coordinating policy interventions becomes exceedingly complex. Quite the opposite, the path to integral development built on the notion of care is essentially simple:[54] care, as the theoretical and practical foundation for action, can be practiced and it is

---

54. "The complexity of the experience of man is dominated by this intrinsic simplicity... the complexity itself of this experience simply shows that the whole experience, and consequently the cognition of man,... tends to compose a whole in cognition rather than to cause complexity." Wojtyla, *The Acting Person*, 8.

easily detected "in action"; its effects can be observed and its effectiveness measured. On the basis of elemental experience, there is a strong presumption that care "works" as a transformative action.[55] For example, accessing anonymous food through well-designed anonymous provision mechanisms may be absolutely necessary to preserve human life in emergency situations; however, that same mechanism cannot provide an answer to the human need for self-esteem, for participation and for social recognition, that only vivid relationships of "care" can provide. Within a caring framework, the support of the best technological tools remains precious—but they are tool, not the centerpiece of impersonal, routinely responses to integral human needs.

c. Reorganizing global governance, with human dignity at the center

Pope Francis, when visiting the UN General Assembly in 2015, gave a speech[56] where he candidly affirmed:

> The number and complexity of the problems require that we possess technical instruments of verification. But this involves two risks. We can rest content with the bureaucratic exercise of drawing up long lists of good proposals—goals, objectives and statistics—or we can think that a single theoretical and aprioristic solution will provide an answer to all the challenges. . . (A)bove and beyond our plans and programmes, we are dealing with real men and women who live, struggle and suffer, and are often forced to live in great poverty, deprived of all rights. To enable these real men and women to escape from extreme poverty, we must allow them to be dignified agents of their own destiny.

Beyond goals and targets, plans and programs, the sustainable development process is a path traded by real men and women. Enabling the most disadvantaged among them to become *dignified agents of their own destiny* in their "home," which is "our common home," remains the only path to truly sustainable development.[57] Thus, the ideal of human dignity,

55. Beretta and Maggioni, "Time, Relations and Behaviors."

56. Pope Francis, Meeting with the members of the General Assembly of the United Nations Organization, *Address of the Holy Father*, United Nations Headquarters, New York, Friday, 25 September 2015 http://w2.vatican.va/content/francesco/en/speeches/2015/september/documents/papa-francesco_20150925_onu-visita.html.

57. Take hunger eradication: we find both the problem (hunger and extreme poverty) and the resources for its sustainable solution (human work, producing adequate food) in the same environment: farming and rural life. Addressing the paradox of rural

foundational of the entire UN structure,[58] provides a possible overarching framework where the 169 "bits and pieces" of the SDG process can converge. This is possible because, as human being, we can discern human dignity and its violations in practice. *A Road to Dignity*[59] was also the title of the Synthesis Report prepared in December 2014 by the United Nations Secretary-General on the Post-2015 Agenda was indeed titled. The word "dignity" summarized both the general inspiration, and the expected outcome of a successful implementation of the post 2015 development agenda.

How can international, national and local institutions and organization that contribute to the *de facto* global governance system support the SDG process, collaborating to enable disadvantaged people to become *dignified agents of their own destiny* in their "home," which is also "our common home"? Compromise and agreement at the global level represent necessary, but not sufficient, conditions for effective action. We experienced decades of international declarations about sustainability, with the connected bargaining about who should do what—with scant results, especially for the most vulnerable members of the human family. Beyond agreeing on ideal principles, the international community is called (which is more important!) to take the necessary operational steps to pursue SDGs as "*a road to dignity*" not to be realized in the future, but building the path of development on the dignified agency of the poor, starting from now.

CONCLUSION

We live in a complex, plural world, which faces unprecedented challenges concerning our common home, that interconnect the material, relational and symbolic space of the living-together of the human family. However complex and plural, the international community is ultimately made up of persons that—as a matter of fact—have so much in common. Our "global

---

hunger can be daunting, but it is possible to reconnect problem and solution in an "integral" perspective: hunger eradication and decent work are originally connected. This example can give the flavor of how different are, in practice, adopting an "integral" perspective rather than a merely "extensive" approach.

58. Human dignity provided the "umbrella" concept underpinning the UN charter and the foundation of universal human rights. For thorough discussion, see Carozza, "Human Rights, Human Dignity."

59. United Nations, *The Road to Dignity by 2030*. The UN Secretary General had previously submitted the Report *A Life of Dignity for All*, in July 2013. That official report identified six keywords: Dignity, People, Prosperity, Planet, Justice and Partnership; it is interesting to note that in the September 2015 UN Declaration adopting the SDG some of the keywords were reformulated into five "P": People, Planet, Prosperity, Peace, Partnership. https://sustainabledevelopment.un.org/post2015/transformingourworld.

commons" are not only material goods, that are to be used and not abused (such as the environment). We also have in common invaluable non-material goods that are co-essential to sustainable development: interpersonal and international relations to be healed and promoted, on the basis of recognizing each other's humanity as the common precious gift we all received. Human dignity is this: the awareness that human beings, each and all of them, are of incomparable value. Every new day offers new opportunities for the international community to take the path of "caring for our common home," abandoning (power-laden) bargaining in favor of humble dialogue, open to encountering the humanity of others, reinforcing the international community's awareness of being one family.

BIBLIOGRAPHY

Acemoglu, Daron, and James Robinson. *Why Nations Fail: The Origins of Power, Prosperity, and Poverty.* New York: Crown, 2012.
Amin, Samir. *L'accumulation à l'échelle mondiale.* Paris: Anthropos, 1970.
———. *Le développement inégal: Essai sur les formations sociales du capitalisme périphérique.* Paris: Minuit, 1973.
Baldwin, Richard. "Trade And Industrialisation after Globalisation's Second Unbundling: How Building and Joining a Supply Chain are Different and Why It Matters." *NBER Working Paper* No. 17716, December 2011.
Balestri, Sara, and Simona Beretta. *Poverty Eradication: Access to Land, Access to Food.* Milano: EDUCatt 2105. http://system.educatt.com/libri/povertyeradication/.
Benedict XVI, Pope. *Caritas in veritate.* June 29 2009.
Beretta, Simona. "Cinquant'anni di politiche per lo sviluppo alla luce della *Populorum progressio*." In *Questione sociale questione mondiale: La permanente attualità del magistero di Paolo VI*, edited by F. Citterio. Centro di Ateneo per la Dottrina Sociale della Chiesa, Studi 3. Milan: Vita e Pensiero, 2017.
———. "Freedom and Agency: Time and Relations Matter for Development." In *Human Dignity and Development*, edited by P. Carozza and C. Sedmak. Notre Dame, Indiana: University of Notre Dame Press, forthcoming.
———. "Wealth Creation in the Global Economy: Human Labor and Development." In *Rediscovering Abundance: Interdisciplinary Essays on Wealth, Income and Their Distribution in the Catholic Social Tradition*, edited by Helen Alford, Charles Clark, Stephen A. Cortright, Michael Naughton, 175–201. Notre Dame: University of Notre Dame Press, 2006.
Beretta, Simona, and A. Mario Maggioni. "Time, Relations and Behaviors: Measuring the Transformative Power of Love-Based Communities." In *Kellogg Institute for International Studies Working Papers* #421. Notre Dame, Indiana: University of Notre Dame, April 2017. https://kellogg.nd.edu/time-relations-and-behaviors-measuring-transformative-power-love-based-community-life.
Burda, Michael, and Charles Wyplosz. *Macroeconomcs—A European Text.* 6th ed. Oxford: Oxford University Press, 2013.

Carozza, Paolo. "Human Rights, Human Dignity and Human Experience." In *Understanding Human Dignity*, edited by Christopher McCrudden, 192. Proceedings of the British Academy. Oxford: Oxford University Press, 2013.

Chenery, B. Hollis et al. *Patterns of Development, 1950–1970.* Vol. 3. London: Oxford University Press, 1975.

"Cumulative Causation." In *Encyclopedia.com.* https://www.encyclopedia.com/social-sciences/applied-and-social-sciences-magazines/cumulative-causation.

Economic and Social Council. *Progress towards the Sustainable Development Goals: Report of the Secretary-General*, E/2016/75. United Nations, 2016 session 24 July 2015–27 July 2016 Agenda items 5, 6 and 18 (a). https://unstats.un.org/sdgs/files/report/2016/secretary-general-sdg-report-2016—EN.pdf.

Emmanuel, Arghiri. *Unequal Exchange: A Study of the Imperialism of Trade.* New York: Monthly Review Press, 1972.

Francis I, Pope. *Laudato si'.* May 24 2015.

———. Meeting with the members of the General Assembly of the United Nations Organization. *Address of the Holy Father.* United Nations Headquarters, New York, Friday, 25 September 2015. http://w2.vatican.va/content/francesco/en/speeches/2015/september/documents/papa-francesco_20150925_onu-visita.html.

Frank, Gunder Andre. "The Development of Underdevelopment." *Monthly Review Press* 18.4 (1966) 17–31.

ILO. *Poverty and Minimum Living Standards: The Role of the ILO*, 1970. Record of Proceedings, Geneva, 1971. http://www.ilo.org/public/libdoc/ilo/P/09616/09616%281970-54%29.pdf.

Jolly, Richard. *United Nations Intellectual History Project*, Briefing Note n.7, Ralph Bunche Institute for International Studies, The CUNY Graduate Center, May 2010, http://www.unhistory.org/briefing/7UNandDevStrategies.pdf.

Jolly, Richard, Louis Emmerij, Dharam Ghai, and Frédéric Lapeyre. *UN Contributions to Development Thinking and Practice*, Bloomington: Indiana University Press, 2004.

Jolly, Richard, Louis Emmerij, and Thomas G. Weiss. *The UN and Human Development.* UN Intellectual History Project, Briefing Note Number 8, July 2009. http://www.unhistory.org/briefing/1Origins.pdf .

Myrdal, Gunnar. *An American Dilemma: The Negro Problem and Modern Democracy.* New York: Harper & Brothers, 1944.

———. *Asian Drama: An Inquiry into the Poverty of Nations.* 1944. Reprint, New York: Pantheon, 1968.

———. *Economic Theory and Underdeveloped Regions.* London: Duckworth, 1958.

———. *The Political Element in the Development of Economic Theory.* Cambridge: Harvard University Press, 1954.

Nurkse, Ragnar. *Problems of Capital Formation in Developing Countries.* New York: Columbia University Press, 1953.

Pasinetti L. Luigi. *Dinamica economica strutturale.* Bologna: Il Mulino, 1993.

———. *Structural Change and Economic Growth: A Theoretical Essay on the Dynamics of the Wealth of Nations.* Cambridge: Cambridge University Press Archive, 1983.

Paul VI, Pope. *Populorum progressio.* March 26, 1967.

Prebisch, Raul. *The Economic Development of Latin America and Its Principal Problems.* Economic Commission for Latin America, Lake Success. New York: United Nations Department of Economic Affairs, 1950.
Sen, Amartya. *Commodities and Capabilities.* Amsterdam: North-Holland, 1985.
Singer W. Hans. "The Distribution of Gains between Investing and Borrowing Countries." *American Economic Review* 40 (1950) 473–85.
UNICEF. *The 1960s: Decade of Development.* https://www.unicef.org/sowc96/1960s.htm.
United Nations. "A Prehistory of the Millennium Development Goals: Four Decades of Struggle for Development in the United Nations." *UN Chronicle* 44.4 (December 2007). https://unchronicle.un.org/article/prehistory-millennium-development-goals-four-decades-struggle-development-united-nations.
United Nations. *The Road to Dignity by 2030: Ending Poverty, Transforming All Lives and Protecting the Planet.* Synthesis Report of the Secretary-General On the Post-2015 Agenda. New York, 4 December 2014. http://www.un.org/disabilities/documents/reports/SG_Synthesis_Report_Road_to_Dignity_by_2030.pdf.
United Nations. *Sustainable Development Goal 2. End Hunger, Achieve Food Security and Improved Nutrition and Promote Sustainable Agriculture.* https://sustainabledevelopment.un.org/sdg2.
United Nations Development Programme. *Human Development Index (HDI).* http://hdr.undp.org/en/content/human-development-index-hdi/.
United Nations Development Program. *Human Development Report,* 1990. http://hdr.undp.org/en/content/what-human-development.
Wojtyla, Karol. *The Acting Person.* Translated by Andrzej Potocki. Analecta Husserliana 10. Dordrecht: Reidel, 1979 (1st Polish ed., 1969).
Young, A. Allyn. "Increasing Returns and Economic Progress." *The Economic Journal* 38/152 (December 1928) 527–42.

3

The Anthropological Bases of Integral Human Development

From Integral Human Development to Integral Ecology; Some Responses to the Challenges of Governance and Sustainability; Considerations on the Encyclical *Laudato Si'* of Pope Francis

Fausto Gianfreda, SJ

ABSTRACT

Pope Francis's encyclical *Laudato Si'* is in continuity with the social teaching of the church in the encyclical *Populorum Progressio* of St. Paul VI, particularly in the way it treats the ideas of sustainable development and *governance* within ecological discourse. By means of a trinitarian theological anthropology, Francis carries out a critical reading of these realities, removing them from the purely economic realm. The theological anthropology which animates and governs the entire discourse shows that, among other things, it has a certain model in the spirituality of the Exercises of S. Ignatius. Such a treatment of the ideas of sustainable development and *governance* frees them from the possibility of being affected by unintended consequences, also establishing an aesth-ethic of creation based on a mystical foundation of ecology beyond the cure for environmental disasters.

After *Octogesima adveniens*—a "discourse on method of the church's social teaching"[1]—*Populorum progressio* (PP) has been recognised as "the fundamental ecclesial document on development"[2] in the wake of *Gaudium et spes* (GS) which is the "*magna carta* of the social magisterium of the contemporary church."[3] In 1988, in a paper on the magisterium of St. Paul VI in PP,[4] A. Acerbi highlights that Pope Montini stated in PP that development requires "the acquisition of a deeper human dimension":[5] authentic development consists in the "leaving behind the security of the material bases of life until communion with God," the "ideal of transcendent humanism."[6] The results of development "are not guaranteed by trust in technical procedures."[7] The encyclical points out the risk of economicism: against this error it brings forward arguments from philosophical and theological anthropology, which leads to the idea of integral development by indicating, in line with GS 35, the superiority of being over having. Hence the critical role which the encyclical's idea of development would play in the theory and praxis of development more widely; the ongoing process would require changes in development to occur which held a non-reductive view of the human being. PP took as its starting point the cultural datum of development which had arisen in the economico-political context and inserted it in a theological context, so that its orientation would not lie, according to the ideology of progress, in the state of development of the industrialised countries of the West but rather in human fullness—PP speaks of a "full-bodied humanism" (n. 42)—in which technical and economic factors are reconciled with ethical and religious values. Thereby indicating the need for the developed countries to perceive the limits of their development.

G. Giraud has described *Laudato Si'* (LS) as "the most important magisterial document of the Catholic Church from the Second Vatican Council to today."[8] It is a prophetic text that listens to the twofold cry of the earth and of those rejected by society (LS 43), affirming that the ecological approach becomes the social approach (LS 49). It sets out the problems concerning pollution and climate change, the question of water, the loss of biodiversity,

---

1. Coste, René. "L'enciclica 'Populorum Progressio,'" 25.
2. Coste, "L'enciclica 'Populorum Progressio,'"23.
3. Coste, "L'enciclica 'Populorum Progressio,'"23
4. Acerbi, "I fondamenti teologici della 'populorum progressio,'" 28–36.
5 Acerbi, "I fondamenti teologici della 'populorum progressio,'"28–36.
6. Acerbi, "I fondamenti teologici della 'populorum progressio,'"30.
7. Acerbi, "I fondamenti teologici della 'populorum progressio,'"32.
8. Giraud, Gaël. "*Laudato Si',*" 33–34.

the deterioration of human life and social degradation, and the global injustice of which the poor are the victims. In a summary judgement Pope Francis gathers up his analysis of the present period which is in need of *governance* for sustainable development:

> These situations have caused sister earth, along with all the abandoned of our world, to cry out, pleading that we take another course. Never have we so hurt and mistreated our common home as we have in the last two hundred years. Yet we are called to be instruments of God our father, so that our planet might be what he desired when he created it and correspond with his plan for peace, beauty and fullness. The problem is that we still lack the culture needed to confront this crisis. We lack leadership capable of striking out on new paths and meeting the needs of the present with concern for all and without prejudice towards coming generations. The establishment of a legal framework which can set clear boundaries and ensure the protection of ecosystems has become indispensable; otherwise, the new power structures based on the techno-economic paradigm may overwhelm not only our politics but also freedom and justice.[9]

In n. 159, the Pope gives a precise illustration of the sustainability of development according to the intergenerational concept the classical definition of which is known as "Brundtland" according to the World Commission for the Environment:

> The notion of the common good also extends to future generations. The global economic crises have made painfully obvious the detrimental effects of disregarding our common destiny, which cannot exclude those who come after us. We can no longer speak of sustainable development apart from intergenerational solidarity. Once we start to think about the kind of world we are leaving to future generations, we look at things differently; we realize that the world is a gift which we have freely received and must share with others. Since the world has been given to us, we can no longer view reality in a purely utilitarian way, in which efficiency and productivity are entirely geared to our individual benefit. Intergenerational solidarity is not optional, but rather a basic question of justice, since the world we have received also belongs to those who will follow us.[10]

---

9. LS 53.
10. LS 159.

My view is that there is continuity in the Social Doctrine of the church between PP and LS, in particular in the mode of treatment of the ideas of sustainable development and *governance* within ecological discourse. In LS, by means of a trinitarian anthropological theology, Pope Francis carries out a critical reading of these realities: withdrawing them from a sphere that is purely economic and thus freeing them from the possibility of being affected by unintended consequences. In two of his recent essays, P. Benanti[11] points out this hermeneutic, illustrating the category of integral ecology as the "conceptual paradigm which is able to reorientate the believer's thought on to some fundamental themes concerning human life and justice,"[12] by contrast with the tecnicho-scientific field of complexity and emergency. Benanti underlines the essentially spiritual dimension of integral ecology[13] which completes and surpasses holistic and reductionist models (understanding the latter as an analytical procedure). In particular, Benanti points out the two-way link between *governance* and development which is such that "the role of ethical reflection in this process of *governance* lies not so much in identifying solutions to the various problems directly but introducing into the debate the critical question on the meaning of the human mediated by *technological innovation* and on the means which can guarantee an authentically human development."[14] In this way, the perspective of discernment and dialogue in LS is itself internal to the anthropological vision in question: bringing to pass already on the formal level what is presented as structural of reality, that is, complexity in interrelationship and interdependence. Benanti writes:

> The response which Francis offers to Christians and to people of good will to take charge of the management and utilisation of technology is in the form of discernment and dialogue. Francis' magisterium does not claim to resolve these tensions by giving lines or directives to be followed by virtue of a role or principle of authority but takes on board the complexity of the problem, indicating the need for a sharing of aspirations and of dialogue to find common solutions so as to be able to orientate

---

11. The volume, Miguel Humberto Yáñez SJ., *Laudato si': Linee di lettura interdisciplinari per la cura della casa comune*. Roma: GBP, 2017, contains the two essays of Benanti Paolo: "L'ecologia integrale: una nuova categoria per la bioetica credente?" (69–95) and "La tecnologia: problema o soluzione della crisi ecologica? Alcune linee di discernimento etico a partire dalla *Laudato Si*'" (171–91).

12. Benanti, "*L'ecologia integrale*," 70.

13. Benanti, "*L'ecologia integrale*," 86–87.

14. Benanti, "*La tecnologia*," 190–91.

technology and its progress towards the common good in forms of authentic human development.[15]

In this connection, to be brief, a second point of contact between LS and PP is the hope which enables us to face up to the unpleasant results of the necessary advance of technology. Paul VI was accused, by some, of technological optimism and of wishing for an economic progress which was a development of being; in the face of ecological instability, the fracturing cultural identities and secularisation.[16] In fact, the expectation of a new humanism which would reconcile technology and spiritual values was at the heart of PP. So, the denunciation of environmental and social disasters as well as the condemnation of technocracy characterises LS, and yet, Francis's view is one of hope in a humanism which allows for integral and integrating living.

In this paper, therefore, I intend to illustrate the structure of the encyclical is founded on as it is on the theological anthropology which is at the heart of the text and animates and governs the whole discourse: an anthropology which, among other things, shows that it has the spirituality of the Exercises of St. Ignatius of Loyola as a certain model. After illustrating this structure, I shall make some personal considerations on the orientation LS gives to the contemporary cultural process.

The Pope introduces the theological argument by claiming for it a legitimate and necessary space within a contemporary society that is threatened by technocracy. The discourse begins with a criticism of the dictatorship of technology and finance over politics. The politics exclude everything which is outside of its interests (LS 54). It is precisely human dignity and the environment that are the object of exclusion in a society dominated by the worship of the market (LS 56). With a reference to the *subprime* crisis which began in the United States mortgage market in 2007, which demonstrated the financialisation of the world economy and put at risk the entire international financial system with the poisoning of the credit markets, the Pope identifies decisively the dominion of money in our society, the progeny of an anthropological crisis. A politics in slavery to finance is not able to produce that good *governance* which is the inescapable precondition of sustainable development (LS 55–56). Given this social situation, we have a clear vision of sustainable development, beyond normativity, as a science of complex systems. So then, the encyclical's greatness lies in including within

---

15. Benanti, "La tecnologia," 186.

16. See Campanini, "Le radici culturali del nuovo umanesimo proposto dalla 'Populorum progressio.'"

this complexity areas which are not taken into consideration by a society which is slave to the logic of finance and technocracy:

> Given the complexity of the ecological crisis and its multiple causes, we need to realize that the solutions will not emerge from just one way of interpreting and transforming reality. Respect must also be shown for the various cultural riches of different peoples, their art and poetry, their interior life and spirituality. If we are truly concerned to develop an ecology capable of remedying the damage we have done, no branch of the sciences and no form of wisdom can be left out, and that includes religion and the language particular to it,[17]

And further:

> It cannot be maintained that empirical science provides a complete explanation of life, the interplay of all creatures and the whole of reality. This would be to breach the limits imposed by its own methodology. If we reason only within the confines of the latter, little room would be left for aesthetic sensibility, poetry, or even reason's ability to grasp the ultimate meaning and purpose of things.[18]

This is how the Pope opens up a space in the discussion on sustainable development for the Christian doctrine of creation which, in the dialogue with science, enables the thought of an integral ecology:

> I am well aware that in the areas of politics and philosophy there are those who firmly reject the idea of a Creator, or consider it irrelevant, and consequently dismiss as irrational the rich contribution which religions can make towards an integral ecology and the full development of humanity. Others view religions simply as a subculture to be tolerated. Nonetheless, science and religion, with their distinctive approaches to understanding reality, can enter into an intense dialogue fruitful for both.[19]
>
> The doctrine of creation accounts for the dignity of the human being which is not just some*thing* but some*one* who is free, capable of self-giving and entering into communion with others (LS 65). The meaning of life lies in a cosmotheandric relationality which has been negated by sin but can be restored

---

17. LS 63.
18. LS 199.
19. LS 62.

through the harmony of universal reconciliation, illustrated by the Poverello of Assisi:

> . . . human life is grounded in three fundamental and closely intertwined relationships: with God, with our neighbour and with the earth itself. According to the Bible, these three vital relationships have been broken, both outwardly and within us. . . . It is significant that the harmony which Saint Francis of Assisi experienced with all creatures was seen as a healing of that rupture. Saint Bonaventure held that, through universal reconciliation with every creature, Saint Francis in some way returned to the state of original innocence. This is a far cry from our situation today, where sin is manifest in all its destructive power in wars, the various forms of violence and abuse, the abandonment of the most vulnerable, and attacks on nature.[20]

Here is how sustainable intergenerational development can be guaranteed by the recognition of this relationality:

> This implies a relationship of mutual responsibility between human beings and nature. Each community can take from the bounty of the earth whatever it needs for subsistence, but it also has the duty to protect the earth and to ensure its fruitfulness for coming generations.[21]

The Pope recalls the biblical foundation of this theology of relationality: "the Bible has no place for a tyrannical anthropocentrism unconcerned for other creatures."[22]

The antidote to the utilitarianism of a degenerate anthropocentrism is to be found in the contemplation of the creation through love which, in the little book of the Spiritual Exercises of St. Ignatius, has a moment of exceptional efficacy which is recalled in the words of the *Catechism of the Catholic Church*:

> The German bishops have taught that, where other creatures are concerned, "we can speak of the priority of *being* over that of *being useful*." The Catechism clearly and forcefully criticizes a distorted anthropocentrism: "Each creature possesses its own particular goodness and perfection . . . Each of the various creatures, willed in its own being, reflects in its own way a ray of God's infinite wisdom and goodness. Man must therefore

---

20. LS 66.
21. LS 67.
22. LS 68.

respect the particular goodness of every creature, to avoid any disordered use of things."[23]

The recognition of omnirelationality is the guarantee of that sustainable development which today takes the name of integral ecology: "everything is interconnected, and that genuine care for our own lives and our relationships with nature is inseparable from fraternity, justice and faithfulness to others."[24]

The Pope reads cosmic interrelationality in an open systemic vision, in an evolutionary perspective:

> In this universe, shaped by open and intercommunicating systems, we can discern countless forms of relationship and participation. This leads us to think of the whole as open to God's transcendence, within which it develops. Faith allows us to interpret the meaning and the mysterious beauty of what is unfolding. We are free to apply our intelligence towards things evolving positively, or towards adding new ills, new causes of suffering and real setbacks.[25]

In this evolutionary-systemic conception, evil can be understood as the stimulus to the human action of response to the creative action of a God who limits himself:

> God in some way sought to limit himself in such a way that many of the things we think of as evils, dangers or sources of suffering, are in reality part of the pains of childbirth which he uses to draw us into the act of cooperation with the Creator.[26]

It is in this personal-dialogic collaborative response that the special nature of the human being in the cosmos is found:

> Human beings, even if we postulate a process of evolution, also possess a uniqueness which cannot be fully explained by the evolution of other open systems. Each of us has his or her own personal identity and is capable of entering into dialogue with others and with God himself. Our capacity to reason, to develop arguments, to be inventive, to interpret reality and to create art, along with other not yet discovered capacities, are signs of a uniqueness which transcends the spheres of physics and biology. The sheer novelty involved in the emergence of a personal

---

23. LS 69.
24. LS 70.
25. LS 79.
26. LS 80.

being within a material universe presupposes a direct action of God and a particular call to life and to relationship on the part of a "Thou" who addresses himself to another "thou."[27]

The special nature of the human being cannot be any excuse for a view in which nature is the object of dominion (LS 82). The delineation of the contemplative horizon of LS bears the marks of Ignatian spirituality which has as one of its pillars the *Contemplatio ad amorem* of the Spiritual Exercises of St. Ignatius of Loyola. This can be detected especially in number 80 of the encyclical where, with quotations from the teaching of St. Thomas Aquinas on creation—hidden source of the *Contemplatio*[28]—it says, with reference to God:

> God is intimately present to each being, without impinging on the autonomy of his creature, and this gives rise to the rightful autonomy of earthly affairs. His divine presence, which ensures the subsistence and growth of each being, "continues the work of creation." The Spirit of God has filled the universe with possibilities and therefore, from the very heart of things, something new can always emerge: "Nature is nothing other than a certain kind of art, namely God's art, impressed upon things, whereby those things are moved to a determinate end . . ."[29]

This is an impressive passage in an argument in which God's action is contemplated according to the evolutionary thought of a Teilhardian type:

> The ultimate destiny of the universe is in the fullness of God, which has already been attained by the risen Christ, the measure of the maturity of all things. Here we can add yet another argument for rejecting every tyrannical and irresponsible domination of human beings over other creatures. The ultimate purpose of other creatures is not to be found in us. Rather, all creatures are moving forward with us and through us towards a common point of arrival, which is God, in that transcendent fullness where the risen Christ embraces and illumines all things. Human beings, endowed with intelligence and love, and drawn by the fullness of Christ, are called to lead all creatures back to their Creator.[30]

27. LS 81

28 See Fausto Gianfreda, "La *Contemplatio ad amorem* di Sant'Ignazio e il neoplatonismo." In *La storia, il dialogo, il rispetto della persona. Scritti in onore del Cardinale Achille Silvestrini*, ed. Luca Monteferrante and Damiano Nocilla Roma: Studium, 2009, 225–253.

29. LS 80.

30. LS 83.

Thus, LS is focused on a theological anthropology which, in its turn, is based on the contemplation of the interconnection and interrelationality in the mutual multiplicity of reality. This is wonderfully expressed in number 86:

> The universe as a whole, in all its manifold relationships, shows forth the inexhaustible riches of God. Saint Thomas Aquinas wisely noted that multiplicity and variety "come from the intention of the first agent" who willed that "what was wanting to one in the representation of the divine goodness might be supplied by another," inasmuch as God's goodness "could not be represented fittingly by any one creature." Hence we need to grasp the variety of things in their multiple relationships. We understand better the importance and meaning of each creature if we contemplate it within the entirety of God's plan. As the Catechism teaches: "God wills the interdependence of creatures. The sun and the moon, the cedar and the little flower, the eagle and the sparrow: the spectacle of their countless diversities and inequalities tells us that no creature is self-sufficient. Creatures exist only in dependence on each other, to complete each other, in the service of each other."[31]

The Pope indicates the immanence of God in nature, the recognition of which is behind the ecological virtues:

> The bishops of Brazil have pointed out that nature as a whole not only manifests God but is also a locus of his presence. The Spirit of life dwells in every living creature and calls us to enter into relationship with him. Discovering this presence leads us to cultivate the "ecological virtues."[32]

This presence of God in the many designates the creation in reference to the paternity of God and accounts for the sacred fabric of reality as a family, moving to a gesture of respect:

> ... called into being by one Father, all of us are linked by unseen bonds and together form a kind of universal family, a sublime communion which fills us with a sacred, affectionate and humble respect.[33].

---

31. LS 86.
32. LS 88.
33. LS 89.

If people withdraw from this communion in order to dominate, their life vanishes[34] This is the danger facing the entire world at the present time, dominated as it is by the technocratic paradigm from which it is absolutely necessary to be freed.[35] Behind the tendency to technocratic dominion, there is a perverse anthropocentrism.[36] The Pope refers to the possibility of climbing back up the slope, appealing to human freedom and calling for the redefinition of progress:

> We have the freedom needed to limit and direct technology; we can put it at the service of another type of progress, one which is healthier, more human, more social, more integral.[37]
>
> All of this shows the urgent need for us to move forward in a bold cultural revolution. Science and technology are not neutral; from the beginning to the end of a process, various intentions and possibilities are in play and can take on distinct shapes. Nobody is suggesting a return to the Stone Age, but we do need to slow down and look at reality in a different way, to appropriate the positive and sustainable progress which has been made, but also to recover the values and the great goals swept away by our unrestrained delusions of grandeur.[38]

Only the contemplation of the creation in its omni-relationality makes the thought of integral ecology possible:

> Ecology studies the relationship between living organisms and the environment in which they develop. This necessarily entails reflection and debate about the conditions required for the life and survival of society, and the honesty needed to question certain models of development, production and consumption. It cannot be emphasized enough how everything is interconnected. Time and space are not independent of one another, and not even atoms or subatomic particles can be considered in isolation. Just as the different aspects of the planet—physical, chemical and biological—are interrelated, so too living species are part of a network which we will never fully explore and understand. A good part of our genetic code is shared by many living beings. It follows that the fragmentation of knowledge and the isolation of bits of

---

34. LS 117.
35. LS 108–109.
36. LS 115–116.
37. LS 112.
38. LS 114.

information can actually become a form of ignorance, unless they are integrated into a broader vision of reality.[39]

In particular, with regard to the environment, it has to be recognised that nature is not separate from us; rather, it permeates us so that, in the relevant research, it is necessary to pay attention to the reality of the ecosystems:

> Ongoing research should also give us a better understanding of how different creatures relate to one another in making up the larger units which today we term "ecosystems." We take these systems into account not only to determine how best to use them, but also because they have an intrinsic value independent of their usefulness. Each organism, as a creature of God, is good and admirable in itself; the same is true of the harmonious ensemble of organisms existing in a defined space and functioning as a system. Although we are often not aware of it, we depend on these larger systems for our own existence. We need only recall how ecosystems interact in dispersing carbon dioxide, purifying water, controlling illnesses and epidemics, forming soil, breaking down waste, and in many other ways which we overlook or simply do not know about. Once they become conscious of this, many people realize that we live and act on the basis of a reality which has previously been given to us, which precedes our existence and our abilities. So, when we speak of "sustainable use," consideration must always be given to each ecosystem's regenerative ability in its different areas and aspects.[40]

Ecological fullness implies a multidisciplinary humanism in the analysis of environmental problems.[41] This multidisciplinary approach must also involve politics.[42] Moreover, integral ecology demands attention to local cultures.[43] In particular, the multidisciplinary approach in the ecology of the environment must bear on town-planning, in consultation with the citizens, creating a fair balance of interrelationality between the urban spaces and human activity.[44] Taking care of the environment refers to taking care of one's own body which is the point of contact with the environment and with other living beings.[45]

39. LS 138.
40. LS 140.
41. LS 141.
42. LS 197.
43. LS 143.
44. LS 150.
45. LS 155.

Human interrelation calls to mind the common good, that is the integral development of the person and the social order. The achievement of this requires the application of the principles of subsidiarity and distributive justice.[46] Interdependence necessitates a global consensus in tackling the contemporary ecological problems.[47] Referring especially to the measures necessary to respond to the problems relating to climate change, the Pope highlights the global common good which should guide international negotiations.[48] In considering the priority to be given to the poor countries, he indicates the importance of international relations and treaties that respect the sovereignty of each state.[49] The conclusion of LS is for an ecological conversion which, with the aim of a necessary balance of relations, involves first and foremost a measure of degrowth in some parts of the world.[50] This ecological conversion is founded on the "omni-relationality" of the real:

> It also entails a loving awareness that we are not disconnected from the rest of creatures, but joined in a splendid universal communion. As believers, we do not look at the world from without but from within, conscious of the bonds with which the Father has linked us to all beings.[51]

Theologically, this is correct from the trinitarian-Christocentric point of view. For a Christian, respect for the environment finds its meaning in the contemplation of the fundamental mysteries of the faith:

> Various convictions of our faith, developed at the beginning of this Encyclical can help us to enrich the meaning of this conversion. These include the awareness that each creature reflects something of God and has a message to convey to us, and the security that Christ has taken unto himself this material world and now, risen, is intimately present to each being, surrounding it with his affection and penetrating it with his light. Then too, there is the recognition that God created the world, writing into it an order and a dynamism that human beings have no right to ignore.[52]

---

46. LS 157.
47. LS 164.
48. LS 169.
49. LS 173–175.
50. LS 193.
51. LS 220.
52. LS 221.

In particular, the creative action of the Trinity determines the trinitarian structure of every creature:

> For Christians, believing in one God who is trinitarian communion suggests that the Trinity has left its mark on all creation. Saint Bonaventure went so far as to say that human beings, before sin, were able to see how each creature "testifies that God is three." The reflection of the Trinity was there to be recognized in nature "when that book was open to man and our eyes had not yet become darkened." The Franciscan saint teaches us that *each creature bears in itself a specifically trinitarian structure*, so real that it could be readily contemplated if only the human gaze were not so partial, dark and fragile. In this way, he points out to us the challenge of trying to read reality in a trinitarian key.[53]

The mutual and communal interrelationality of creation is to be attributed precisely to the matrix of the trinitarian dynamic:

> The divine Persons are subsistent relations, and the world, created according to the divine model, is a web of relationships. Creatures tend towards God, and in turn it is proper to every living being to tend towards other things, so that throughout the universe we can find any number of constant and secretly interwoven relationships. This leads us not only to marvel at the manifold connections existing among creatures, but also to discover a key to our own fulfilment. The human person grows more, matures more and is sanctified more to the extent that he or she enters into relationships, going out from themselves to live in communion with God, with others and with all creatures. In this way, they make their own that trinitarian dynamism which God imprinted in them when they were created. Everything is interconnected, and this invites us to develop a spirituality of that global solidarity which flows from the mystery of the Trinity.[54]

The spiritual-theological vision of St. Ignatius of Loyola is implicitly infused in LS. This is proved in n. 233 where the Pope points to the encounter with God in all things within an evolutionary concept of the creation, quoting the thought of St. Bonaventure who—together with the already considered St. Thomas Aquinas—is also a hidden source of the *Contemplatio ad Amorem* mentioned above:[55]

---

53. LS 239.
54. LS 240.
55. LS 239.

The universe unfolds in God, who fills it completely. Hence, there is a mystical meaning to be found in a leaf, in a mountain trail, in a dewdrop, in a poor person's face. The ideal is not only to pass from the exterior to the interior to discover the action of God in the soul, but also to discover God in all things. Saint Bonaventure teaches us that "contemplation deepens the more we feel the working of God's grace within our hearts, and the better we learn to encounter God in creatures outside ourselves."[56]

Finally, this cosmic-mystical vision of the presence of God in every creature summons the various believers on the planet to an interreligious dialogue of concern and care just as, equally, it evokes a dialogue among the sciences on behalf of the environment.[57]

LS lays the foundations for a contemporary spiritual ecological theology which fosters a *governance* of plenary development that goes beyond seeking just to remedy environmental disasters. In this sense, it is the implementation of the social magisterium of the church in direct communication with the PP's concept of integral development and, even earlier, with the Second Vatican Council,[58] with an awareness of the current anthropological crisis and looking to the hope of a future of a universe that is on the way to the Pleroma. LS sets the world with its ecological problems in a cosmic contemplative horizon according to the revelation of Jesus Christ in collaborative dialogue with science, with culture and with the non-Christian religions. The power of this process is really notable and opens up paths of theoretical study and practical activity to people and institutions. LS teaches us that to serve the human means asking ourselves again about humanity and the whole of creation. Founded on relation and reciprocal communication, Francis's reflection makes the centre of attention the cosmo-ontological question so that anthropology cannot avoid the transcendent reference of man to being in its totality.

My suggestion is that this question could result in an aesth-ethic of the creation based on a mystical foundation of ecology in a sacramental-symbolic approach to creation: following in the direction of Francis's magisterium, perhaps in the perspective of the Spiritual Exercises of St. Ignatius of

---

56. LS, 233

57. LS 201.

58. GS, 59: "For the above reasons, the Church recalls to the mind of all that culture is to be subordinated to the integral perfection of the human person, to the good of the community and of the whole society. Therefore it is necessary to develop the human faculties in such a way that there results a growth of the faculty of admiration, of intuition, of contemplation, of making personal judgment, of developing a religious, moral and social sense."

Loyola which enable the believer to see God in everything. This aes-ethetic would have as its object the salvation of the creation (in the double sense of the genitive: subjective and objective) that is to say, at one and the same time, the working of God in creation on our behalf and our responsibility in recognising that the creation is inhabited by the presence of God: this is a single process in which God expresses himself in the creation so as to bring about our recognition. This aesth-ethic would aim at developing a sense of sacrality, of marvel and of mystery: through the symbol that leads to the supernatural so as to enable the recognition and the favouring of order and grace. Sacramentality would be the characteristic of this aesth-ethic, where religion and rite form part of the ordered make-up of the world. Finally, the centre of this aesth-ethic of creation would be the gracious human response to the divine grace. In fact, as an alternative to the cult of efficiency and power, it is necessary to promote a culture of grace/gratuity in sympathetic relation.

Such an aesth-ethic can come about only in the recognition of the grace of existing. More than ever, contemporary people need to rediscover praise as joy at the fascination of the world, to share, through collaboration with God, in the care and development of the creation, the pleasure of God in creating the world. Through wonder, they must be able to share in the re-creation of God who is Love, dynamic, interrelational, compassionate. Thus, by overcoming the instrumental and objectifying conception of nature, it is necessary to recognise the creation as *locus theologicus* in that it is the (place of) encounter with God. In addition to St. Bonaventure and St. Thomas Aquinas, there are other teachers who share this way of thinking: St. Maximus the Confessor, John Scotus Eriugena, St. Hildegard of Bingen and Meister Eckhart. Francis has affirmed the interconnection of the world as a reflection of the trinitarian perichoresis and has, in fact, called for the consideration of the evolution of the cosmos as a process through multiple levels of complexity and communion. Therefore in the aesth-ethic of creation, in dialogue with science, theology is called to come to terms with the dynamic history of the universe: with its pan-relationality and self-transcendence through which, in humanity, the universe arrives at self-awareness.

The ethic contained within this aesth-ethic begins with the humility to recognise the need for a different language from that of the rational sphere which is part of eurocentric culture. A language of an integral ecology founded on an integral anthropology, that is, one that integrates the human, cosmic and divine: open to the multiple rationalities and different cosmologies of the various cultures of the world. That involves the abandonment of the Western economic model based on the commodification of the other and on an all-pervasive technology. Francis is asking us to leave a society of environmental and human disorder, dominated by deregulated finance, to arrive at a society directed to the common good: this is to begin from a politics of control of the financial markets and of investments. This order—he teaches us—responds to the structure of harmonious reality because it is relational and can be read in the circularity of the natural ecosystems. Furthermore, Francis calls for the construction of a global community of solidarity through interreligious dialogue: with especial concern for the peoples and species that are most vulnerable. Hence the appeal for a new eco-justice, a new asceticism consisting of eco-compatible lifestyles: for a just, bioethical and spiritual management of our limited natural resources.

There follows, on the epistemological level, the passage from an understanding of reality that aims at the control over nature to one that is relational, holistic and evolutionary: integrating analytic and instrumental with symbolic reason, overcoming the philosophical and theological dualisms characteristic of the West. Beyond discursive-analytical thought and the mechanistic vision of nature and the cosmos, it necessitates a holistic approach based on systemic thought.

In this connection, it is impossible to overlook the necessary reform of the academic institutions: to introduce the youth to a new ecological awareness through new pedagogic models. Education should consist not so much in the accumulation of information as in a transformative process which enables a creative interaction with others and with nature: forming an empathetic sensitivity with the object of knowledge. This would mean developing perception before conceptualisation, contemplation before analysis. An understanding that is holistic and intuitive has to replace the primacy of reductionist scientific rationality. Intuition would precede discursive and analytic thought: grasping the interconnection among the different problems. Education of the spirit and education of the body should proceed in tandem. There is an obligation to stimulate mimetic learning and participatory knowledge by means of art, meditation and play.[59] All this makes up a free education which has its finest realisation in the harmonious beauty of the liturgy as once again the words of Francis clearly show us:

Encountering God does not mean fleeing from this world or turning our back on nature. This is especially clear in the spirituality of the Christian East. "Beauty, which in the East is one of the best loved names expressing the divine harmony and the model of humanity transfigured, appears everywhere: in the shape of a church, in the sounds, in the colours, in the lights, in the scents." For Christians, all the creatures of the material universe find their true meaning in the incarnate Word, for the Son of God has

---

59. For these concluding observations, see Boff, Leonardo and Hathaway, Mark. *Il Tao della liberazione. Esplorando l'ecologia della trasformazione* Roma: Fazi, 2014.

incorporated in his person part of the material world, planting in it a seed of definitive transformation. "Christianity does not reject matter. Rather, bodiliness is considered in all its value in the liturgical act, whereby the human body is disclosed in its inner nature as a temple of the Holy Spirit and is united with the Lord Jesus, who himself took a body for the world's salvation."[60]

BIBLIOGRAPHY

Acerbi, Antonio. "I fondamenti teologici della 'populorum progressio.'" In *Il magistero di Paolo VI nell'enciclica "populorum progressio"*, 28–36. Brescia—Roma: Istituto Paolo VI—Studium, 1989.

Benanti, Paolo. "L'ecologia integrale: una nuova categoria per la bioetica credente?" In *Laudato si': Linee di lettura interdisciplinari per la cura della casa comune*, edited by Miguel Humberto Yáñez, SJ, 69–95. Rome: GBP, 2017.

Benanti, Paolo. La tecnologia: problema o soluzione della crisi ecologica? Alcune linee di discernimento etico a partire dalla *Laudato Si.*" In *Laudato si': Linee di lettura interdisciplinari per la cura della casa comune*, edited by Miguel Humberto Yáñez, SJ, 171–91. Rome: GBP, 2017.

Boff, Leonardo, and Mark Hathaway. *Il Tao della liberazione: Esplorando l'ecologia della trasformazione*. Rome: Fazi, 2014. See: *The Tao of Liberation: Exploring the Ecology of Transformation*. Maryknoll, NY: Orbis, 2009.

Campanini, Giorgio. "Le radici culturali del nuovo umanesimo proposto dalla 'Populorum progressio.'" In *Il magistero di Paolo VI nell'enciclica "populorum progressio"*, 37–53. Brescia—Roma: Istituto Paolo VI—Studium, 1989.

Coste, René. "L'enciclica 'Populorum Progressio' nel contesto del pontificato di Paolo VI." In *Il magistero di Paolo VI nell'enciclica "populorum progressio,"* 25. Brescia—Rome: Istituto Paolo VI—Studium, 1989.

Francis, *Laudato si'* 2015. http://w2.vatican.va/content/francesco/en/encyclicals/documents/papa-francesco_20150524_enciclica-laudato-si.html.

Giraud, Gaël. "*Laudato si*': un appello decisivo". In Boff, Leonardo, Costa, Giacomo, Giaccardi, Chiara, Giraud, Gaël, Magatti, Mauro, Zanotelli, Alex. *Curare madre terra. Commento all'enciclica* Laudato si' *di papa Francesco*, Bologna: Emi, 2015.

---

60. LS 235.

4

Challenges to Solidarity
Governance and Democracy in a Sustainable European Union

SILVANA SCIARRA

ABSTRACT

Compelling priorities in policies of sustainability, prioritised by the Catholic Church, are recalled in this paper in order to highlight parallel developments in European Union social policies, with a special emphasis on choices to be made as a follow up to austerity measures. The concept of subsidiarity inspired both past and contemporary Christian social doctrines and has kept an unchanged value as a means of participation and democratization of political processes. The shortcomings of the approaches adopted in European Union social policies in the aftermath of the economic and financial crisis are outlined. In particular, governance techniques, mainly deprived of solid political bases, have increasingly set aside the principle of solidarity and have given rise to marginalisation, social conflict and inequalities, which, in the long run, may put at risk social cohesion and democracy. The active role of judicial bodies—and of constitutional courts above all—is recalled, with the caveat that they should avoid occupying the domain of politics. They should rather act as guardians of solidarity, reconciling economic and financial constraints with social justice through legal instruments and reasoning. Two distinct though complementary systems of representation are examined, both working as vehicles of solidarity: intermediary groups rooted in civil society, holders of collective interests, preventing inequalities and enhancing fairness and justice; states and supranational institutions, translating demands of solidarity into binding norms. The encyclical letter *Laudato si* is recalled for its many connections with current legal analysis, which permeates interdisciplinary methodologies. Openness to law and science and commitment to enhance international organizations are strong messages sent to policy-makers and to states throughout the world.

1. SUBSIDIARITY VERSUS GOVERNANCE

Principles of subsidiarity and proportionality are foundational principles in European Union (EU) law. They deal with the distribution of competences and consequently with the attribution of powers. Beyond the law, they have philosophical and even ethical implications, since they challenge hierarchies in organisations, as well as in politics.

The Charter of Fundamental Rights of the European Union (CFREU), which has acquired the same legal value as the Treaties[1] is inspired by the principle of subsidiarity. The provisions of the CFREU are addressed to "the institutions, bodies, offices and agencies of the Union with due regard for the principle of subsidiarity and to the Member States only when they are implementing Union law" (art. 51). Hence, different levels of accountability are at stake for the enforcement of fundamental rights

Although EU law enshrines "human dignity, freedom, democracy, equality, the rule of law and respect for human rights, including the rights of persons belonging to minorities" among its values (art. 2 TEU), a constant need is observed to connect this legal statement with the practices put in place by governments and institutions. The latter must be constantly active in establishing very close links with citizens, valuing their needs and aspirations.

On the occasion of the sixtieth anniversary of the signature of the Treaty of Rome, which gave birth to the then European Economic Community, a declaration, delivered by the leaders of 27 Member States, reiterated all commitments for a "Union that is safe and secure, prosperous, competitive,

---

*I am grateful to Dr. Angelo Jr. Golia, an intern at the Italian Constitutional Court at the time of writing this chapter, currently Senior Research Fellow, Max Planck Institute for Comparative Public Law and International Law, Heidelberg. He read a first draft of this chapter, commented on it, and helped me in the editing of quotations. Gratitude implies that all responsibilities for mistakes and omissions are exclusively mine.

1. Art. 6 TEU, entered into force in 2009, explicitly refers to the Charter of Fundamental Rights of the European Union of 7 December 2000, as adapted at Strasbourg, on 12 December 2007, which is now part of primary EU law.

sustainable and socially responsible," open to European countries that respect the fundamental values of the Union.[2] Beyond the rhetoric inspiring a remarkable historic event, it is not difficult to detect the message that the project of an integrated Union is still to be completed and some of its goals still to be accomplished. The example of Europe as a unitary democracy framed within the "postnational constellation" has not vanished and efforts to re-legitimize it have not disappeared.[3]

At a different level, the same urgency to link mere statements with concrete demonstrations of political will is underlined in the UN Agenda 2030 on sustainable development.[4] Relying on similar aspirations, the Brundtland Commission drafted the 1987 Report, "Our common future,"[5] which opened the way to considerations and proposals on issues crucial for humanity as a whole. Pope Paul John II, celebrating the twentieth anniversary of the encyclical letter *Populorum Progressio*, was outspoken on similar issues and his views were influential for the UN Commission.[6] In that Report the emphasis, among other priorities, is on poverty and on the compelling task to meet basic needs of all for a better life. Equity, acquired by political systems as a common good, should be pursued by "effective citizen participation in decision making and by greater democracy in international decision making."[7]

A common ground of analysis and similar recommendations connect auspices for sustainable development and for enhanced democracy in the EU and in the global scene. Looking at both angles, so that sustainability and democracy stay interconnected, the discourse of policy-makers must be addressed to states and, at the same time, to international organizations.

Appeals to improve democracy in the EU take into account a peculiar legal system, which has, since its origins, tried to set up an institutional

---

2. See: http://www.consilium.europa.eu/en/press/press-releases/2017/03/25/rome-declaration/ .

3. Following the inspiring ideas of Jürgen Habermas, see Habermas, *The Postnational Constellation*, 96.

See also Joerges, et al. "A New Type of Conflicts Law as Constitutional Form in the Postnational Constellation," 153–65.

4. See, in particular, point 8: "We envisage a world of universal respect for human rights and human dignity, the rule of law, justice, equality and non-discrimination; of respect for race, ethnicity and cultural diversity; and of equal opportunity permitting the full realization of human potential and contributing to shared prosperity."

5. Report of the World Commission on Environment and Development: Our Common Future, http://www.un-documents.net/wced-ocf.htm.

6. The encyclical letter *Sollicitudo rei socialis*, published in 1987, intends to be in a line of continuity with *Populorum progressio*. See: http://w2.vatican.va/content/john-paul-ii/en/encyclicals/documents/hf_jp-ii_enc_30121987_sollicitudo-rei-socialis.html.

7. Report of the World commission, n. 28.

framework, combining unity and diversities of Member States. Diversity continues to be an asset of the EU and must be preserved. In different stages of European integration the church shared this goal and promoted principles of subsidiarity and solidarity, paying respect to all people "valuing their historical and cultural distinctions," as the Union should not be "reduced to its merely geographic and economic dimensions."[8] However, there is widespread awareness of the drawbacks that are inherent in the European legal architecture, especially when democracy is endangered and claims for solidarity are not transposed into actions.

In the early 2000s the European Commission supported academic research—carried on, among others, by philosophers and political scientists, some of them operating at the Catholic University of Louvain—to construct a theory of governance tailored on deliberative democracy. Openness towards civil society was intended as a move towards an expanded circle of stakeholders with the intention to listen to voices coming from different groups. "Proceduralisation" of law and self-learning within organisations were keywords in that discussion. The ambition was to find ways of "governing well" in specific contexts of society and to enhance democracy.[9]

Efforts to overcome an excessive centralization in technocratic bureaucracies were translated into growing attention towards autonomous orders put in place by non-state actors. A possible implication for this attractive hypothesis was to go beyond black letter law approaches and promote soft law techniques. These ideas were transposed into certain European policies, in particular employment policies, which should have developed innovative methods of coordination among national administrations. Harmonization, the alternative regulatory technique provided for in EU law, prevails for the enforcement of social policies and has binding effects on Member States. In promoting mere coordination of employment policies, proximity to those who had lost their jobs or never entered the labour market and to interest groups capable to interpreter their aspirations, was perceived as a symptom of renewal and a way to enhance social justice. However, harmonized measures were explicitly excluded.

8. For example, in the Post-synodal apostolic exhortation *Ecclesia in Europa*, delivered by Pope John Paul II in 2003. See: *http://w2.vatican.va/content/john-paul-ii/en/apost_exhortations/documents/hf_jp-ii_exh_20030628_ecclesia-in-europa.html#fnref172*, n. 110.

9. De Schutter et al. *Governance in the European Union*.
This publication is part of the 'Cahiers' of the Forward Studies Unit of the European Commission. An example of how this discussion was echoed outside European scholarship may be found in Joshua Cohen and Charles Sabel, "Directly-Deliberative Polyarchy," *European Law Journal* 3 (1997): 313–42.
See also Zürn, *Law and Governance in Postnational Europe*.

Unless properly contextualised, European governance can be a misleading concept and, at the same time, a distorted practice. As a concept, it may weaken the notion of democracy and representation; as a practice it may dilute consultation and involvement into empty procedures. Deliberative processes, detached from democratic principles of representation and based on soft law procedures without the support of enforceable sanctions, may lead to the unintended result of diminishing the role of supranational institutions and narrowing their political powers.

Current debates in the EU require, on the contrary, a strong emphasis on institutional responsibility and a return to transparent principles of democracy. This implies re-legitimizing politics via stronger links with citizens.

In the discussion on the urgency to reform the EU the following passage of the encyclical letter *Laudato si'*—related to environmental issues and yet attentive to other disputes in society—is the right key to hold in order to enter some of the most controversial points I want to address:

> Let us keep in mind the principle of subsidiarity, which grants freedom to develop the capabilities present at every level of society, while also demanding a greater sense of responsibility for the common good from those who wield greater power. Today, it is the case that some economic sectors exercise more power than states themselves. But economics without politics cannot be justified, since this would make it impossible to favour other ways of handling the various aspects of the present crisis.[10]

Doctrines put forward in the encyclical letter are illuminating and open up wider spaces for reflection to both lawyers and policy-makers. Lack of concern for the environment runs parallel to disregard for social issues in a broad sense. The indifference of politics in all fields is negatively reflected upon the most vulnerable and marginal groups in society. For Francis an ecological approach becomes a social approach, hence "it must integrate questions of justice in debates on the environment, so as to hear *both the cry of the earth and the cry of the poor*."[11]

Concern expressed in this passage is generated by the awareness that very often the poor and the excluded, despite the fact that they are the majority of the world's population, are mentioned in international fora in a ritual manner, with no real commitment to act.

In the perspective to provide concrete approaches to worldwide problems, the semantic in *Laudato si'* is coherent with legal scholarship arguing for the

---

10. Francis, *Laudato Si'*, para. 196.
11. Francis, *Laudato Si'*, para. 49.

openness of legal systems and for enhancing communications among law and science.[12] Pope Francis looks at a "universe shaped by open and intercommunicating systems," which allows us to discern numerous "forms of relationship and participation."[13]

His message calls for transparency and efficiency in decision-making processes and, at the same time, acknowledges the limits of local authorities to intervene effectively. This is why the adoption of enforceable international agreements is recalled as an indication to states that should be facing their primary responsibilities.[14] The idea is that the openness of systems—to be interpreted as legal and political systems in constant communication to one another—brings about shared commitments, combined with powers to sanction all deviations from these compelling goals.

Further on, this passage is equally illuminating:

> The twenty-first century, while maintaining systems of governance inherited from the past, is witnessing a weakening of the power of nation states, chiefly because the economic and financial sectors, being transnational, tends to prevail over the political. Given this situation, it is essential to devise stronger and more efficiently organized international institutions, with functionaries who are appointed fairly by agreement among national governments, and empowered to impose sanctions.[15]

In the open public space portrayed by Frances in *Laudato si'* subsidiarity acquires a scope wider than a "social philosophy." It invigorates the church's social doctrine transferring to a transnational level the urgent demand for protection, coming from individuals who feel deprived and hopeless. One of the propositions is that civil society organizations should, at national and international levels, continue to act as intermediate aggregations ready to oppose excesses in centralization and to prevent negative interferences of the states. Even at this regard, the semantic adopted in the letter echoes notions of legal pluralism, which have expanded the field of analysis for scholarship interested in learning how law is produced beyond nation states, in a transnational dimension.[16]

---

12. See Habermas, *Between Facts and Norms*. More generally see also Sibley *Law and Science*

13. Para. 79.

14. Para. 173.

15. Para. 175.

16. An account in Maduro et al., Transnational Law.

From a historical perspective, see in particular the works of the continental thinkers Louis Salleron, Denis du Rougemont and Alexandre Marc, theorists of federalism,

Soon after the tragedy of the Second World War, drafters of the Italian Constitution interpreted the catholic social doctrine of subsidiarity as a powerful tool against oppressive regimes and as a mean to empower lower levels of the state and guarantee fundamental freedoms. Subsidiarity also acknowledged the innovative contribution of intermediary bodies, which best exploited the newly established democratic freedoms and flourished in a pluralist society.[17] The language of constitutional law, in Italy as in other Western European countries, absorbed the many notions of subsidiarity and adapted them to the peculiarities of state administrations and to the dynamic expansion of autonomous orders, in which both individual and collective interests should be heightened.

The tension in all such cases was between a state-centred constitutionalism and the empowerment of sub-systems, which were created as a result of individual freedoms. A similar tension can be perceived today if one looks at the dynamic interrelationship among national constitutions and international law. In all circumstances the main concern is for an effective guarantee of fundamental rights.

In the overall construction of the encyclical letter subsidiarity becomes a powerful reference to states as responsible actors in international law, when they exercise their powers to sanction illegal behaviours and when they select competent élites.[18] Such a reference can also be read as a parallel notion to pluralism, since it specifies that actions to be taken in the international scene are multiple and interdependent. Pope Francis recalls all objective responsibilities, in all places in which decisions are taken and results are foreseen. For all these implications, *Laudato si'* creates a space of continuity with messages of hope spread around the world by the Catholic Church.

---

subsidiarity and political pluralism, which played a leading role on the construction of European post-war institutions, e.g. Aron and Alexandre Marc, Principes du fédéralisme.

17. For example, Dossetti, Funzioni e ordinamento dello Stato moderno a paper presented in 1951 at a national meeting of the association of Italian catholic lawyers, now reprinted as Dossetti, "Non abbiate paura dello Stato!"

18. In contemporary legal theory these concepts have been developed, among others, by Benvenisti.

See Benvenisti "States as Trustees of Humanity," 295–33; and Benvenisti, *The Law of Global Governance*.

2. GOVERNANCE IN THE AFTERMATH OF THE ECONOMIC AND FINANCIAL CRISIS

I move now to analyse the consequences attached to institutional changes, which are meant to add new levels of decision-making and expand deliberative processes in the EU.

In the burst of the economic and financial crisis a very technical combination of norms was set up in order to foster economic governance. "Governance by numbers"[19] in some crucial passages of institutional developments within the EU, displaced all significant connections with occupational groups, putting solidarity at risk and diminishing the impact of consolidated social allegiances. Furthermore, an increased mobility of companies and the dislocation of workers across national frontiers may, in the long run, end up breaking all connections with territories and favour phenomena of social dumping.

This point is strictly related to issues of representation, especially for weaker and peripheral groups, the ones most severely hit by the crisis. Challenges to solidarity, a fundamental principle supporting the EU, lead to unintended outcomes. They affect individuals in their awareness of belonging to local communities and to associations; they confuse priorities and plans for life; they insinuate unnatural comparisons among clusters of people having in common low incomes and little hope to improve their living standards.

Such challenges to solidarity have been sidelined and possibly under evaluated when adopting measures to counterbalance the economic and financial crisis.

For example, in the framework of the so-called European Semester[20] the aim to coordinate national economic policies is presented as a precondition to launch growth and employment, as well as to simplify procedures on fiscal policies and put forward plans for the consolidation of public debt. In the original format of economic governance hinted in the European semester, no specific mention was made of representative groups, neither there were attempts to include them in the different stages in which the soundness of national economies was constantly and rigorously tested. The voice of groups at risk of marginalisation in national labour markets should have been heard and priorities should have been set, taking into account

---

19. Supiot, *Governance by Numbers*.

20. The European Semester was formalised through Regulation (EU) No 1175/2011 of the European Parliament and of the Council of 16 November 2011 [2011] OJ L306/12.

a fair balance between financial constraints and fundamental social rights brought forward by representative organizations.[21]

In providing financial assistance to countries put under pressure by the crisis—one paramount example is Greece—a legal mechanism was created whereby, in order to receive such an assistance, governments had to enter agreements, called Memoranda of Understanding, which imposed severe cuts on spending for social protection, pensions, salaries and health. This meant intervening in already weak and destabilised social contexts, imposing sacrifices on parts of the population which were poor and deprived of support for essential needs.

For all these reasons, it is of utmost importance to reflect on the consequences emerged in the aftermath of the economic and financial crisis, which hit the EU and the rest of the world. Austerity measures inflicted sacrifices on poor and marginal groups, in exchange for financial help, whenever situations of excessive deficits were ascertained. Memoranda of Understanding, subscribed by euro-area Member States with the European Commission, the European Central Bank and the International Monetary Fund, departed from a more traditional European method and introduced asymmetries,[22] which can only be corrected, prospectively, by way of renewed synergies towards reforms of the Treaties.

Theories on economic governance, displayed at an institutional and supranational level, were unproductive in such emergencies. However, intermediary bodies—unions and various other groups active in civil society—were proactive at national levels, in collecting demands coming from people deprived of essential social benefits and suffering for wage and pension cuts. They were also realistic in promoting strategic litigation, referring to international organisations different from the EU, in particular the Council of Europe and the International Labour Organisation.

During the crisis, the move towards a technocratic system of decision-making ended up weakening the role of organisations—such as those representing management and labour—which are indicated in the Treaty on the functioning of the European Union (TFEU) as the holders of a quasi-institutional role in law-making[23].

---

21. It is noteworthy that the European Council and the European Commission should reconsider this option and expand opportunities to include the social partners in discussions on economic governance. See European Commission, *A new start for social dialogue*.

22. See generally Baraggia, "Conditionality Measures in the Euro area crisis," 268-88.

23. Art. 152 TFEU enshrines the notion of social dialogue, to be considered original in a comparative perspective, since it empowers European level organizations

This is yet another sign of the dangers inherent in politics, when it disconnects from social spheres. The social doctrine of the church reminds us of the vital part assigned to intermediary bodies in support of individuals who try to overcome marginalisation and to emancipate from exclusion and poverty.

In Western European traditions solidarity has been shaped around collective interests interpreted by unions. Unions translate representation into enforceable rights and prepare the ground for standard-setting procedures, which are meant to protect weaker parties, promoting collective bargaining and enhancing consultation and participation. There are good reasons to believe that this practice is still relevant. Solidarity should be reinforced, among other means, by empowering representative groups and making them responsible for the enforcement of standards. Legitimacy in representation should be the outcome of democratic criteria set by states, either adopting ad hoc legislation or promoting concerted negotiations with the social partners.

Several Member States of the EU have chosen to go into this direction and to enforce democratic criteria of representation for the unions. The ultimate result of such choices is to strengthen European social partners' legitimacy and to consolidate their role as representatives of management and labour at the EU level. This double track of representation exemplifies the complexities of the interests at stake, which are inexorably national and transnational.

At an international level an interesting solution is the one adopted by the Council of Europe. The 1995 Protocol annexed to the European Social Charter (ESC) introduced procedures for collective complaints, empowering organizations—not individuals—to address a committee of independent experts. In order to lodge a complaint, organizations need to be "representative," in accordance to article 2.1 of the Protocol, and must show evidence of their competence in areas dealing with the social rights covered by the European Social Charter (ESC). The committee of experts has elaborated criteria of "representativeness," autonomous from the ones described at national levels. For example, for an organization complaining to have been denied the fundamental right to organize, the Committee looked not so much at the number of associated members, but rather to its "real, active and independent" role.[24] This pragmatic approach to collective representation has been helpful to national organizations active in countries

---

representing management and labour to participate in law-making processes on social matters. I have developed this analysis in Sciarra, *Solidarity and Conflict*.

24. Complaint no. 103/2013, points 13 and 14.

severely hit by austerity measures, the ones that chose to lodge complaints to the Committee of experts. The ESC and the 1995 Protocol on collective complaints in particular put them in the position to ascertain violations of fundamental social rights in international law, since the legal basis in EU law was uncertain.

The proclamation of the "European Pillar of Social Rights" goes into the direction of finding inspiration in other international law sources and giving new impetus to social rights, following the years of austerity.[25] The symbolism of the "pillar" suggests that construction, instead of destruction, is the pathway to follow in the EU.

3. WAGE POLICIES AND SOCIAL DUMPING

Challenges to solidarity are, at the same time, challenges to fundamental principles of international law, EU law and national constitutional law. The partial convergence of standards of protection is a sign of growing interconnection among legal systems. It generates multiple levels of enforceability for individual and collective rights.

Shortages in public finances and the urgency to adopt selective measures may, unless thoughtfully conceived, introduce unacceptable divides among groups of the population: younger workers counterweighted to older ones; men treated differently from women; holders of modest pensions opposed to low-income people. Such distortions should all be corrected: whenever the principle of equal treatment is attacked legal systems are shaken in their foundations.

Courts—and constitutional courts in particular—have been central in the burst of the economic and financial crisis in the EU, since most challenges to solidarity display constitutional implications. Hence, courts may acquire an activist role in setting the borders of solidarity, while taking into account financial constraints. The concept of "reasonable" legal measures inspires constitutional adjudication, whenever the principle of equal treatment is at stake. Principles are by no means weaker than rights in the harmonious construction of constitutional values.[26]

Constitutional courts, however, should not occupy the scene of the legislature and should wisely express their margin of appreciation, avoiding interferences with politics. They should be guardians of solidarity and constantly monitor that fundamental rights be respected. Judicial activism,

---

25 See http://www.consilium.europa.eu/en/press/press-releases/2017/11/17/european-pillar-of-social-rights-proclamation-and-signing/pdf/.

26. See Sciarra, *Solidarity and Conflict*, passim.

if taken to an extreme, is not a successful method to enhance solidarity. The way for constitutional courts to acquire reputation is to act independently from politics in adjudicating on fundamental rights and in interpreting international and EU standards.

One very sensitive subject matter is related to wage policies. The ILO Global wage report contributes to the UN 2030 Agenda for sustainable development and is a remarkable resource to understand how wage inequalities—both within companies and among companies—are at the origin of broader inequalities in societies.[27] Furthermore, wages are at the centre of regime competition, when companies move to countries with a lower labour cost and even when they move temporarily across frontiers, for the provision of services.

In countries where collective bargaining, with or without the support of the law, is a widespread practice, wage policies are better monitored and still portray forms of occupational solidarities. However, wage cuts have been proposed and enacted in several EU countries as part of austerity measures, with special emphasis on the public sector. These issues have been under the lenses of constitutional courts because they may collide with equal treatment or even with the fundamental right to dignity. It is not a coincidence that the abovementioned European Pillar of social rights should indicate the right to fair wages: dignity is translated into a decent standard of living for individuals and for their families.[28]

Wage inequalities are reported in the EU and are an obstacle to transnational solidarity. In the Baltic countries, where a very high proportion of people are at risk of poverty and social exclusion, a significant wage gap has been measured with the neighbouring countries of Northern Europe. Precisely in this part of the EU wage dumping is recurring, for companies crossing the frontiers on temporary provisions of services. This practice has implications on sustainable development, because it insinuates differential treatments as a result of a legitimate mobility of workers within the European single market. It is a paradox that dignity should be detached from freedom to move, when it comes to paying fair wages.

At the origin of conflicting standards of sustainability—national and sub-national, national and transnational, regional and international—one can see an unsolved dilemma among "hybrid norms." Sustainable development is spreading well beyond environmental issues and includes all social areas in which individuals are exposed to uncontrolled economic strategies.

27. The latest Global wage report 2016/2017 IS available at http://www.ilo.org/global/research/global-reports/global-wage-report/2016/lang—en/index.htm. Useful information in Lübker and Schulten, "Price inflation."

28. At point 6.

This is why fundamental rights are recurrently treated as human rights and attracted into the widest possible area of protection. They represent, together with popular sovereignty "the two normative perspectives from which an enacted, changeable law is supposed to be legitimated as a means to secure both the private and civic autonomy of the individual."[29]

The fundamental right to dignity is a good example of how to combine multiple levels of protection enhancing transnational regimes of solidarity and making them converge towards common standards. Decent wages are a significant paradigm of how pluralism of legal and autonomous sources—for example autonomous systems of collective bargaining—are projected towards the enactment of positive rights and the consolidation of fair standards. Once more, pluralism stands as a resource parallel to subsidiarity and favours the combination of policies based on the legitimacy of those who pursue them.

4. CONCLUDING REMARKS: FOR A SUSTAINABLE GOVERNANCE IN THE EU

I have highlighted two systems of representation, which should be vehicles of solidarity. On the one hand there is space for groups rooted in civil society, holders of collective interests, responsible for the enforcement of standards. They must qualify as representative groups, in order to prevent inequalities and enhance fairness and justice. On the other hand states and supranational institutions should translate solidarity into binding norms, establish the right priorities, select the relevant measures to be adopted and provide support to the ones most in need. Within the EU states are responsible for the enforcement of European law. At an international level they must respect international standards and be accountable for the protection of human rights.

The accent put in *Laudato si'* on states' primary responsibilities for the enforcement of fundamental human rights is in line with directions impressed by international organizations—which also recall private actors' responsibilities, those of multinational companies in particular[30]—and by international courts. Networks of solidarity should emerge through

---

29. Habermas, *The Postnational Constellation*, 116.

30. For example in the UN Report of the Special Representative of the Secretary-General on the issue of human rights and transnational corporations and other business enterprises, Ruggie"Protect, Respect and Remedy";

in as well as the 2011 Guiding Principles on Business and Human Rights Implementing the United Nations "Protect, Respect and Remedy" Framework.

democratic processes and be the outcome of real and concrete interests in society, which are transposed to an international scenario.

In legal theory emphasis has been put on the multitude of "societal orders," which are autonomous from central welfare states and even self-determined in modelling their own constitutional ground. Hence, the vision of "multilateral constitutionalism" has been suggested: it respects the specific features of the places in which rights will be enforced and justice will be made.[31] The peculiarities of different orders should make marginal groups perceive—more than it now happens—the vicinity of EU institutions and should enable them to find access to international organizations and claim for their rights.

The reference made in my opening remarks to the principle of subsidiarity comes back in its essential feature and so does the call for pluralism, in its manifold significances. Pluralism of legal sources is a tool to strengthen all actors involved in normative processes. It is essential to construct the widest possible notion of sustainability, inclusive of social policies addressed to the most vulnerable in society.

At the periphery of supranational legal systems, we find some answers to all challenges that austerity measures have raised, whenever the excluded and the ones at risk of poverty felt abandoned. Peripheries can be found in lower levels of state administrations, in local communities populated by non-state actors and by organizations representing those most in need of support.[32] A critical review should imply an *ex ante* evaluation of the economic and social grounds in which the addressees of austerity legislation are located. The implication of this methodology should be that some minimum standards of welfare and social protection be considered untouchable. Respect for human rights should create a barrier against the incursion of legislators who have not previously balanced economic and financial measures against the essential needs of the weakest.

BIBLIOGRAPHY

Aron, Robert, and Alexandre Marc, *Principes du fédéralisme*. Paris: Le Portulan, 1947.
Baraggia, Antonia. "Conditionality Measures in the Euro Area Crisis: A Challenge to the Democratic Principle?" *Cambridge Journal of International and Comparative Law* 4 (2015) 268–88.

---

31. Teubner, *Constitutional Fragments*. See also Teubner, "Transnational Economic Constitutionalism."

32. Teubner, *Constitutional Fragments*, 88–102. See also Teubner, "Global Private Regimes," 71–87.

Benvenisti, Eyal. "States as Trustees of Humanity: On the Accountability of States to Foreign Stakeholders." *American Journal of International Law* 107 (2013) 295–33.

Benvenisti, Eyal. *The Law of Global Governance*. Leiden: Brill-Nijhoff, 2014.

Cohen, Joshua, and Charles Sabel. "Directly-Deliberative Polyarchy." *European Law Journal* 3 (1997) 313–42.

De Schutter, Olivier, et al. *Governance in the European Union*. Luxembourg: Office for Official Publications of the European Communities, 2001.

Dossetti, Giuseppe. *'Non abbiate paura dello Stato!'* Milan: Vita e Pensiero, 2014.

European Commission. *A New Start for Social Dialogue*. Luxembourg, 2016.

Francis I, Pope. *Laudato Si'*. Rome: Vatican Press, 2015.

Habermas, Jürgen. *Between Facts and Norms: Contributions to a Discourse Theory of Law and Democracy*. Translated by William Rehg. Studies in Contemporary German Social Thought. Cambridge: MIT Press, 1996.

———. *The Postnational Constellation: Political Essays*. Translated, edited, and with an introduction by Max Pensky. Studies in Contemporary German Social Thought. Cambridge, MA: Polity Press, 2001.

Joerges, Christian, Kjaer, Poul Fritz, and Tommi Ralli. "A New Type of Conflicts Law as Constitutional Form in the Postnational Constellation." *Transnational Legal Theory* 2 (2011): 153–65.

Joerges, Poul F. Kjaer, and Tommi Ralli. "A New Type of Conflicts Law as Constitutional Form in the Postnational Constellation." *Transnational Legal Theory* 2 (2011) 153–65.

Lübker, Malte and Thorsten Schulten, "Price Inflation Suppresses Real Minimum Wage Growth." *WSI Minimum Wage Report* 39 (2018). https://www.boeckler.de/pdf/p_wsi_report_39e_2018.pdf.

Maduro, Miguel et al., eds. *Transnational Law: Rethinking European Law and Legal Thinking*. Cambridge: Cambridge University Press, 2014.

Ruggie, John. "Protect, Respect and Remedy: A Framework for Business and Human Rights." A/HRC/8/5, 7 April 2008.

Sciarra, Silvana. *Solidarity and Conflict: European Social Law in Crisis*. Cambridge: Cambridge University Press, 2018.

Sibley, Susan S., *Law and Science: Epistemological, Evidentiary, and Relational Engagements and Regulation of Property, Practices, and Products*. Aldershot, UK: Routledge, 2008.

Supiot, Alain. *Governance by Numbers. The Making of a Legal Model of Allegiance*. Hart Studies in Comparative Public Law 20. Oxford: Hart, 2017.

Teubner, Gunther. *Constitutional Fragments. Societal Constitutionalism and Globalisation*. Oxford: Oxford University Press, 2012.

———. "Global Private Regimes: Neo-spontaneous Law and Dual Constitution of Autonomous Sectors in World Society?" In *Globalization and Public Governance*, edited by K.-H. Ladeur, 71–87. Aldershot, UK: Ashgate, 2004.

———. "Transnational Economic Constitutionalism in the Varieties of Capitalism." *Italian Law Journal* 1 (2015) 219–48.

Unione giuristi cattolici italiani. *Funzioni e ordinamento dello Stato moderno*. Quaderni di "Iustitia" 2. Rome: Studium, 1953.

United Nations, *Transforming Our World: The 2030 Agenda for Sustainable Development* (2015). https://sustainabledevelopment.un.org/content/documents/21252030%20Agenda%20for%20Sustainable%20Development%20web.pdf .

Zürn, Michael, and Christian Joerges. *Law and Governance in Postnational Europe: Compliance beyond the Nation-State*. Themes in European Governance. Cambridge: Cambridge University Press, 2005.

5

Promoting Sustainable Integral Human Development and Rural Poverty Reduction in Developing Countries through Bottom-Up Approaches and Grassroots Institutional Building[1]

Monica Romano

The new Agenda 2030 for Sustainable Development,[2] specifically the Sustainable Development Goal (SDG) 16, calls for building effective, accountable, inclusive and transparent institutions at all levels as a means to achieve sustainable development and peace.[3] Well-functioning institutions are critical to building peaceful, just and inclusive societies that provide equal access to justice and are based on respect for human rights, effective rule of law and good governance.[4] From national to local level, institutions play an important role in fostering inclusive development, delivering public services, and enhancing governance and people's participation in decision-making and development processes. By promoting the principles of solidarity and subsidiarity, encouraging political participation, and valuing civil society, the Social Doctrine of the church also recognizes the importance of institutions

---

1. The views expressed in this paper are those of the author only and do not necessarily represent any of the institutions mentioned.

2. The 2030 Agenda for Sustainable Development is a plan of action unanimously adopted by the 193 Member States of the United Nations in September 2015. It comprises 17 Sustainable Development Goals (SDGs) and 169 targets to be achieved during a 15-year timeframe (2016–30); http://www.un.org/ga/search/view_doc.asp?symbol=A/RES/70/1&Lang=E

3. UN, *Transforming our World.* 9, 25, 26.

4. UN, *Transforming our World.*

(including small, local entities) in developing "the social dimension of the person," "exercising personal rights," and bringing about "a qualitative enrichment of democratic life."[5] Inclusive and well-governed institutions can therefore be conducive to "integral human development," a concept dating back to 1967 with the publication of Paul VI's encyclical letter *Populorum Progressio*. At that time, the Pope challenged the dominant paradigm of development as equivalent to economic growth and introduced a holistic concept whereby authentic development is "the development of each man and of the whole man."[6] Later on, the "human development approach," which was proposed in the 1990s by the United Nations Development Programme (UNDP) and is now widely accepted by the international community, also argued for a new definition and measurement of development, centered on people, viewed as improvement of people's wellbeing, opportunities and choices, with income growth being a means, rather than an end in itself.[7]

But what is meant by "institution"?[8] According to North,[9] "institution" is a broad and multi-faceted term encompassing a range of formal regulatory frameworks (e.g. laws, constitutions, policies, rules...), which are "humanly devised" or "explicitly and intentionally created"[10] and enforced by official authorities, and informal norms or socially prescribed or proscribed patterns of behavior (beliefs, customs, traditions, mind-sets, worldviews, values, practices...), which "are part of the heritage that we call culture,"[11] are tacitly accepted, and whose underlying assumptions are generally ignored or not questioned. Formal and informal institutions are "constraints" (North) and "systems of established and prevalent social rules" (Hodgson)[12] that shape human and organizational action and social interactions; determine people's access to resources, opportunities, livelihoods, as well as their participation in decision-making and political processes (hence power relations and people's inclusion/exclusion); and serve collective valued purposes. North also distinguishes between institutions as the "rules of the

---

5. Pontifical Council for Justice and Peace, "Compendium of the Social Doctrine of the Church."

6. Jean Paul II, "Populorum Progressio," n. 14.

7. United Nations Development Programme, "About Human Development."

8. There is a rich literature on the concept and definition of "institutions." The paper only provides an overview of some insights from the literature, without attempting to be exhaustive. Please refer to the bibliography for more information through some specific publications on the topic.

9. North, *Institutions, Institutional Change and Economic Performance*.

10. Avner and Kingston, "Institutions: Rules or Equilibria?," 15.

11. North, *Institutions*, 37.

12. Hodgson, "What Are Institutions?," 2.

game," defining how the game is played, and organizations as the "players of the game," consisting of "groups of individuals bound together by some common purpose to achieve certain objectives."[13] Organizations, however, can also be considered as "special institutions," with their own players and rules of the game, so that they can provide institutional rules for individuals or act within the broader institutional framework.[14] Like institutions, organizations can also be formal and informal.[15]

Institutions may include customary norms and religious beliefs and practices, marriage, influencing, for example, gender-differentiated systems, behaviors, access to assets and resources. According to the Compendium of Social Doctrine of the church, institutions, represented by laws, customary norms and civil constructs, have the "capacity to influence and condition the choices of many people over a long period of time."[16] Organizations are entities, structures, associations that are formed and act under the given institutional framework, implement the rules or exercise power, and advance the interests of their members. According to Hodgson, organizations are special institutions with clear boundaries, distinction between members and non-members, and definition of leadership and responsibilities.[17] Organizations can be categorized as public (e.g. ministries, government departments, schools, hospitals), private (e.g. commercial firms), and civil society (such as member-based associations, cooperatives, trade unions, political movements, NGOs). They can be established and operate at various levels—macro (national, regional, international, such as ministries or multilateral or bilateral or regional organizations), meso (sub-national, provincial, district levels), and micro (local or village, such as community-based or grass root organizations or village committees, which often have an informal status).[18]

The Compendium refers to a wide range of organizations, mostly of associative nature or belonging to civil society, such as volunteer groups, cooperatives, unions, community and local self-government entities, "territorial realities," "smaller" or "intermediate" social units, often emerging from the creativity of citizens and having "something original to offer to the

---

13. North, "Economic Performance through Time," 361.

14. Hodgson, "What Are Institutions?" 10.

15. This paper does not necessarily apply the distinction between "institution" and "organization" and may use the term "institution" also to refer to "organization."

16. Pontifical Council for Justice and Peace, "Compendium of the Social Doctrine of the Church," n. 163.

17. Hodgson, "What Are Institutions?" 18.

18. Lobo, "Institutional and Organizational Analysis for Pro-poor Change: Meeting IFAD's Millennium Challenge."

community."[19] Based on the principle of subsidiarity, introduced by Pope Pius XI in the encyclical letter *Quadragesimo Anno* (1931), the State or larger and more complex organizations, whenever possible, should transfer decision-making powers, functions, and responsibilities to the lowest or smallest levels, while providing them with "economic, institutional or juridical assistance" (*subsidium*).[20] Experience emerging from development and poverty reduction programs confirms that involving institutions that are closer to the beneficiaries can enhance beneficiary participation in project activities and the likelihood that their priorities are taken into consideration and project benefits accrue to them.[21] Even when these institutions are not well managed and have governance issues, they often tend to represent their membership's interests better than any other entity.[22] Working through local smallholder institutions is also instrumental to reducing delays and avoiding cumbersome processes (e.g. for approvals, fund transfers, procurement of goods and services) often associated to centralized or larger public entities.

The Compendium also highlights that groups, associations, and local organizations constitute a "network of relationships," an "aggregate of economic, social, cultural, sports-oriented, recreational, professional and political expressions to which people spontaneously give life and which make it possible for them to achieve effective social growth."[23] In the past few decades, development discourse has increasingly recognized the important role of institutions, particularly smallholder institutions at the grassroots and community level, in reducing poverty and fostering development. Experience has shown that poverty, especially in rural contexts where most of the poor live, rather than being (only) an issue of scarcity of resources (lack of food, land, water. . .) or of low income is often the result of institutional factors that undermine the ability of poor people (especially the most vulnerable groups such as women, youth, indigenous communities and ethnic minority groups) to access assets, services, resources, and opportunities, and to make or influence decisions that affect their lives.[24] Poverty is, also, vulnerability, exclusion, and powerlessness.[25] Poor rural people, primar-

19. Pontifical Council for Justice and Peace, "Compendium of the Social Doctrine of the Church," no. 185, 187.

20. Pontifical Council for Justice and Peace, "Compendium of the Social Doctrine of the Church," no. 186.

21. Bamberger et al., *"The Design and Management,"* 150.

22. IFAD, "Rural Poverty Report 2011," 226.

23. Pontifical Council for Justice and Peace, "Compendium of the Social Doctrine of the Church," no. 185.

24. Lobo, *Institutional and Organizational Analysis*, 13, 17, 18.

25. IFAD, "Transforming Rural Institutions," 3.

ily found among smallholder farmers, fishers, livestock keepers and pastoralists, and forest users, often live in marginalized, fragile, and geographically dispersed areas. They face considerable constraints in accessing timely and quality inputs; productive assets, primarily land, due to insecurity of tenure and limited rights; training opportunities and rural advisory services; and secure and profitable markets for their produce. Although smallholder producers and family farmers produce most of the food, they are voiceless in decision-making and policy processes. Grass root, community-level and membership-based organizations can mediate poor people's access to opportunities and resources, represent their voice and interests in decision-making and development processes, and influence formal and informal institutions and policy, thus tackling the root causes of poverty. However, developing countries, especially rural areas, are often characterized by a weak institutional environment. Poor rural communities often have limited organizational capacity and their institutions are characterized by poor management and governance mechanisms, have limited financial and skilled human resources, may not be fully accountable and representative of their communities or membership base, and may not always be inclusive. It is, therefore, necessary to invest in strengthening the individual and collective capabilities of poor rural people so that their institutions can achieve "effectiveness, inclusiveness, and accountability"(SDG 16) and "responsive, inclusive, participatory and representative decision-making at all levels" (target 16.7).[26] Smallholder institutions also need to be provided with support and capacity building to aggregate and federate at meso and macro levels to pool together resources, achieve economies of scale, and reduce transaction costs; gain voice and representation to establish dialogue with government, private sector, civil society, and donor community; forge partnerships and alliances; raise funds; and influence policy for pro-poor change.[27] Achieving grass root organizational development and institutional transformation is a long, complex, time-consuming and often sensitive process, which can lead to poverty reduction[28]. It can also contribute to make development interventions more relevant and inclusive; ensure a higher degree of ownership among target communities; and enhance the likelihood of sustainability.

As mentioned, poor rural communities are often marginalized and poorly organized. However, in every village, one could find some community institution or group, even small in size, not fully active, of informal

---

26. Lobo, *Institutional and Organizational Analysis*, 18.
27. Lobo, *Institutional and Organizational Analysis*, 34.
28. IFAD, *Transforming Rural Institutions*, 16.

nature. There is a wide range of smallholder rural organizations that could be found at the community or grass roots level, often formed around a common interest, of economic or social type, mostly being membership-based and having an informal status. These include: village level institutions for local governance and development (such as local or village councils and development committees); activity-based organizations for production and/or marketing of a given commodity (e.g. farmer groups and associations, agricultural and rural cooperatives, pastoral and small-scale fisher organizations); community-based financial organizations (e.g. self-help groups, saving and credit associations, village banks, etc.); and organizations to manage water or common land or rural infrastructure facilities (e.g. water user groups and associations, forestry groups, road maintenance groups...). When adequately supported and capacitated, these organizations have proven to be powerful platforms of aggregation and collective action of poor people, smallholder producers, marginalized groups, mediating for their members' access to inputs, services, productive assets, and markets; ensuring a better and sustainable management of common natural and productive assets; facilitating the provision of more relevant and responsive public agricultural research and rural advisory services; establishing more transparent, accountable, and participatory governance mechanisms as well as planning and development processes; exercising pro-poor policy influence at national and regional levels; and bringing about institutional and social transformation.

AFFINITY-BASED AND MICRO-FINANCE GRASS ROOT INSTITUTIONS

Saving and Credit Groups (SCGs) are small-scale community-managed financial institutions that have been in existence for long time and are found almost everywhere in the world. The primary purpose of SCGs is providing simple savings and loan facilities under low transaction costs to communities or people with poor asset base, who have no access to formal financial services. These groups can be called differently—such as, in Africa, rotating savings and credit associations (ROSCAs), village savings and loan associations (VSLAs), accumulating saving and credit associations (ASCAs), (rural) savings and credit cooperatives (RU)SACCOs), and—mostly in India and South/South-East Asia—self-help groups (SHGs). The main commonalities of SCGs are that they are generally simple, self-governed, member-based, voluntary and transparent institutions whereby members pool individual savings through regular cyclical contributions and rotate a common fund for internal lending. The loans are generally of a short duration and used to start up individual or joint income generating activities and enterprises, or to meet the members' daily needs or emergencies. After taking the loan, the member then pays back the amount in regular contributions with an interest rate and service charge that is set by the group. Like most of the other grass root organizations, SCGs generally entail that members elect their leaders and determine the group policies, regulations, and operating procedures.

In India, the SHGs model was introduced in mid-1980s by MYRADA, a local NGO, which piloted a program to enhance access to financial services for the poor. This approach went far beyond the provision of credit and became a powerful social, economic, and political empowerment movement for poor women and a catalyst of institutional change within villages and communities. A SHG consists of 10–20 women from the same village, with similar social and economic conditions. Group members self-select themselves based on affinity, proximity, and common interest, and make decisions collectively. The women agree to regularly make savings and contribute to a group fund, from which they start to borrow on a rotational basis, without collateral, after some capital is accumulated, paying back with a small interest. Women can use the loan for emergency needs or to make an investment to start an income-generating activity or a micro-enterprise—on individual basis or collectively. It is important for group success and continuity that it is cohesive and enforces strict rules (regular savings and timely repayments; regular meetings and compulsory attendance; rotation in leadership). Through the SHG Bank Linkage Programme (SBLP),[29] SHGs with a track record of regular, well-managed resources can access formal credit through linkages with banks or other formal financial institutions. As of 2014, over 4 million SHGs had outstanding loans and over 7.4 million savings accounts with banks under the SBLP.[30]

By participating in the SHG and strengthened by the mutual solidarity, women build their self-confidence, share their common concerns and interests, and develop skills to manage their savings and credit, become microentrepreneurs and earn their livelihoods on a sustainable basis. SHGs also become catalysts of change within their communities, actively participating in or contributing to village development interventions (e.g. for building or rehabilitating community infrastructure and other facilities, change laws, etc.), or taking up collective action to address social issues such as sanitation,

---

29. It was a program launched in the 1990s by the National Bank for Agriculture and Rural Development (NABARD) to link the informal financial institutions with the formal banking sector. For information on NABARD please visit www.nabard.org.

30. Sharma and Chatterjee, "Revitalizing the Self-Help Group Movement in India."

alcoholism, domestic violence, gender inequality, child marriage or the dowry system. It is not rare that SHG members are even elected in local village committee and *Gram Panchayat*.[31] Although there are challenges associated to group sustainability, mainly due to low literacy rate of women members and poor financial management, requiring long-term external support to the groups before they graduate into self-sustaining institutions, the SHG approach has proven to be an important tool for poverty reduction and empowerment of marginalized women, tribal communities, and scheduled castes. It was adopted by the Government of India and scaled up in a number of national and donor-supported programs.[32] Today, there are about 4 million SHGs in India, with 70 million members and over 300 million people indirectly involved.[33] Some SHGs started to aggregate and federate at cluster or village level, block or sub-district level, and at district level to provide support and services to the SHGs to enhance the likelihood of sustainability of the groups. The various services that are generally provided by federations to member SHGs include provision of credit and other financial products; auditing and financial management; training and capacity building; group performance monitoring; facilitation in establishing linkages with banks; input supply and bulk purchases; business plan preparation and marketing services; and social support to address issues such as child marriage, domestic violence, gender and social discriminations as well as to promote development initiatives (drinking water, health, etc.).[34]

In 2005, in Mali, Oxfam America started to support Saving for Change (SfC) groups of women, with similar features as the SHGs (regular savings, internal lending with a small interest rate and no collateral, and management of a common fund).[35] When group members decide, often in times of high expenditures (such as festivals or the planting season), the resources from the funds are shared among the members based on the individual savings. Each member is generally able to obtain an annual return on savings of at least 30 percent. According to data from OXFAM America, as of April 2013, the program supported 18,804 SfC groups in Mali, with total 423,654 members. An evaluation study carried out by the Bureau of Applied Research in Anthropology, University of Arizona, and Innovations for Poverty Action[36]

31. The *Gram Panchayat* or Village Council is the lowest-level local government institution in India.

32. Ravi, "The Growth of Self Help Groups in India: A Study," 168.

33 Prayer, "IFAD's Experience with Rural Finance and Self-Help Groups in Asia."

34. Salomo et al., "A Study of SHG Federation Structures in India," 8–25.

35. Innovations for Poverty Action, "Evaluating the Saving for Change Program in Mali."

36. University of Arizona, "Final Impact."

found out that SfC groups had a positive impact on poor people's asset building (financial assets and livestock) and on improving food security. Specifically, the SfC groups contributed to a 31 percent increase in savings, 12 percent increase in the amount of money borrowed from savings groups by women in SfC villages, and 13 percent increase households' livestock holdings.[37] Additionally, households in villages with SfC groups were 10 percent less likely to be chronically food insecure and all of those accessing loans from SfC groups indicated to have become more resilient. Women also believed that the solidarity and social ties have been strengthened by participating in SfC groups. However, the study found weak and limited evidence of SfC's contribution to increased income, agricultural inputs or assets, health and education expenditures, or business development and expansion. There are also divergent findings on SfC's impact on social capital and intra-household decision-making.

ACTIVITY- OR COMMODITY-BASED GRASS ROOTS INSTITUTIONS

It is well known that smallholder producers have limited access to inputs, technologies, credit, information, training, and marketing facilities, which severely constrains their ability to produce in quality and quantity and to market their produce. Smallholder producers are often unable to adequately respond to a growing demand for consistent and regular agricultural supply with stringent quality and safety standards required by more sophisticated consumers and modernized retail markets. Unless small producers are organized, it is challenging to address power asymmetries with other stakeholders in the value chains (e.g. traders, middlemen, private entities) and to access market information. Organizing producers into associations or cooperatives can be an effective tool to overcoming these challenges. Producer organizations can help members take advantage of economies of scale while reducing risks and transaction costs; provide credit, inputs and services; organize bulk marketing of produce and enhance the producers' bargaining power in the market place; and represent their members' interests in policy processes.

In Sao Tome e Principe, the Participatory Smallholder Agriculture and Artisanal Fisheries Development Programme (PAPAFPA), funded by the International Fund for Agricultural Development (IFAD) and implemented during 2003–2015, facilitated the organization of cocoa and coffee producers into cooperatives and the establishment of partnership arrangements

---

37. University of Arizona, "Final Impact," 13.

with the private sector. According to IFAD,[38] before the project started, about 700 farmers were producing and locally trading only 50 MT tons of cocoa beans. To enhance cocoa production, the cooperative engaged in partnership with KAOKA (a French company), which imports organic cocoa, and Cafédirect (a UK company), which imports Fairtrade certified cocoa. KAOKA provided technical assistance to farmers on how to produce, process, dry, and pack cocoa beans for export markets. It purchased all certified organic cocoa directly from farmers' associations through their cooperative (the Export Co-op for Organic Cocoa—CECAB) and financed the organic cocoa certification process through the certification company ECOCERT. As of 2013, CECAB had 1,800 members, generating revenues of approximately USD 1.40 million. It rehabilitated 690 hectares of cocoa tree land and grafted 40,000 cocoa trees. Cafédirect buyed Fairtrade certified cocoa directly from farmers' associations through their cooperative (CECAQ-11), which is made up of 17 farmers organizations representing 830 smallholders, 290 of whom are women. Cultivating 840 hectares of cocoa trees, in 2011 the cooperative nearly produced and exported 90 tons of high-quality certified cocoa, ten times more than in 2009. Government also had a role to play, including provision of technical assistance to organize farmers through local service providers; building infrastructure and facilities, such as roads, warehouses, drinking water systems, solar panels, and cocoa nurseries; ensuring access to inputs (seedlings, fertilizers, tools for tree maintenance and equipment) and credit to producers; and supporting CECAB in cocoa tree rehabilitation. In addition to its financial contribution, IFAD provided supervision and implementation support to the project, supported farmer associations, and acting as broker between the government, private partners, and farmer' cooperatives. As of 2013, nearly 2,200 farmers were growing cocoa certified as organic or Fairtrade for the international chocolate industry, and due to the average increase in annual income, those living below the poverty line were reduced from 25 to 8 percent.[39] About 8,000 people have directly or indirectly benefited from the creation of new jobs.

The Amul dairy cattle model[40] consists of a three-tier cooperative structure under which a dairy cooperative society at the village level is federated under a milk union at the district level, which in turn is aggregated into a milk federation at the state level. The village dairy cooperative society

38. IFAD, "Small-scale Producers."

39. The *Gram Panchayat* or Village Council is the lowest level of institution of local government in India.

40. See: Amul, "About Us—The Amul Model" and Amuldairy.

is formed by small milk producers, who can become members by buying a share and committing to sell milk only to the society. Each village cooperative has a milk collection center where every day milk is taken by each member and tested for quality, which is the basis of payment. At the end of each year, from the profit generated by the cooperative, each member is given a bonus based on the quantity of milk poured. At the district level, a union of village cooperative societies is formed and owned by them. The union provides inputs and services to village-level cooperative societies, such as feed, veterinary care, artificial insemination; organizes training to cooperative members and leaders; buys milk from village-level cooperatives; and processes milk and milk-derived products. Milk and related products are then marketed by the state-level apex body, the *Gujarat Cooperative Milk Marketing Federation (GCMMF)*. The model has then cut out middlemen for procuring and selling milk, so that the benefits accrue directly to the primary producers. The main feature of this model is that the milk producers control all stages of production, processing and marketing of milk and milk products. They collectively manage the entire cooperative structure to ensure that the higher-tier organizations serve the purpose of the lower levels and that the gains flow back to the milk producers. GCMMF has an annual turnover (2016–17) US$ 4.1 billion. *Its daily milk procurement is about 18 million litres per day from 3.6 million milk producer members organized in 18,549 village milk cooperative societies and 18 member unions covering 33 districts.*

The Kenya National Farmers' Federation (KENAFF)[41] is a non-political, non profit, democratic, membership-based, registered organization of 2 million Kenyan farmers. It is an umbrella organization or apex body comprising farmer associations from the grass root to the national level. Formed in 1946, initially it used to represent only the interests of large-scale farmers. The federation went through a process of institutional and structural transformation, becoming more inclusive, opening up membership to smallholder farmers (who now constitute the majority), and improving its services.[42] According to KENAFF website, membership consists of *10,868* farmer groups or associations in 44 counties, 51 cooperative societies, 38 commodity associations, and 7 farming companies, for over 550,700 farming families. The federation has been active to enhance farmers' voice, articulating issues affecting them through lobby and advocacy, identifying research issues and preparing studies, and organizing dialogue platforms

---

41. The federation changed name from Kenya National Farmers' Union (KNFU), when it was created in 1946, to Kenya National Federation of Agricultural Producers (KENFAP), in November 2003, and now to KENAFF starting from August 2012. http://www.kenaff.org/node/5.

42. See: ESFIM and KENAFF.

for policy change. For example, with support from the Empowering Smallholder Farmers in Markets (ESFIM) program,[43] the federation made a critical assessment of government interventions in input and output markets under the National Agricultural Accelerated Input Access Programme (NAAIAP), particularly assessing the use of a voucher system for subsided maize seed and fertilizer put in place by NAAIAP and its impact on yield and on farmer income.[44] Based on the findings from this study, the federation proposed changes to the NAAIAP policy through the preparation of a memorandum to the Government on food insecurity. The federation also sought to strengthen mechanisms to improve smallholder produce marketing through the use of the warehouse receipt system and contract farming.

The Pacific Organic and Ethical Trade Community[45] (POETCom) is a regional membership movement of small-scale producers whose secretariat is housed at the Pacific Community (SPC) in Suva (Fiji), a regional technical and development organization.[46] The organization now has 44 members in 17 Pacific Countries. Although farmers in the Pacific have been using organic farming methods for centuries, strict international requirements for organic products often prevent them from exporting their produce, hence benefit from profitable overseas markets.[47]

POETCom has developed and facilitated access to sound and recognized organic certification systems that are affordable and appropriate to small organic producers.[48] Through support from IFAD, POETCom has developed the Pacific Organic Guarantee Scheme, which recognizes group certification through internal control systems for certification to regulated export markets, and also Participatory Guarantee Systems for local and regional markets. Since 2014, POETCom has signed agreements with three internationally accredited certifying bodies to create the Pacific Organic Standard (POS). By meeting this standard, smallholders have access to

---

43. ESFIM (www.esfim.org) is co-funded by IFAD, the European Alliance on Agricultural Knowledge for Development European Economic Interest Grouping (AGRINATURA-EEIG), the Dutch Ministry of Economy, Agriculture and Innovation, Agriterra and CTA—the ACP-EU Technical Centre for Agricultural and Rural Cooperation.

44. *Linking Research to Advocacy in Farmers' Organizations: Building on Country Experiences*, Side event organized by AgriNatura and the ESFIM project in the context of the Farmers' Forum held in conjunction with the thirty-fifth session of IFAD's Governing Council (23 February 2012), https://www.ifad.org/documents/10180/535b2f9f-8532-49d0-b89e-8735e4b6aa0c.

45. See POETCom Secretariat Update.

46. See: Pacific Community.

47. See FIDA, "Organics offer."

48. Hazelman, "PGS, "May," Toolkit for building organic," 4.

high-value niche markets and premium price and increased their incomes. By 2015, 19,000 smallholder farmers had gained certification and 70,000 hectares of lands were put under organic production.

It has been increasingly recognized that top-down centrally administered approaches to common property resource management have often been disappointing, hence the progressive transfer of management of common land, water, forest, and fishery resources to local communities and their institutions on the part of governments, through support of the donor community.[49] While the experience shows that local communities and community-based natural resource management organizations tend to manage common resource better, there are still considerable challenges to accomplish this in an effective, inclusive, and sustainable manner. Some of the factors may include the incomplete transfer of power to the local level institutions; lack of inclusive, representative, accountable, and well governed and managed institutions; risk of elite capture and conflict; and a non-conducive policy environment.[50]

In the 1990s in Morocco, more than 12 per cent of rangelands were degraded, putting at risk the livelihoods of millions of pastoral households if the trend was not to be reversed. It was in this context that an IFAD-supported project in the Eastern part of the country developed successfully a community-based rangeland management approach in an area covering four communes with 3 million hectares and a population of about 58,000 people.[51] The project facilitated the re-organization of tribal institutions into 44 pastoral management cooperatives of 9,000 households. Members were required to purchase "social shares" to access cooperative's health and veterinary services and improved pastures. The model also envisaged the implementation of a new and flexible livestock management system to support pastoralist mobility. As a result of this community-based management approach, rangelands considerably improved, with positive impact also on the environment, nomadic pastoral systems, and animal health. The model was adopted by Government of Morocco for all rangeland development initiatives and was replicated in other countries in the region.

In Nepal, leasehold forestry was introduced as a new kind of property rights regime over 20 years ago, with the aim of regenerating degraded forest land while alleviating rural poverty. Between 1978 and 1994, forest area decreased at an annual rate of 1.7 per cent and from 1964 to 1991,

---

49. Lee and Neves, "Rural Poverty"

50. IFAD, "How to Strengthen Community-based Natural Resource Management Organizations," 2.

51. IFAD, "Rural Poverty Report," 93.

570,000 hectares of forest were lost.[52] Under the leasehold forestry management system, small plots (4–10 ha) of degraded state forestland are handed over by Government on 40-year lease to very poor and/or socially excluded households forming leasehold forest user groups (LFUGs), usually made up of 7–15 members.[53] Several programs have been supporting this approach, including IFAD and the Food and Agriculture Organization (FAO) of the United Nations.[54] As of 2015, there were about 7,000 LFUGs with 65,400 household members in 40 out of the 75 districts in Nepal.[55] Different evaluations and studies confirm that the approach was successful in regenerating degraded forestland; improving livelihoods, income and food security of rural poor people (especially women); increasing access to forest products and availability of animal feed, thus reducing women's workload and time spent to collect forest-based fodder; promoting leadership among women and ethnic minority groups, traditionally voiceless and marginalized; and enhancing women's self-esteem and confidence.[56] Still, a number of issues affect the sustainability of the model. A study carried out in 2012 by FAO indicated that most of the LFUGs were still institutionally weak and only about 20–25 percent were still fully active, with the majority (50–60 percent) being moderately active.[57] Other issues pertain to conflict over forestland; the slow process of granting leasehold certificates; the legal status of the LFUGs; and persistence of food insecurity and limited sustainable livelihoods generated for group members.

In many parts of developing countries, water is a major constraint to rural development. Often, it is not or not only an issue of scarcity, but rather or also of access and governance. Water User Groups (WUGs) and Water User Associations (WUAs), if properly capacitated and operating in a conducive policy environment, play a vital role in enhancing access to and sustainable management of water resources and related infrastructure, while conserving water, protecting the environment, and enforcing legislation for

---

52. Adhikari, "Regenerating Forests," 31.

53. IFAD, *Nepal, Country Programme Evaluation*, 13–20.

54. The Hills Leasehold Forestry and Forage Development Project (HLFFDP), implemented between 1992 and 2002, was financed by an IFAD loan and by a grant from the Netherlands to finance technical assistance implemented by FAO; a post-project follow-up phase by Government of Nepal between 2002 and 2005; the Leasehold Forestry and Livestock Programme (LFLP), implemented from 2005 to 2014, supported by IFAD; and the IFAD-funded Western Uplands Poverty Alleviation Project (WUPAP) with technical assistance provided by FAO through Finnish Government's financial support.

55. Adhikari, "Regenerating Forests," 37.

56. IFAD, *Nepal, Country Programme Evaluation*, 37, 41, 72.

57. Adhikari, "Regenerating Forests," 36.

sustainable water management. In Tanzania and Zambia, Fair Water Futures (known as *Uhakika wa Maji* in Swahili) was a project implemented by Water Witness International to support equitable and effective water resource management.[58] An evaluation conducted by Oxford Policy Management[59] on the first phase of the project implemented in Tanzania with funds from DFID's Global Poverty Action Fund (GPAF) indicated that the project contributed to increased water security for 159,000 people. One of the main features of the project was strengthening existing WUAs or, when not existing, establishing new ones at community level. The Government of Tanzania set up a decentralized system of governance of water resources, divided into watersheds managed by Basin Water Boards (BWB). Under the Integrated Water Management Framework (IWMF),[60] WUAs are the lowest decentralized structures delegated by BWBs for local water use management, including monitoring that local water users are compliant with the individual water use permits (WUPs), coordinating water users and use arrangements, ensuring that all users get an equal share of water, and helping to resolve conflicts. Members of the WUAs pay membership entry and regular fees, and penalties are charged to those breaking the rules. According to OXFAM evaluation, WUAs contributed to greater communities' understanding of legal rights over water, obligations and responsibilities relating to water security, increasing the voice of community-level marginalized water users. Communities also indicated that collective water use allocation and management reduced water conflict or misuse of water resources. Examples of improvements in water security include the reduced dumping of solid waste, supporting processes for the construction of a new water treatment facility, and a more equitable water supply through issuance of WUPs and involvement of WUAs. Still, while a number of donor programs support WUAs based on principles of decentralization, participation, and full cost recovery, experience shows that establishing effective WUAs is a long and challenging process and it takes time to build institutionally sound and well-functioning WUAs. The main issues include the lack of a genuine consultative or participatory process in forming WUAs or their limited inclusiveness; lack of a real delegation of authority to WUAs by upper formal institutions; and weak institutional, financial, and human resource capacity

---

58. The project was implemented in two phases: phase 1 (in Tanzania only) from April 2013 to March 2016 and phase 2 from January 2015 to July 2017. For more information, please see *https://waterwitness.org/fair-water-futures*.

59. Tincani and Mwaruvanda, *Final Evaluation*.

60. The Integrated Water Resources Management (IWRM) approach was introduced in the early 1990s by international donors for a coordinated development and management of water, land and related resources to ensure environmental sustainability.

of WUAs, requiring long-term and continuous support by upper-level public institutions, beyond the (often short) life of donor-funded programs.

In Bangladesh, since the 1990s, IFAD programs have been implementing community-based approaches for inland open water fisheries management, which is quite complex because of physical conditions and the variety of stakeholders around water resources.[61] The Government of Bangladesh had managed the inland fisheries by leasing lakes to fishers' groups by auction on an annual basis. However, the auctions tended to be monopolized by rich and influential people in the community, excluding poor fishers, who used to work as share-catchers, which limited their rights to only 25 per cent of their catch.[62] Moreover, securing tenure for one year only did not provide users with incentives to invest in the lakes in terms of building or improving infrastructure. IFAD's approach envisaged decentralized management of the water bodies through long-term leases to groups of poor fishers that could manage the water resource based on equal sharing of costs and benefits among group members. More recently, IFAD also supported the Ministry of Land in transferring the rights over public water bodies or "*beels*" to community fisher groups (*beel* user grups or BUGs). Each BUG receives the user rights over one *beel* and elects a Beel Management Committee (BMC), made up of 7–9 members, one-third of whom being women. The BMC is accountable for overall management of the *beel* following strict guidelines and laws on conservation of the fish and water bodies. Penalties are enforced if the guideline are violated. Decentralizing and transferring responsibilities to fisher groups resulted in overall better management of water bodies, earlier often found in deteriorating conditions and with low levels of stocking of fish; increased fish production and diversity of fish species as a result of better management practices; empowerment and improved livelihoods of poor fishers, including women; and better maintained or improved infrastructure.[63] The main challenges are associated to the sustainability of BUGs beyond project support, including through their institutionalization and/or policy formulation; risk of elite capture; delays in organizing leases and fees; and social conflicts when forming groups.[64] As a post-project exit strategy, the current IFAD-supported Haor Infrastructure

---

61. About four million hectares of open water in Bangladesh are the rivers, *beels* (permanent and seasonal lakes and wetlands), *baors* (oxbow lakes), *haors* (large deeply flooded depressions), and floodplains provides more than 264 fish species. Khan et al., "Effective Supervision."

62. IFAD, "Community-based Natural Resource," 23.

63. Nathan and Niaz, "Case Study of the Oxbow Lakes Small-Scale Fishermen's Project (OLSSFP) Bangladesh—1990–1997," 11–12.

64. IFAD, *People's Republic of Bangladesh*, 61.

and Livelihood Improvement Project (HILIP) is supporting a process of institutionalization of BUGs into production and marketing cooperatives. As of March 2017, 143 BUGs have been registered as production and marketing cooperatives under the Department of Cooperatives.[65]

As noted, despite challenges, supporting grass root, smallholder, community-level institutions can result in deep social and institutional transformation and sustainable, integral human development as people are put at the center. These institutions can be the entry point for and drivers of bottom-up, participatory, and inclusive development processes, successfully addressing the root causes of poverty. A last example to illustrate this is the *Shaurya Dal* or "Courage Brigades,"[66] launched in India by the Government of Madhya Pradesh in 2014 to challenge and address social issues, gender-based inequality, and caste-based discrimination through community-based solutions. "Courage Brigades" are informal groups of five women and five men respected in their communities working on a voluntary basis to exercise social pressure and raise awareness about issues affecting girls and women, including discrimination, domestic abuse, rape, gender disparities, dowry, and child marriage. The groups also proactively take action to resolve issues regarding sanitation, malnutrition, and joint property ownership, alcoholism, gambling, and corruption. According to IFAD, which has scaled up the model through the ongoing Tejaswini Rural Women's Empowerment Project, the groups continue to exercise a leading role in all the villages covered by the program and have been scaled up to become a state-wide movement being replicated in all the 51 districts.[67] Through the work of Courage Brigades, a reduction in violence against women has been recorded and a high number of cases presented to them have been resolved.[68] The groups are recognized by their communities as a forum to address violence against girls and women. The Ministry of Women and Child Development is considering to scale up this model to the entire country.[69]

Building sustainable, representative, inclusive and accountable institutions and bringing about community-driven social and institutional

---

65. IFAD, *Haor Infrastructure and Livelihood*, 5.

66. http://mpsdc.gov.in/shaurya/ Non serve IFAD, "India," https://www.ifad.org/web/operations/country/id/india; Directorate of Women Empowerment, Department of Women & Child Development Madhya Pradesh, *Transforming lives, (A document on Shaurya).*

67. IFAD, *Tejaswini*, 11–14.

68. Directorate of Women Empowerment, Department of Women & Child Development Madhya Pradesh, *Transforming lives (A document on Shaurya).*
IFAD, "Republic of India Country Programme Evaluation," 48.

69. IFAD, "Republic of India Country Programme Evaluation," 45–48.

change require long time and may entail a sensitive and complex process. It is about working with poor, sometimes marginalized communities and groups of people, socially and economically disadvantaged, and living in institutionally weak environments. Intense support, capacity building, and mentoring, combined with holistic approaches, are required to nurture and accompany these groups so that they can become institutionally robust and self-sustaining entities with a strong and inclusive membership base that is able to lead its pathway out of poverty, towards sustainable and integral human development.

BIBLIOGRAPHY

Adhikari, Ram Bala et al. "Regenerating Forests and Livelihoods in Nepal: A New Lease on Life." FAO and IFAD 2015. http://www.fao.org/3/a-i5013e.pdf.
Amul. "About Us—The Amul Model." http://www.amul.com/m/about-us.
Amuldairy. www.amuldairy.com.
ANGOC, CIRDAP, and IFAD. *CSO Experiences in Strengthening Rural Poor Organizations in Asia*. Quezon City: ANGOC, 2006.
Anyonge, Tome. and others. *Strengthening Institutions and Organizations*. Rome: IFAD, 2013. https://www.ifad.org/documents/10180/a4c30900-e274-4c97-81e7-595256b3441c.
Bamberger, Michael et al. *The Design and Management of Poverty Reduction Programs and Projects in Anglophone Africa: Proceedings of a Seminar Sponsored Jointly by the Economic Development Institute of the World Bank and the Uganda Management Institute*. Washington, DC: World Bank eLibrary, 1996. https://doi.org/10.1596/0-8213-2767-4.
Bureau of Applied Research in Anthropology, University of Arizona Innovations for Poverty Action. *Final Impact Evaluation of the Saving for Change Program in Mali, 2009-2012*. April 2013. https://www.freedomfromhunger.org/sites/default/files/SavingforChangeMaliResearchFullReportMay2013.pdf.
Directorate of Women Empowerment. *Transforming Lives (A document on Shaurya)*, http://www.projecttejaswini.com/WCD/Publication/Transforming%20Lives,%20A%20Document%20On%20Shaurya.pdf.
ESFIM. http://www.esfim.org/kenfap-kenya-in-house-research-capacity-to-monitor-government-policy.
FIDA, "Organics Offer New Opportunities to Young Farmers in the Pacific Islands." https://www.ifad.org/web/latest/story/asset/39380176.
Greif, Avner, and Christopher Kingston. "Institutions: Rules or Equilibria?" In *Political Economy of Institutions, Democracy and Voting*, edited by Gonzalo Caballero and Norman Schofield, 45-74. Heidelberg: Springer, 2011.
Hazelman, Stephen David. *PGS: Revolutionising Organics in the Pacific. Enhancing Pacific Farmer's Access to Certification*. Practitioners' Track, IFOAM Organic World Congress 2014, "Building Organic Bridges." 13-15 Oct., Istanbul, Turkey; http://orgprints.org/23055/7/23055.pdf.

Herbel, D., E. Crowley, N. Ourabah Haddad and M. Lee. *Good Practices in Building Innovative Rural Institutions*. Rome: FAO/IFAD, 2012. http://www.fao.org/docrep/015/i2258e/i2258e00.pdf.

Hodgson, M. Geoffrey. "What Are Institutions?" *Journal of Economic Issues* 40.1 (march 2006):1–25. http://www.geoffrey-hodgson.info/user/bin/whatareinstitutions.pdf.

IFAD. *A Field Practitioner's Guide: Institutional and Organizational Analysis and Capacity Strengthening*. Rome: IFAD, 2014. https://maintenance.ifad.org/documents/10180/9b01ec72-77c4-4b55-a456-7f459d57e2c9.

———. *Community-based Natural Resource Management: How Knowledge Is Managed, Disseminated and Used*. Rome: IFAD, 2006. https://www.landcoalition.org/sites/default/files/documents/resources/cbnrm-ifad.pdf.

———. *Community-Driven Development Decision Tools for Rural Development Programmes*. Rome: IFAD, 2009. https://www.ifad.org/documents/38714170/39150184/Community-driven+development+decision+tools+for+rural+development+programmes.pdf/93dfocc9-e122-49f3-b7d6-9111c01e7f3f.

———. *Guidance Notes for Institutional Analysis in Rural Development Programmes*. Rome: IFAD, 2009. https://maintenance.ifad.org/documents/10180/bbc0deeo-cdc8-4372-97fd-41ad88aeeb80.

———. *Haor Infrastructure and Livelihood Improvement Project (HILIP) Supervision and Climate Adaptation and Livelihood Production (CALIP) Mid-Term Review Report*. Rome: IFAD, 2017. https://operations.ifad.org/documents/654016/3f810a0f-74c5-4cd6-84c7-85d6743fd292.

———. *How to Strengthen Community-based Natural Resource Management Organizations*. Rome: IFAD, 2014. https://maintenance.ifad.org/documents/10180/b77e8cc4-b49f-4fbe-9605-0c2280c0e17e.

———. *Teaser: Strengthening Smallholder Institutions and Organizations*. Rome: IFAD, 2014. https://maintenance.ifad.org/documents/10180/da81a38b-747b-433c-8149-d8ccc5ce439c.

INAFI and PROCASUR. *Community Based Fisheries Management under Sunamganj Community Based Resource Management Project (SCBRMP) in Bangladesh*.

———. *Nepal Country Programme Evaluation*. Rome: IFAD, 2013. https://www.ifad.org/documents/38714182/39714055/nepal.pdf/58c575dc-e6a9-439b-bb2b-420c0f1b9203.

———. *People's Republic of Bangladesh Country Programme Evaluation*. Rome: IFAD, 2016. https://www.ifad.org/documents/38714182/39713659/CPE_Bangladesh.pdf/504ffb3e-e8ff-4b47-b575-4e285ad19c9d.

———. *Republic of India Country Programme Evaluation*. Rome: IFAD, 2016. https://www.ifad.org/documents/38714182/39713847/india_cpe_2016.pdf/ccc8b662-a9cf-4e6e-bd2e-6223500c4a5c.

———. *Rural Development Report 2016: Fostering Inclusive Rural Transformation*. Rome: IFAD, 2016. https://www.ifad.org/documents/38714170/39155702/Rural+development+report+2016.pdf/347402dd-a37f-41b7-9990-aa745dc113b9.

———. *Rural Poverty Report 2011*. Rome: IFAD, 2011. https://www.ifad.org/documents/10180/c47f2607-3fb9-4736-8e6a-a7ccf3dc7c5b.

———. *Smallholder Livestock Development: Scaling up Note*. Rome: IFAD, 2015. https://www.ifad.org/documents/10180/3016058c-043d-49ad-ae03-3cd28acc0831.

———. *Small-scale Producers in the Development of Cocoa Value-Chain Partnerships*. Rome: IFAD, 2013. https://maintenance.ifad.org/documents/10180/b8249b3d-7733-4f4b-951c-a80aa6d8619e.

———. *Tejaswini: Madhya Pradesh Rural Women's Empowerment Programme Supervision Report*. Rome: IFAD, 2017. https://operations.ifad.org/documents/654016/eb54bade-30c4-457c-8e54-ada33b4dd1f8.

———. *Transforming Rural Institutions in Order to Reach Millennium Development Goals*, Roundtable Discussion Paper for the Twenty-Fifth Anniversary Session of IFAD's Governing Council. Rome: IFAD, 2003. https://www.ifad.org/fr/web/latest/event/asset/39007714.

Innovations for Poverty Action (IPA). "Evaluating the Saving for Change Program in Mali." https://www.poverty-action.org/study/evaluating-saving-change-program-mali.

John Paul II, Pope. *Populorum Progressio*. 1967. http://w2.vatican.va/content/paul-vi/en/encyclicals/documents/hf_p-vi_enc_26031967_populorum.html.

Kenya National Farmers' Federation (KENAFF). http://www.kenaff.org/node/5.

Khan, A. K. M. Firoz et al. "Effective Supervision of Inland Capture Fisheries of Bangladesh and Its Hurdles in Managing the Resources." *Bandung: Journal of the Global South* (2016) 3–17. https://link.springer.com/article/10.1186/s40728-015-0026-6.

Lee R. David, and Bernardete Neves. "Rural Poverty and Natural Resources: Improving Access and Sustainable Management." *ESA Working Paper* No. 09–03. Background Paper for IFAD 2009 Rural Poverty Report. http://www.fao.org/3/a-ak422e.pdf. https://www.ifad.org/documents/10180/289f2f0e-deab-470a-8900-f300c0fd134a.

Leftwich, A., and K. Sen. *Beyond Institutions: Institutions and Organisations in the Politics and Economics of Poverty Reduction—a Thematic Synthesis of Research Evidence*. IPPG Research Consortium on Improving Institutions for Pro-Poor Growth, University of Manchester, 2010. http://www.ippg.org.uk/8933_Beyond%20Institutions.final%20(1).pdf.

Linking Research to Advocacy in Farmers' Organizations: Building on Country Experiences. Side event organized by AgriNatura and the ESFIM project in the context of the Farmers' Forum held in conjunction with the thirty-fifth session of IFAD's Governing Council (23 February 2012). https://www.ifad.org/documents/10180/535b2f9f-8532-49d0-b89e-8735e4b6aa0c.

Lobo, Crispino. *Institutional and Organizational Analysis for Pro-poor Change: Meeting IFAD's Millennium Challenge*. Rome: IFAD, 2008. https://www.ifad.org/documents/38714170/39144386/Institutional+and+organizational+analysis+for+pro-poor+change_meeting+IFAD%27s+millennium+challenge+-+A+sourcebook.pdf/9ccc9570-1732-4473-bc9c-14efa0e595ec.

May, Christopher. *Toolkit for Participatory Guarantee Systems in the Pacific Island*. POETCom, with assistance of the Pacific Community, European Union Increasing Agricultural Commodities Trade Project and the International Fund for Agricultural Development. September 2015. http://www.organicpasifika.com/pasifikapolicytoolkit/wp-content/uploads/sites/5/2016/11/pacific-pgs-toolkit.pdf

Nathan, Dev and Niaz Ahmed Apu. *Case Study of the Oxbow Lakes Small-Scale Fishermen's Project (OLSSFP) Bangladesh—1990–1997*. IFAD Innovation Mainstreaming Initiative. Rome: IFAD, 2004. https://www.ifad.org/documents/10180/32855f32-1b9c-46b5-8778-2f02c3fee54b.

North, Douglass C. "Economic Performance through Time." *American Economic Review* 84.3 (June 1994) 359–68.

———. *Institutions, Institutional Change and Economic Performance*. Cambridge: Cambridge University Press, 1990.

Pacific Community. http://www.spc.int.

Pontifical Council for Justice and Peace. *Compendium of the Social Doctrine of the church*. Rome: Libreria Editrice Vaticana, 2004. http://www.vatican.va/roman_curia/pontifical_councils/justpeace/documents/rc_pc_justpeace_doc_20060526_compendio-dott-soc_en.html.

POETCom, *POETCom Secretariat Update*. http://www.organicpasifika.com/poetcom/news/poetcom-secretariat-update.

Prato, Bettina, and Longo, Roberto. "Empowerment of Poor Rural People through Initiatives in Agriculture and Natural Resource Management." *Promoting Pro-poor Growth: the Role of Empowerment*. Paris: OECD Publishing, 2012. https://www.oecd-ilibrary.org/development/poverty-reduction-and-pro-poor-growth/empowerment-of-poor-rural-people-through-initiatives-in-agriculture-and-natural-resource-management_9789264168350-5-en.

Prayer, Mattia. *IFAD's Experience with Rural Finance and Self-Help Groups in Asia*. http://www.masterhdfs.org/masterHDFS/wp-content/uploads/2014/05/IFAD-experience-with-SHG-in-microfinance-Master-HDFS.pdf.

Ravi, S. "The Growth of Self Help Groups in India: A Study." *Indian Journal of Applied Research* 1.7 (April 2012) 168–70.

Salomo, Wolfgang et al.. *A Study of SHG Federation Structures in India: Core Elements for Achieving Sustainability*. Deutsche Gesellschaft für Internationale Zusammenarbeit (GIZ) GmbH GIZ NABARD Rural Financial Institutions Programme. 2012. https://www.dgrv.de/webde.nsf/7d5e59ec98e72442c1256e5200432395/38efe94db3eefd11c1257b47004f83c1/$FILE/SHG-Federations%20Report.pdf.

Sharma, Misha, and Shreya Chatterjee. *Revitalizing the Self-Help Group Movement in India*. CGAP (Consultative Group to Assist the Poor), 2016. https://www.cgap.org/blog/revitalizing-self-help-group-movement-india.

Tango International. *Sustainability of Rural Development Projects. Best Practices and Lessons Learned by IFAD in Asia*. Rome: IFAD, 2009.

Thierry, Benoit. *Regenerating Forests and Livelihoods in Nepal: A New Lease on Life*. Boston, MA: CABI, 2015. http://www.fao.org/3/a-i5013e.pdf.

Tincani, Lucrezia and Willie Mwaruvanda. *Final Evaluation of the Fair Water Futures Project (Uhakika wa Maji) in Tanzania*, Final Report. June 2016. https://static1.squarespace.com/static/5627894ce4b0a834a45c5cec/t/5797782929687f7f82454abe/1469544518377/Fair+Water+Futures+Phase+I+-+Final+evaluation.pdf.

UN General Assembly. *Transforming our World: the 2030 Agenda for Sustainable Development*. 21 October 2015. http://www.un.org/ga/search/view_doc.asp?symbol=A/RES/70/1&Lang=E.

United Nations. *Global Sustainable Development Report 2016*. New York: Department of Economic and Social Affairs, 2016. https://sustainabledevelopment.un.org/content/documents/2328Global%20Sustainable%20development%20report%202016%20(final).pdf.

United Nations Development Programme. "About Human Development." http://hdr.undp.org/en/humandev.

University of Arizona, Bureau of Applied Research in Anthropology, *Final Impact Evaluation of the Saving for Change Program in Mali, 2009-2012.* https://www.freedomfromhunger.org/sites/default/files/SavingforChange MaliResearchFullReportMay2013.pdf.

WEBSITES

http://mpsdc.gov.in/shaurya/;
http://www.amul.com/m/about-us
http://www.amuldairy.com
http://www.cgap.org/blog/revitalizing-self-help-group-movement-indiawww.esfim.org
http://www.esfim.org/kenfap-kenya-in-house-research-capacity-to-monitor-government-policy/.
http://www.kenaff.org/node/5 http://www.hdr.undp.org/en/humandev
http://www.ifad.org/web/latest/story/asset/39380176
https://www.ifad.org/web/operations/country/id/india
http://www.nabard.org
http://www.organicpasifika.com/poetcom/news/poetcom-secretariat-update/
http://www.poverty-action.org/study/evaluating-saving-change-program-mali
www.projecttejaswini.com/WCD/Publication/Transforming%20Lives,%20A%20Document%20On%20Shaurya.pdf
www.spc.inthttps://waterwitness.org/fair-water-futures/.

6

Structural Challenges to the Realization of the Sustainable Development Goals
JEFFREY SACHS

It's a pleasure and an honour to speak about the Sustainable Development Goals and the challenges that we face in meeting them. The concept of Sustainable Development is the most important public policy concept in our world today. Sustainable development signifies *economic development* that is *socially inclusive* and *environmentally sustainable*, or what Pope Francis calls integral human development.

Sustainable Development calls for a holistic vision of the development process. It's not good enough for nations to have rising income if the national income is very unequally distributed. It is certainly not adequate to have economic development if the very process of economic growth destroys biodiversity, dangerously alters the climate, and poisons the land, air, and water.

The core problem is that the global economic system today does not produce sustainable development on its own. There is no "invisible hand" (using Adam Smith's famous description of the market economy) that guides the world to sustainable development. The global market economy is actually quite good at promoting economic growth; it is quite good at creating the incentives to make profits; it is quite effective at motivating hard work and entrepreneurship. Yet, it is not at all good at delivering fairness, promoting justice, fostering a sense of community, or ensuring environmental sustainability.

These limitations of the market system are of course why the church's social teachings for the last 128 years are so essential. Ever since Pope Leo XIII delivered the remarkable encyclical *Rerum Novarum* ("of the New Things") in 1891, where he referred to "the new things" of industrialization, the church has wisely taught that we do need a market economy but one that operates within a *moral framework* that ensures human dignity, provides justice for all, and protects the Earth. The great social teachings have all followed in this line: a market system operating within a moral framework. These crucial teachings including *Quadragesimo Anno* (1931), *Pacem in Terris* (1963), *Populorum Progressio* (1967), *Centesimus Annus* (1991), *Laborem Exercens* (1981), *Caritas in Veritate* (2009), and now *Laudato Si'* (2015).

Two excerpts of this unique body of thought, so vital for our times, capture the essence of the church's remarkable moral guidance. In *Populorum Progresio*, Pope Paul VI summarizes the obligations of the rich to the poor this way:

> Everyone knows that the Fathers of the church laid down the duty of the rich toward the poor in no uncertain terms. As St. Ambrose put it: "You are not making a gift of what is yours to the poor man, but you are giving him back what is his. You have been appropriating things that are meant to be for the common use of everyone. The earth belongs to everyone, not to the rich." These words indicate that the right to private property is not absolute and unconditional.
>
> No one may appropriate surplus goods solely for his own private use when others lack the bare necessities of life. In short, "as the Fathers of the church and other eminent theologians tell us, the right of private property may never be exercised to the detriment of the common good." When "private gain and basic community needs conflict with one another," it is for the public authorities "to seek a solution to these questions, with the active involvement of individual citizens and social groups."

In *Laudato Si'*, Pope Francis also teaches that property rights must be set within a moral order:

> The Christian tradition has never recognized the right to private property as absolute or inviolable, and has stressed the social purpose of all forms of private property. Saint John Paul II forcefully reaffirmed this teaching, stating that "God gave the earth to the whole human race for the sustenance of all its members, *without excluding or favouring anyone.*" These are strong words. He noted that "a type of development which did not respect and promote human rights—personal and social, economic and political, including the rights of nations and of peoples—would not be really worthy of man." He clearly explained that "the church does indeed defend the legitimate right to private property, but she also teaches no less clearly that there is always a social mortgage on all private property, in order that goods may serve the general

purpose that God gave them." Consequently, he maintained, "it is not in accord with God's plan that this gift be used in such a way that its benefits favour only a few." This calls into serious question the unjust habits of a part of humanity.

The reality of our world today is a very wealthy global economy that is deeply divided between the rich and poor. The reality is a very dynamic global economy that is causing devastating damage to the natural environment in three major ways: global warming; the destruction of other species and ecosystems; and massive chemical pollution of the air, freshwater, land and oceans.

The governments of the world have recognized these profound dangers, yet they still do not act on them satisfactorily. Back in 2015, all 193 member governments of the United Nations adopted the 17 Sustainable Development Goals (SDGs) in order to shift the world economy towards sustainable development. They are part of the overall framework of global cooperation for achieving sustainable development.[1] Agenda 2030 and the 17 SDGs were adopted on September 25th 2015, a wonderful day at the United Nations that opened with a riveting speech by Pope Francis to the world leaders, calling on them to choose the moral course for the sake of the poor, human dignity for all, and the planet.

Let me highlight a few of the splendid ambitions of the SDGs. SDG 1 calls on the world to end extreme poverty by 2030. SDG 3 calls on the world to ensure Universal Health Coverage (UHC), thereby securing for all the human right to health. SDG 4 calls for every child, rich or poor, urban or rural, to complete at least a secondary education. SDG 8 commits the world to decent work for all, and the end of to all forms of modern slavery and human trafficking. SDG 13 calls on every country to take decisive steps to end global warming and to ensure resiliency to climate change. SDG 14 calls on every government to protect the world's marine environment. SDG 15 calls for protection of the world's terrestrial environment. SDG 16 highlight the need for peaceful and inclusive societies. SDG 17 calls for global cooperation to achieve the 16 SDGs, including through means such as development assistance, debt relief, technology transfer, and capacity building.

The key point is that the SDGs are in complete alignment with *Laudato Si*. They constitute a bold but also realistic global program for holistic sustainable development. Yet the SDGs will certainly not succeed unless we work hard at success, scaling up our investments in people, the environment, and infrastructure. Governments and businesses must redirect their efforts from now till 2030 to succeed in achieving the goals set forth in Agenda 2030.

1. United Nations, "Transforming Our World."

I often describe the SDGs as our generation's "moonshot," referring to the bold initiative of President John F. Kennedy to reach the moon. On May 25, 1961, President Kennedy said the following to the American people:

> First, I believe that this nation should commit itself to achieving the goal, before this decade is out, of landing a man on the moon and returning him safely to the earth. No single space project in this period will be more impressive to mankind, or more important for the long-range exploration of space; and none will be so difficult or expensive to accomplish.[2]

The US public rallied to this challenge. The US federal government spent amply. NASA, America's space agency, went to work, recruiting thousands of idealistic and talented people out to succeed on the great adventure of getting to the moon and back. In July 1969, the US accomplished the seemingly impossible: landing Neil Armstrong and Buzz Aldrin on the moon, and returning them and crew member Michael Collins safely to the Earth.

In our own time, we have the advanced technologies in information and communications, advanced materials, renewable energy, health care, conservation biology, and many other cutting-edge areas, needed to achieve the SDGs. We have the necessary wealth, both public and private. The world has set 17 bold goals. Now we must follow through to meet the sustainable development challenge. If we choose to do so, this generation can end extreme poverty, ensure universal health coverage, and guarantee a quality education for every child on Earth.

The extent of vast private wealth today is absolutely staggering. The rich can make a marked contribution to the SDGs if they put their enormous wealth to good use. According to the most recent comprehensive data, there are now an estimated 2,208 billionaires with a combined net worth of around $9.1 trillion (as of March 2018). If these 2,208 individuals give (or are taxed) just 1 percent of their net worth each year, that would mobilize around $91 billion per year, an amount sufficient to ensure healthcare coverage and education for every poor child on the planet!

Let me summarize some of the specific SDG challenges that lie ahead. The first challenge I'll mention is to transform the world's energy system from one that is based on fossil fuels (coal, oil, and natural gas) to one that is based overwhelmingly on renewable energy (solar, wind, hydro, geothermal, and others). The conversion to renewable energy (as called for by SDGs 7 and 13) is essential to slowing and then halting human-made global warming. One piece of very good news is that many of the poorest countries in the world

---

2. Kennedy, "Special Message to Congress."

have massive renewable energy potential, such as the vast solar energy available to the Sahel of Africa, including Mali, Niger, Central African Republic, Burkina Faso, Senegal, and others. These countries will be able to build modern twenty-first century energy systems based largely or entirely on renewable energy, and even to become large-scale renewable energy exporters.

The second challenge is shift farm practices towards sustainable agriculture, as emphasized by SDGs 2, 14, and 15. Current farm practices are leading to land degradation, deforestation, and freshwater depletion. Farm systems around the world need to shift to sustainable practices.

The third challenge is to make the world's cities productive, inclusive and sustainable, as called for by SDG 11. All over the world, rural populations are now flocking the cities, especially as farming and mining become heavily mechanized, with machines replacing workers on the farms and in the mines. The new jobs will be urban based.

Yet are the cities ready to absorb billions more people in the coming decades? Do they have adequate water and sewerage systems? Do they have adequate roads and light rail? Do they have adequate power supplies based on renewable energy? Are there enough teachers and classrooms for the children? Considerable efforts and investments will be needed to ensure that the world's cities are cities are prosperous, socially inclusive, and environmentally sustainable.

The fourth and fifth challenges, respectively, are universal access to healthcare (SDG 3) and to education (SDG 4). These goals are especially vital in Africa, where both healthcare and education still fall far short of universal coverage.

The sixth challenge is to deploy the new Information and Communications Technologies (ICTs) for the common good. The new ICTs, including wireless broadband, artificial intelligence, and low-cost high-powered devices such as computers, tablets, and smartphones, offer breakthroughs for healthcare, education, e-commerce, e-finance, e-payments, e-governance, and many other online applications. Yet at the same time, the ICTs present new and serious challenges. Some are economic, such as when advanced technologies replace existing jobs. Many relate to human rights, including the rights to privacy and safety from cyberwarfare. Our global challenge is to harness the new ICTs for sustainable development while insuring that these very technologies do not gravely undermine human rights.

What are the practical obstacles to achieving the SDGs?

The first obstacle is corporate impunity. Many powerful multinational companies simply do not behave themselves, despoiling the environment while also evading taxes and exploiting local communities. Think of how Shell Oil Company long behaved in the Niger Delta, leaving behind a long trail of corruption, illegality, and pollution.³ Or think too about how they and their rich owners *hide their wealth in tax havens*, such as those in the US and UK Caribbean.⁴ These tax havens are indeed controlled by the world's richest countries on behalf of their richest citizens. It is past time to close these tax havens and to insist that the world's multinational companies pair their fair share in taxes.

A second monumental obstacle is the plutocratic bias of many rich and powerful countries, including my own, the United States. The rich countries have long promised to give the poor countries a mere 0.7 percent of GDP as development aid, yet they fail to give even this modest amount. The average level of development aid is only around 0.3 percent of donor-country GDP, and for the United States, a measly 0.17 percent of GDP. If the US were to give 0.7 percent rather than 0.17 percent, the boost in US development aid would amount to around $100 billion per year!⁵

A third structural obstacle to the SDGs is inter-ethnic violence and violence more generally. Recent estimates suggest that the *global cost of violence* is a staggering $14.8 trillion per year, or 12.4 percent of global income, a sum easily enough to fund the SDGs many times over.⁶ Here we need the religious leaders always to be saying very clearly: "No violence in the name of religion." Demagogic politicians misuse religion, exploit religion, by preaching hatred and fear. We see the ethnic chauvinism all around us, the gross abuse of religion by the nationalistic, populistic politicians.

A fourth obstacle is what Pope Frances powerfully terms "the globalization of indifference."⁷ Here Pope Francis is pointing to a world society trapped by the superficial imagery of mass advertising, all designed to attention towards luxury goods and away from social justice and concern for the poor. The urgency of sustainable development is drowned in the superficiality of consumerism.

In *Laudato Si'*, Pope Francis called rightly for a common plan for our common home. Soon afterwards, governments adopted the SDGs. Now they need to follow through on their promises.

The world is blessed with profound technical knowledge, vast wealth, and shared goals. The SDGs are indeed within reach. Our greatest challenge is a moral one: to choose our purposes and use our resources justly and

---

3. "Niger Delta Villagers Lose."
4. Alstadsæter et al. *Tax evasion and inequality.*
5. OECD, *Country Programmable Aid (CPA)*
6. Institute for Economics & Peace. *The Economic Value of Peace 2018.*
7. *Evangelii Gaudium.*

wisely, in accordance with the virtue of *phronesis* or practical wisdom, in Aristotle's terms.

Laudato Si', and indeed all of the church's great social teachings, are vital guideposts and deep inspirations for our generation's journey to sustainable development and to the world we seek for our children and for generations to come.

BIBLIOGRAPHY

Alstadsæter, Annette, Niels Johannesen, and Gabriel Zucman. *Tax Evasion and Inequality*. No. w23772. National Bureau of Economic Research, 2017.

Francis I, Pope. *Encyclical Letter Laudato si' of the Holy Father Francis*. 1st ed. 2015.

———. *Evangelii Gaudium*. St Paul's Publishing, 2013.

Institute for Economics & Peace. *The Economic Value of Peace 2018: Measuring the Global Economic Impact of Violence and Conflict*, Sydney, October 2018. http://visionofhumanity.org/ reports.

Kennedy, John F. "Special Message to Congress on Urgent National Needs." 25 May 1961. Speech. https://catalog.archives.gov/id/193914.

"Niger Delta Villagers Lose UK Court Bid to Sue Shell over Pollution." *BBC News*, 26 Jan. 2017. http://www.bbc.com/news/world-africa-38759643.

Organisation for Economic Co-operation and Development. *Country Programmable Aid (CPA) (indicator)*. OECD (2019). doi: 10.1787/69d8099b-en.

TWI2050—The World in 2050 (2018). *Transformations to Achieve the Sustainable Development Goals. Report Prepared by The World in 2050 Initiative*. IIASA Report. International Institute for Applied Systems Analysis (IIASA). Laxenburg, Austria.

United Nations. "Transforming Our World: The 2030 Agenda for Sustainable Development Sustainable Development Goals Knowledge Platform." *United Nations*. http://sustainabledevelopment.un.org/post2015/transformingourworld.

7

Good Governance, Leadership and Social Justice In Africa

Ludovic Lado, SJ

INTRODUCTION

Governance is all about the exercise of power in an organisation or a society. It is fine when it is at the service of the common good, that is, the good of all the members of the community.[1] We are addressing here the governance of the African States, that is to say, governance at the national level as a question of the quality of leadership. Good governance supposes good governors, or good leaders, those who have an "ethical goal," a term which Ricoeur defines as being "a good life, with and for the other, in *just institutions*."[2] The search for and preservation of good governance is the desire of every contemporary society, and the African States are no exception. In the present paper, I shall maintain that the question of governance in Africa is less a problem of the existence of appropriate institutions than that of the political leadership's lack of ethical concern, namely, its inability to put the service of the common good above the pursuit of its own interests. In the first part, we shall address the elements of the political context, setting the question of governance in Africa today within its colonial matrix. In fact, after the slave trade, which dehumanised Africa for almost four centuries, colonisation, under the cover of the ideology of civilisation, was an attempt to recreate Africa in the image of the West in every aspect. This scheme of recreation was decided outside Africa and without the Africans during the

1. Hollenbach, *Bien Commun et Ethique Chrétienne.*
2. Ricoeur, *Soi-même Comme un Autre*, 202.

Congress of Berlin in 1884/1885. The present political map of Africa is the distant result of this and bears the arbitrary marks of this heteronomy. In the second part, we shall revisit the convulsions of governance in postcolonial Africa in terms of the ethical poverty of the political leadership. Finally, in the third part, we shall explore the outlines of the contribution of the church to governance in Africa.

ELEMENTS OF THE POLITICAL CONTEXT

Africa is a vast continent, very diversified in every way. However, in order to speak of the issues of governance and leadership in Africa today, some general considerations are essential concerning the political context which governs the structure of the nations. Here, I have chosen to highlight the challenge which ethnic awareness represents for the consolidation of a national awareness. Hence the fragile nature of a certain number of African states. A certain idyllic picture of the politics of precolonial Africa can give the impression that, before colonisation, Africa was politically uniform and consisted of a juxtaposition of ethnic groups living together peaceably. According to this perspective, it was the colonist who introduced the destabilising factor in gathering together within the modern State disparate groups who found it hard to live together. If it is true that the colonial carving-up of Africa was arbitrary, it is wrong to think that precolonial Africa was an island of homogeneous peace before its encounter with the West.

Historians and anthropologists have shown well enough that the political organisation of precolonial Africa was not only pluriform but also dynamic. For example, they have identified societies with diffused power (*band societies*, segmentary and tribal organisations) as well as societies that are strongly hierarchical (societies with chiefs, kingdoms, empires).[3] The anthropologist, Francis Dupuy, even maintains that the phenomenon of the state in Africa is prior to colonisation.[4] According to him, Africa already had powerful and expansionist states like the Empire of Ghana, which existed from the third to the eighth century, or, again, that of Mali from the thirteenth to the fourteenth century. The precolonial state appeared in Africa as a centralised political unity, based on territorial sovereignty and watching over the maintenance of order and peace. On the economic level, the work for the common good was expressed through the achievement of works of general interest possible thanks to the taxes paid by the population. Besides, these political units made war on one another: in precolonial

---

3. See Rivière, *Anthropologie Politique*.
4. Dupuy, *Anthropologie Economique*, 114.

Africa, slavery on a reduced scale was a means of expansion and enrichment. The victor annexed the vanquished, stole their goods and enslaved them as a workforce.[5]

However, it was colonisation that imposed on the whole of Africa the modern state as a territorial unit of governance marked by the principle of sovereignty. In imposing on Africa the form of the state with rigid frontiers, colonisation superimposed an extra referent of identity which covered over the lines of kinship that structured the ethnic groups and the clans. I shall not dwell here on the ambiguity inherent in using the terms "tribe" or "ethnic group" in Africa. It is a subject that has been explored abundantly in the anthropological and philosophical literature.[6] It will suffice to recall that the ethnic affiliations in Africa were reshaped by the colonial and postcolonial matrices and so are not simple copies of precolonial units. This is a mark of the historicity of African societies.

Thus, the young states had to take care to see to the emergence of a national awareness able to supersede the logic of kinship. The indirect mode of colonisation practised by the English shows that they did not necessarily think up the political reconfiguration of their colonies at the expense of the pre-existing forms of organisation. The specialists in ethnogenesis in Africa even affirm that the colonial processes, especially the practice of settling the populations in order to identify them and control them better, did not only crystallise the ethnic identities, despite these being characterised by a certain fluidity, but even created them.[7] That is to say that instead of diluting ethnic awareness, the colonial and even postcolonial processes reinforced them to the extent that certain ethnic labels which some today believe to go back to precolonial Africa were in fact created by colonisation and used by the poor postcolonial governance.

History attests that the majority of postcolonial African states began their political life with a multiparty system. However, the first generation of African rulers, with only a few exceptions, very quickly replaced this with a one-party system. The main argument given by the first African rulers for replacing the initial multiparty system with the authoritarian one-party system which was familiar from the end of the 1960s to the beginning of the 1980s was that political pluralism formed a threat to national integration. According to them, political pluralism risked favouring ethnic awareness at the expense of national integration. It is true that, since independence, a good number of civil wars in Africa have been linked with inter-ethnic

---

5. Dupuy, *Anthropologie Economique*, 114.
6. See Amselle and M'bokolo, *Au Cœur de l'Ethnie*.
7. Thomson, *An Introduction to African Politics*, 58–59.

conflict. The most tragic of our days is that of the interethnic clashes in Southern Sudan. A similar tendency can be seen in the functioning of the political parties, the tendency to associate with the ethnic groups of their leaders. Hence the problem of the expression of ethnic diversity, of political pluralism and "national integration." National integration is understood here as the process by which common citizenship supersedes the other forms of belonging.

As the extreme case of the genocide in Rwanda in 1994 illustrates well, the resilience of precolonial identitary primordialisms compromises the awakening of national conscience in Africa. As J. F. Bayart writes,

> The systems of inequality and domination which prevailed before colonisation were not erased by it. Still today, they follow their historical course under the cover of "modern" institutions: the ancestral connections between the elders and youngsters in society, the unequal relations between ethnic groups, intensified by an unprecedented dimension and by new content, find themselves transposed within the political and economic apparatus of the state, and mediated by it in a particular way.[8]

Once again, however, ethnicity is displayed today in Africa in a context different from that of precolonial Africa. This context is that of globalisation and multiculturalism which reshapes group identities.[9] Arjun Appadurai, who is interested in the reasons for the resilience of the ethnic lines at the expense of national awareness, seems to attribute the persistence of ethnic sentiments to the contradictions of modernity in what it is useful to call the "thesis of unequal development":

> This maintains the point of view that the project of development, such as been imposed on the non-Western world, has generally given rise to the creation of new elites and new divisions between castes and classes, sometimes emerging only in response to different neo-colonialist projects in the new states. Modernisation is held responsible for the friction provoked by rising expectations and the contradictions between economic and political participation. The latter foster mass frustration which can easily be translated by demagogues of all shades into racist speech and actions.[10]

---

8. Bayart, *L'Etat au Cameroun*, 14. See also Warnier, *Régner au Cameroun*, 295; Munoz, "Au nom du développement," 67–85.

9. See Warnier, *la mondialisation de la culture*.

10. Appadurai, *Après le colonialisme*, 212.

Moreover, we live in a world where the electronic media and the movements of population have assumed a global scale. They share in the construction of local, national and transnational identities. It is within this context of the entanglement of multiple identities that the problem of good governance and leadership in Africa is set.

THE CRISIS OF POLITICAL AND ETHICAL LEADERSHIP IN AFRICA

I am depending here on Franz Fanon's concept of the "colonised intellectual." In his work, *Les damnés de la terre*,[11] which has become a classic, Fanon distinguishes three principal stages in the trajectory of intellectuals who have experienced colonisation. The first stage is that of assimilation where "the colonised intellectual proves that he has assimilated the culture of the occupier." The second is that of memory, when the colonised intellectual who, until then, has maintained relations of exteriority with his people, re-members his past and is haunted by it. This is a "period of anguish, malaise, experience of death, experience too of nausea." The third stage is that of combat when he becomes aware of his alienation and is transformed into fighting for freedom, for his own freedom and that of his people. This time of combat was embodied in Sub-Saharan Africa by the nationalist movement which took off in the 1940s. It is embodied in the first generation of African intellectuals a good number of whom are attracted by the pan-Africanist ideal to the North American origins.[12]

It was only after the Second World War that the nationalists of the countries colonised by France embraced nationalism fed by the first African academics in Europe: "6000 km from their country, these young people discovered the values of ancestral Africa and claimed them with a pride that was all the more aggressive as the colonisers had taught them to disdain them and to loose themselves from them. This was the era of literary pan-Africanism and a triumphant black culture."[13] If in the Anglophone areas, pan-Africanism took on a more political orientation, in the Francophone areas it was cultural for preference. After independence, however, the pan-Africanist goals were relegated to the second level in favour of the urgency of the national construction of the young states.

On the morrow of independence, starting from the middle of the 1960s, the governance of the African countries turned to authoritarianism

11. Fanon, *Les damnés de la terre*, 207–12.
12. Yabara, *Africa Unite! Une histoire du Panafricanisme*.
13. Hebga, *Les étapes des regroupements africains*, 117.

and made a pact with violence. In fact, before the end of the 1960s, the majority of African countries passed from a multiparty to a one-party system. This change had nothing to do with the will of the African peoples. On the contrary, almost everywhere, it was imposed by every means, including violence, by a handful of autocrats who immediately put their power at the service of their own egoistical interests. In other words, the famous "fathers of the nation" succumbed to the temptation of absolute power and set up oppressive regimes, bloody and merciless dictatorships, in order to retain it.[14]

As underlined in the previous section, these leaders justified this passage to political monolithism by the desire for national integration. According to them, political pluralism in Africa favours tribalism. However, the reality is, instead of national integration, the one-party system has masterminded and preserved state tribalism, state terrorism, corruption, the embezzlement of public money, etc. In suppressing or muzzling the political opposition, the autocrats have consecrated the reign of one-track thinking. Totalitarianism has been built only on the ruins of the exercise of the critical spirit. In this context, writes A. Mbembe, "the free spaces and the critical viewpoint are almost forced to follow clandestine paths, preferring to use symbols, popular codes and disguised language"[15] Today, there are few African countries which can claim to have risen to the challenge of national integration and development. This is not always the fault of material and human resources. Bad governance is one of the principal breaks on development in Africa. It shows itself in the bad administration of natural and human resources by corrupt and irresponsible rulers. All this engenders social injustice, the resentment of the excluded and violence.

In other words, "the authoritarian one-party state" has given rise only to lack of economic productivity and social injustice. However, one of the catalysts of this bad governance which it is appropriate to mention is "the colonial pact," which is manifested by the maintenance of the trading economy and the sacred nature of the interests of the Western powers safeguarded by every means which include the protection of dictators and the orchestration of civil wars. International relations are marked here by the unhealthy complicity which subordinates respect for human dignity to the economic interest of the great powers in Africa.

However, the wind of democracy which began to blow in Eastern Europe towards the end of the 1980s did not spare Africa. Thirsty for freedom, the African peoples too have become involved in the claims of democracy: national conferences, multiparty systems, free elections, street movements,

14. Nyanchoga et al., *Governance in Africa*.
15. Mbembe, *Les Jeunes*, 14–15.

etc. Supported by some of their Western sponsors, after repeated manœuvres of resistance, the autocrats have finally been "converted without conviction and without enthusiasm" to the multiparty system. We have then seen the proliferation of political parties and a timid return to multiparty elections. However, with a few exceptions, the experience of these recent years has shown that the multiparty system is not synonymous with democracy; the multiparty system in Africa has found it hard to integrate the idea of political changes in power, the main reason being that in the majority of cases there is only a facade of democracy. The autocrats of the *ancien regime*—and some of them are still in power—cling on to power by every means and do everything to torpedo attempts at openness and political transparency.

THE CHALLENGE OF GOOD GOVERNANCE

A careful reading of the work of Karl Popper shows that the paradigm of intersubjectivity structures both his philosophy of the sciences and his political philosophy. His critical rationalism supposes a community of individuals who are free and able to discuss, each of them putting his ideas to the test by submitting them to the criticism of the others. Scientific and socio-political progress occur necessarily by the rejection of monologue, openness to the other and tolerance, the only bulwarks against superstition and violence. Finally, what he calls democracy is a political system which integrates human plurality and privileges intersubjective control, this control being the sole guarantee against tyranny.[16]

It is appropriate, then, to free political practice in Africa from the providentialism that encourages the monopolisation of power, thus depriving it of the indispensable right of looking at the other from a critical point of view. Politics embodies the greatest possibility of evil, and it is necessary to control it tirelessly so that human passions do not metamorphose it into a "thanatocracy." The controlling institution has to be a collective and plural enterprise. Hence the need for rethinking the relation to the other in African politics in the light of the paradigm of intersubjectivity. J. Y. Calvez insists on the need to base political action on mutual recognition. He writes thus:

> The democratic dialogue certainly makes sense correlatively only when it returns to the living recognition among the members of society. Maximum respect for this recognition and not its abandonment constitutes democracy . . . And democracy in the sense of its procedures does not replace recognition if that

16. Popper, *Misère de l'historicisme*, 90.

> is missing ... If it is true that one does not have to submit to a pre-established truth, one has at least to submit to liberty as a common goal, one has to recognise and respect the liberty of the other ... a practical truth, once again, but fundamental.[17]

In 1990, Bechir Ben Yahmed, who is not unknown to assiduous readers of the African weekly *Jeune-Afrique*, observed that it was vital for Africans not to confuse the multiparty system with democracy:

> The major, not to say unique, concession which the African powers make when they feel obliged to change is to renounce the single party to adhere to the ideology of the multiparty system ... They have nothing to fear from the multiparty system for, I repeat, if the single party is dictatorship, the multiparty system is not democracy, not by a long shot ... Those African peoples who content themselves with the multiparty system as their democratic food will not be slow to notice that they are still hungry.[18]

In fact, many African peoples have reclaimed and obtained the return of the multiparty system but they are still waiting for democracy. Post-electoral violence multiplies, and alternation remains a dream in a good many countries. There are few African countries which deserve to be called "lawful states" from the fact that they respect human rights. J. Y. Calvez states that "the *lawful state*, the state of human rights must open up into the democratic state" because it embodies the "the right of participating, having a share, taking part, beyond everything that one can simply receive."[19]

The path which leads to democracy is still a long one. However, with regard to the evolution of the indices of good governance in Africa, there are some glimmers of hope. According to the index of good governance for the year 2017, produced by the *Fondation Mo Ibrahim* which publishes an annual report appraising the states over the question of good governance, there is some progress in this matter on the continent even if it is slow. The report puts it like this:

> Although the majority of countries (40) have improved their overall governance in the course of the last ten years, more than half of these are showing that this progress has either slowed down, or a regression is observed in certain areas, with a fall in these last five years. During this time, eight of the twelve

17. Calvez, *Politique*, 169–70.
18. Yahmed, *Jeune-Afrique*.
19. Calvez, *politique*, 104–6.

countries which register a decline in overall governance during the last decade show no sign of a reversal of this tendency, dropping at a still more rapid pace in the course of the last five years. Consequently, the average improvement in governance in Africa has slowed down ... In the course of the last five years, more countries have declined than in the last ten years in all the categories of governance of the *Ibrahim Index of African Governance (IIAG)*, with the exception of security and the rule of law.[20]

As for the average score of all the African countries, the following table gives the details :

Sectors	Score /100
Safety and rule of law	52,8
Participation and human rights	49,4
Sustainable economic opportunity	45,1
Human development	56,1
Average	50,8

Sources: Report of the Ibrahim Index of African Governance (IIAG), 2017.

The first five in the list are : Mauritius (81,4), Seychelles (73,4), Botswana (72,7), Cape Verde (72,2) and Namibia (71,2) ; while the last five on the list are Sudan (32.2), the Central African Republic (30.5), Eritrea (29.2), South Sudan (20.2) and Somalia (11.6). What are we to take from these figures? First, that Africa, as a whole, attains just the average when it comes to good governance (50,8/100); second, it is below average in the areas of participation, human rights and sustainable economic opportunity; third, the results vary from one country to another. Above all, however, the report highlights the fact that even if there are countries which are developing well, in general, one notes a slowing down of the progress of African states in the area of good governance.

Faced with the persistence of political violence, the question arises as to the link between morality and politics: is evil inherent in politics? We wish to answer this question in the negative with the support of Aristotle who maintains that politics is not only one of the most noble of human occupations but also that it is inseparable from morality. For Aristotle, as we know, "the virtue of justice is of the essence of civil society, for the administration of justice is of the same order as the political community."[21] The crisis

---

20. Mo Ibrahim Foundation, *Report*.
21. Aristote, *La Politique*, 31.

of good governance is fundamentally the crisis of the good administration of the common good in society, the bad administration of the public good which is the good of the whole community.

CHURCH, GOOD GOVERNANCE, AND SOCIAL JUSTICE IN AFRICA

In the area of leadership and governance, the church and society are both confronted with the challenges of the primacy of the promotion of the common goods[22] in a globalised society where individualism often goes along with individual or collective egoisms. This concern for the common good is the necessary result of the establishment of institutions of governance which favour the effective control of the exercise of power by the governed. In fact, even the hierarchical church must learn again to account to the faithful for its management of this common good which is the church while working to make it more inclusive and more participatory. It is rightly in preaching, for example, that it will have the moral authority necessary to play its prophetic role with a view to the improvement of governance in society.

Speaking then of leadership and governance in the church, we start from the postulate that it concerns a church incarnated in the society which it aspires to transform thanks to the values of the Gospel. In fact, as historical community and social body, the church is not outside society but within society, for its members always belong to a society which they are called on to transform in witnessing the gospel values to it. For Jesus, the church, as community of his disciples, is in his place in the world, in society (John 17:14–16). However, this rooting of the church in society, which is a demand of the mission of redemption, is not without risks. For, in the world, the church always runs the risk of being of the world. Christ calls on the community of his disciples to distance itself from the practices of domination in the world, espousing the religion of service, the gift of self for others (John 10:42–45). Thus, this religion of service, as gift of self for others appears as the cardinal value of the model of leadership and governance which Jesus recommends to the church. However, in order to rise to this challenge of an ethical and evangelical leadership able to establish it as "salt of the earth" (Matt 5:13) and "light of the world" (Matt 5:14), the church must not only exorcise the pathologies of clericalism as the matrix of power at its heart, but also sign up to the perspective of a governance based on accountability.

---

22. The *Laudato Si* of Pope Francis employs the happy expression "our common house." Here, nature is being perceived as a common good.

More than a half century after independence, democracy, reconciliation, justice and peace, as culture and socio-political values, remain veritable challenges to establish on the African continent. As we have noted, there was a glimmer of hope in the 1990s with the wind of democracy. However, instead of democracy and justice, many African countries had only a loose multiparty system. Despite the timid emergence of a clear civil society, the game of politics in most of the countries is still in the grasp of a corrupt and kleptocratic political élite which is somewhat indifferent to the elementary demands of social justice. The second African synod, which took place in Rome from 4 to 25 October 2009, studied the contribution of the Catholic Church in Africa to the building up of African societies that are reconciled, fairer and more peaceful. Subsequently, on 19 November 2011, in Benin, Pope Benedict XVI gave the post-synodical apostolic exhortation *Africae Munus* (AM) to the Catholic Church in Africa. From the first chapter of this document, the Pope signals that in taking up the themes of reconciliation, justice and peace, the synod was looking at *"the church's public role and her place in Africa today."*[23]

With regard to the public role of the church, the pastoral constitution *Gaudium et Spes* from Vatican II, privileges the leadership of the laity in the governance of society, discouraging direct interventions by the members of the clergy:

> Secular duties and activities belong properly although not exclusively to laymen . . . Laymen should also know that it is generally the function of their well-formed Christian conscience to see that the divine law is inscribed in the life of the earthly city; from priests they may look for spiritual light and nourishment. Let the layman not imagine that his pastors are always such experts, that to every problem which arises, however complicated, they can readily give him a concrete solution, or even that such is their mission. Rather, enlightened by Christian wisdom and giving close attention to the teaching authority of the church, let the layman take on his own distinctive role.[24]

As religious, not "political, guides," pastors must devote themselves chiefly to the spiritual formation of the laity so that the latter may make their faith a contribution to the sanctifying of the temporal order. According to Pope Benedict XVI, "one of the tasks of the church in Africa consists in forming upright consciences receptive to the demands of justice, so as to produce men and women willing and able to build this just social order by their

---

23. Benedict XVI, *Postsynodal Apostolic Exhortation Africae Munus*, n.17.
24. Vatican II, *Pastoral Constitution Gaudium et Spes*, n. 43, §2.

responsible conduct."[25] However, the visibility of the engagement of the laity in political and social life remains a challenge to take up in today's world.

If for Pope Benedict XVI, "there is no doubt that the building of a just social order is part of the competence of the political sphere, *yet one of the tasks of the church in Africa consists in forming upright consciences receptive to the demands of justice,* so as to produce men and women willing and able to build this just social order by their responsible conduct."[26] The political sphere is clearly distinguished here from the other spheres of society in an approach which takes for granted the social differentiation trumpeted by the theories of modernity. Each sphere would thus have its specific competence to be respected. Turning, for example, to the scandal of the economic injustice suffered by Africa, Benedict XVI states that "given the chronic poverty of its people, who suffer the effects of exploitation and embezzlement of funds both locally and abroad, the opulence of certain groups shocks the human conscience."[27] That is why, "acting in concert with all other components of civil society, *the church must speak out against the unjust order that prevents the peoples of Africa from consolidating their economies . . ."*[28]

Addressing the clergy, and particularly the bishops who, as successors of the apostles, are at the summit of the pyramid of the local ecclesial hierarchy, Benedict XVI recalls, in the spirit of the Gospel, that "the moral authority and the prestige that uphold the exercise of your juridical power can only come from the holiness of your life."[29] In other words, they must preach by example. This example involves holiness of personal life, the promotion of communion and collegiality on the level of international, national and regional conferences, the good administration of the human and financial resources of the church, etc. In fact, Benedict XVI does not fail to recall that the service of reconciliation, justice and peace has to begin within the very bosom of the church: "The church, for her part, is committed to promoting within her own ranks and within society a culture that respects the rule of law."[30]

The Pope calls on the bishops especially to be "good pastors and servants of the flock entrusted to your care, exemplary in life and conduct. The good administration of your dioceses requires your presence. To make your message credible, see to it that your dioceses become models in the conduct of personnel, in transparency and good financial management. Do not

---

25. Benedict XVI, *Postsynodal Apostolic Exhortation Africae Munus*, n. 22.
26. Benedict XVI, *Postsynodal Apostolic Exhortation Africae Munus*, n. 22.
27. Benedict XVI, *Postsynodal Apostolic Exhortation Africae Munus*, n. 79.
28. Benedict XVI, *Postsynodal Apostolic Exhortation Africae Munus*, n. 79.
29. Benedict XVI, *Postsynodal Apostolic Exhortation Africae Munus*, n. 100.
30. Benedict XVI, *Postsynodal Apostolic Exhortation Africae Munus*, n. 81.

hesitate to seek help from experts in auditing, so as to give example to the faithful and to society at large."[31] In other words, the church will not know how to give lessons of good governance to society if it is not exemplary in this area itself.

CONCLUSION

Colonisation has turned Africa into a veritable laboratory of the Western neoliberal model which consists in the transplantation of the Western school, the modern state and its centralised system of governance, political rivalry through political parties, the market economy, new forms of sociality and cultural practices, etc. All this has shaken the socio-political universe of Africa, the precolonial models of governance. After independence, the first African rulers were faced with the management of the ethnic and political pluralism within their young nations. They claimed that this political pluralism was prejudicial to the task of national construction. In the name of national unity or national integration, they gradually suppressed political pluralism in favour of monolithism and authoritarianism. Since the 1990s, Africa has taken up again with the multiparty system but still aspires to political regimes that are truly democratic. As the statistics have shown, the level of good governance in Africa remains very average even if there are signs of hope.

For a long time, the future of Africa has been thought of in terms of imitation of the West. After the first decade of independence, an African philosopher, Marcien Towa, wrote, correctly, that, to escape from its situation of inferiority and perpetual defeat, Africa had to seize this "secret weapon," which enabled, and still enables, the West to have the upper hand over her, notably, its science.[32] For several decades, and without success, Africa has tried out the ideology of development, hoping thus to catch up on the West.[33] It is within this matrix of imitation of the West that the questions of governance and leadership in Africa are included. Today, after all these experiences, there is good reason to think that everything that is good or has worked for the West is not necessarily good for Africa. However, at the end of the day, everything depends on the Africans themselves. It is a question of responsibility and dignity. It is to them that comes back the responsibility to evangelise the leadership in Africa. If the church in Africa succeeds in rising

31. Benedict XVI, *Postsynodal Apostolic Exhortation Africae Munus*, n. 104.

32. Towa, *Essai sur la Problématique Philosophique dans l'Afrique actuelle*, 39

33. For a critique of the ethnocentrism of the concept of development, see Rist, *Le Développement*.

to the challenge of good governance within itself, then it will have the moral authority necessary to inspire that governance in society.

BIBLIOGRAPHY

Amselle Jean-Loup et *Elikia M'bokolo*, eds. *Au Cœur de l'Ethnie. Ethnies, tribalisme et État en Afrique. Afrique.* Paris: La. Découverte, 1985.

Appadurai, Arjun. *Après le colonialisme : Les conséquences culturelles de la globalisation.* Paris: Payot, 2001.

Aristotle. *La Politique.* Paris: Vrin, 2005.

Bayart, Jean François. *L'Etat au Cameroun.* Paris: Presses de la Fondation Nationale des Sciences Politiques, 1979.

Benedict XVI, Pope. *L'exhortation apostolique postsynodale Africae Munus*, 2011.

Boukari-Yabara, Amzat. *Africa Unite! Une histoire du Panafricanisme.* Paris:La Découverte, 2014.

Calvez, Jean-Yves. *Politique: Une Introduction.* Paris: Alto-Aubier, 1995.

Dupuy, Francis. *Anthropologie Economique.* Paris: Armand Colin, 2008.

Fanon, Frantz. *Les damnés de la terre.* Paris: La découverte, 2002.

Giraud, Gaël. "Laudato si': un appello decisivo." In *Curare madre terra: Commento all'enciclica* Laudato si' *di papa Francesco*, Leonardo Boff et al. Bologna: Emi, 2015.

Hebga, Meinrad. *Les étapes des regroupements africains.* Dakar: Collection Afrique Documents, Dossier spécial 98–99, 1968.

Hollenbach, David. *Bien commun et éthique chrétienne*, Paris: Editions Facultés Jésuites de Paris, 2017.

Mbembe, Achille. *Les Jeunes et l'Ordre Politique en Afrique*, Paris: L'Harmattan, 1985.

Mo Ibrahim Foundation. *Report of the Ibrahim Index of African Governance, 2017.* https://sun-connect-news.org/fileadmin/DATEIEN/Dateien/New/2017-IIAG-Report.pdf/.

Munoz, José-Maria. "Au nom du développement : Ethnicité, Autochtonie et promotion du secteur privé au Nord Cameroun." *Politique Africaine* 112 (2008) 67–85.

Nyanchoga, Samuel.A., Francis Muchoki, and P. O. Ogula, *Governance in Africa: Historicaland Contemporary Perspectives.* Nairobi-Kenya: CUEA Press, 2010.

Popper, Karl Raimund. *Misère de l'historicisme.* Paris: Plon, 1961.

Ricoeur, Paul. *Soi-même Comme un Autre.* Paris: Seuil, 1990.

Rist, Gilbert. *Le Développement : Histoire d'une Croyance Occidentale.* Paris: PUF, 1987

Rivière, Claude. *Anthropologie Politique.* Paris: Armand Colin, 2000.

Towa, Marcien. *Essai sur la Problématique Philosophique dans l'Afrique actuelle.* Yaoundé: Clé, 1971.

Thomson, Alex. *An Introduction to African Politics.* London: Routlege, 2000.

Vatican II. *Constitution Pastorale Gaudium et Spes*, 1965.

Warnier, Jean-Pierre. *la mondialisation de la culture*, Paris: La Découverte, 2004.

———. *Régner au Cameroun*: le roi-pot. Paris: Karthala, 2009.

Yamed, Bechir Ben. *Jeune-Afrique.* n° 1530 du 30 avril 1990.

8

The Ethical Challenge of Convergent Technologies
STEFANO ZAMAGNI

1. INTRODUCTION

The aim of this paper is to throw light on some ethical consequences associated with the current rapid diffusion of convergent technologies. It is sloppily reductive to identify the Fourth Industrial Revolution simply with a new technological paradigm. To emphasise this dimension alone, as, unfortunately, is the case with most of the literature on this subject, does not enable us to grasp the elements of rupture on the social and cultural fronts which are being revealed by this emerging phenomenon. This does not allow us to devise strategies of intervention deep enough to face the contemporary challenges. Right from the beginning, I would like to clarify the perspective from which I am going to investigate these realities. The present author does not see himself either in the position of the "*laudatores temporis acti*," the so-called techno-pessimists, or in that of the uncritical admirers of the "magnificent progressive destiny" of humanity. If those who praise the Fourth Industrial Revolution are wrong, those who disparage it are not right. In fact, I regard the present techno-scientific trajectory as something positive in itself, and, moreover, unstoppable. However, it is something that has to be governed with wisdom (that is, with reasonableness) and not only with competence (that is, with rationality).

To understand better my position, I deem necessary to clarify the notion of development, a word very much overused today. In its etymological sense, development indicates the action of freeing somebody from the entanglements, traps and chains which inhibit his/her freedom of action. (The prefix "s" in the Italian "sviluppo" (development) stands for "dis" and confers an opposite sense on the word to which it is joined). It is above all to St. Paul VI that we owe the emphasis on the connection between development and freedom: development as a process of expansion of the real freedoms enjoyed by human beings.[1] In biology, development is synonymous with the growth of an organism. In the social sciences, on the other hand, the term indicates the passage from one condition to another and, therefore, refers to the notion of change (as when one says: that country has passed from the state of an agricultural society to that of an industrial one). In this sense, the concept of development can be associated with that of progress. Bear in mind, however, that the latter is not a merely descriptive concept since it involves an implicit yet indispensable value judgement. In fact, progress is not simply change but rather change towards the better, and so it implies an increase in value. It follows that the judgement of progress depends on the value which one intends to take into consideration. In other words, a valuation of progress and, therefore, of development requires the determination of what it is that has to proceed towards the better. Even if endowed with artificial intelligence, robots are not, and never will be, adequate to such a task.

The central point to be observed is that development cannot be reduced solely to economic growth—still measured today by that indicator well known to all, the GDP (Gross Domestic Product). In fact, growth is only one of its dimensions, and certainly not the only one. The other two dimensions are the socio-relational and the spiritual. However: the three dimensions stand in a multiplicative relation, not an additive one. This means that it is not possible to sacrifice, say, the socio-relational dimension in order to cause an increase of growth—as it is happening today, unfortunately. In a multiplication, even if a single factor is zero, the whole product becomes zero. This is not the case in a sum-total where the annulment of an addendum does not cancel the total; it could even increase it. This is the great difference between the notions of total good (the sum of the individual goods) and of common good (the product of the individual goods). Strictly speaking, it is impossible to speak of integral and inclusive growth whereas one can and ought to speak of integral and inclusive development. Basically, integral human development is a transformational project which has to do with the change of people's lives in the sense of their betterment. Growth, on the other hand, is not transformative in itself. It is for this reason that, as history teaches us, there have been examples of communities or nations which declined even though they were growing. Development belongs to

---

1. See *Populorum Progressio*.

the order of ends whereas growth, which is an accumulative project, belongs to the order of means. An ironic fable, of unknown authorship, enables us to grasp the point in question. An economist was seeking to demonstrate that growth is the decisive factor for development. "This is a law of both the economy and of nature: all growth is good in itself." Among the audience at the conference, someone raised his hand and a hesitant voice called out: "Unfortunately, the cancerous cell thinks that too"!

2. THE "RES NOVAE" OF THE 4TH INDUSTRIAL REVOLUTION

The promise of an empowering and so a transformation both of man and society which is made today by the converging technologies of the NBIC group explains the extraordinary attention that technoscience is receiving in a number of areas, from the cultural to the scientific, from the economic to the political. The end being pursued is not only the empowering of the mind, and not even just the enlargement of diagnostic and therapeutic capacity when it comes to the whole spectrum of pathologies, and, still more, not the improvement in the means of controlling and manipulating information. What is intended is the artificialisation of human beings and, at the same time, the anthropomorphisation of the machine. It is to Julian Huxley that we owe the invention of the word "transhumanism" to describe a future world in which, instead of oppositions between beings, we shall have a continuous hybridisation of the human. As a global movement, transhumanism started in the Silicon Valley, thanks to the efforts of Google and Apple, whose aim is to construct an "enhanced human" with increased abilities. It is on this that it is urgent today to lift the veil of silence, opening a high-profile debate. In fact, the question concerns the anthropological dimension. There are two conceptions of the human which are confronting each other: that of the human-person and that of the human-machine. The latter is gaining ground over the first. That explains, among other things, why the ideal of the human machine is today causing a real emergency in education: training/instruction is replacing education. The human machine "seeks" instruction; education is no use to it. The reference here is to the theory of equilibration, according to which the engine of the mental development of the child and of the young person is a process of cognitive adaptation to impulses coming from outside them.[2]

---

2. For a stimulating critical treatment, I refer to L. Palazzani, *Il potenziamento umano*, where the A. also tackles the problem of the editing of the genome, that is, the deliberate restructuring of one or more chapters of the genetic inheritance contained in cells.

Nothing could be more mechanistic. This is a vision inspired by the principle of homoeostasis, the same one that is at the basis of cybernetic theories. A worrying signal of this reductionism is the gradual disappearance of the figure of the educator. The master-teacher is reduced to the role of facilitator or mediator who must not educate but only assist the process of self-learning or self-training because only what one does by oneself is of value. This is one of the most devastating consequences of libertarian individualism, of which I shall speak in the final section. (It comes to mind the thought of H. Arendt, according to which the master is the one who takes responsibility of the world in which the pupil lives). Not only that, but the professed anti-authoritarianism—according to which, it is not permitted to condition or guide the "free" choices of the subject—is actually hiding an authoritarian vision: only the expert in self-training can speak about education. But didactic methods do not lead to knowledge or are able to measure it objectively, as one tends to believe. It could be of interest to note that we have evidence today which denounces the dependence of an increasing number of young people on the iPhone—depressive syndromes, decreased capacity for concentration, especially among those young people for whom the smartphone is a "drug"[3]—(). So much so that two of the largest American investment funds (Calstrs, the pension fund for the Californian teachers, and the Jana Partners hedge fund) have publicly invited Apple to modify the intensity and the way of using their new machine and to prepare measures specifically directed at teachers.

Let us look at another important novelty associated with the phenomenon at stake. It concerns the new method of organising production (not solely in the manufacturing sphere) known as Industry 4.0. This is an expression coined by the German firm, Bosch, and presented for the first time at the Hannover Trade Fair in 2011. Artificial intelligence, robotics, genomics and information technology are literally revolutionising both the means of production and the meaning of human work. The fusion between the real world of *plants* and the virtual world of information, between the physical world of people and the digital world of data, has given birth to a mixed cyber-physical system which aims at solving those problems which the models of the past have not been able to: like reducing waste; gathering information from the working process and redeveloping it in real time; anticipating project errors by virtualising the production; valuing fully the creativity of the worker; and incorporating the specific requests of the client in all the stages of the production process.[4]

3. Twenge, *iGen*.
4. For an incisive description, I refer to Magone, *Tecnologia e fattore umano nella*

Clearly, in order that the *Cyber-Physical System* (CPS)—the heart of the Industry 4.0 project—can produce the expected results, it is essential that the firm includes a radical organisational innovation which abandons the obsolete Ford-Taylorist model based on hierarchy and an excessive specialisation of tasks. It is of little use to acquire the new machines and to activate their technological operating systems unless there is a management change which knows how to value and develop a participatory culture among all who work in the firm. That is why, for some time, there has been talk of bringing into firms new professional figures such as the "Digital Innovation Officer" responsible for digital innovation; the "Technology Innovation Manager," to facilitate innovation; the "Data Protection Officer" in charge of the protection of data and privacy; the "Coding expert" who teaches how to order the machine to carry out a specific task through the programing language (the coding, to be precise); and yet others. These are indispensable professions for managing better the changes imposed by the use of "big data," of the "internet of things"—an expression used first by Kevin Ashton in 1999—and, in the near future, the "internet of beings," which represents the third phase of the life of the net. It is precisely the lack of such figures which explains some paradoxes that would be otherwise inexplicable. An empirical confirmation of the validity of this observation comes from a recent enquiry of the OECD (*Productivity Trends*, Paris, 2014) which has served to confirm the so-called "Solow paradox": notwithstanding the enormous increase in the power of computers and digital technologies, overall productivity has not increased as much as ought to have been expected. Utilising the data of the G7 countries, the OECD researchers have calculated that in the twenty years 1970–1990, productivity in the seven most advanced countries increased by an average of 2,6% per year; on the other hand, in the period 1991–2013, marked by the general diffusion of the new technologies into the world of business, productivity rose in the same countries by an average of 1,7 % per year.

A few explanations have been advanced to explain the paradox. The most plausible refers to the so-called "great war management problem." In the years preceding the outbreak of the First World War, there was an awesome advance in military technology while military strategy remained basically the same as that which prevailed at the time of the Franco-Prussian War of 1870. *Mutatis mutandis*, the analogy with the present situation is perfect. The new technologies have been adopted so rapidly as to render business strategies irremediably obsolete. Bear in mind that what has happened corresponds to the phenomenon of the "displacement of ends" which takes place

---

fabbrica digitale.

in bureaucracy. Some time ago, the American sociologist, Robert Merton, explained that rules and procedures which were initially meant to prevent administrative chaos became ends in themselves. People work as if sticking to the rules were an end in itself and not, rather, a tool for the end which the business is supposed to be pursuing, i.e. the creation of shared wealth. (To tell the truth, it is fair to say that the decrease in productivity is, at least in part, due to statistical methods still used to measure the GDP. Such methods continue to reflect the transition from agriculture to industry and so are not adequate to represent the misalignment between output increases and improvement in human well-being brought about by the new technologies).

As F. Venier[5] has made quite clear, the principal factor responsible today for the increase in productivity is digital fluency, consisting of the body of new skills made possible by the introduction of the new technologies. This is a metaskill which goes beyond mere digital literacy, that is, the simple knowledge of programmes and applications. When, in 2001, Marc Preusky traced the difference between digital natives and digital immigrants, he could certainly not imagine that his distinction would become obsolete within the span of the following decade. Today, the important distinction is not between digital firms and non-digital ones but between firms which are digitally fluent—and which succeed—and fiirms which are not—and, therefore, simply survive. The former, in fact, have workers who are able to integrate marketing within design, making use of the feedback from sales, something which translates into keeping down costs and increasing the levels of competitiveness.

Basically, today, we are faced with a new division in the labour market, that between the digital workforce and the non-digital workforce. We shall speak of the anthropological and economic consequences of this in the next section. Here I shall limit myself to reiterating the urgency of updating the managerial culture inherited from the recent past, a culture which is incapable of filling the profound gap between the logic of participation demanded by digital fluency, which encourages horizontal collaboration oblivious to hierarchical relations, and the model still dominant in businesses, which privileges linear processes and hierarchical control of a bureaucratic nature. Thus, it happens that, thanks to the possibility of employing a digital workforce, firms that started off as digital and have not been subject to the limits represented by organisational models of the past, end up enjoying an advantage compared with digitally immigrant ones. Consider, in short, of what could happen with the huge-scale employment of 3D printers, applied not only on the production side but extended also to the consumption

---

5. Venier, *La forza lavoro digitale e il futuro dell'organizzazione*.

side. As is well known, the model of the 3D printer—the so-called Rep Rap (*Replication Rapid Prototyper*)—is self-replicating and free. Potentially, a 3D printer could enable firms to produce batches of a single unit of production. That means that it could reproduce its own parts (those that are of plastic) and since the schemes are available to all with a few clicks, each one can in time contribute his own improvements and share them with others.

The printer's way of conceiving and producing is the opposite of the careful operations of the craftsman. This new way proceeds through "additive manufacture": the three dimensional model is broken down into very thin horizontal layers so that the object is constructed from bottom to top, like a superimposition of plates. Work no longer encounters the resistance of wood or stone. The result is that work is no longer a place but a flow, an activity which can be carried out in different places. Creativity and innovation are required from all the workers and not just those in managerial positions. The American AT&T has introduced a system of "gathering ideas" within the company. It works as follows: arranged in groups, the workers present the managers with their own project, as if they were before a "venture capitalist" who has to decide whether to finance it or not. The workers are thus encouraged to take on the risk, at least in part—something that gives rise to new problems in that it concerns the assets both of governance and of ownership. It is worth recalling that Adrian Bowyer—the inventor of the 3D printer—had it in mind to bring about with his machine what Marx believed he could achieve with a political revolution. "The Rep-Rap—he wrote—will enable a revolutionary appropriation of the means of production on the part of the proletariat" because the consumer can also become the producer—this is the figure of the so-called *prosumer*. In every neighbourhood—Jeremy Rifkin has written—3D printers will be found with higher performance than those which a single individual could acquire and handle, and, in these places, the neighbours will be able to help themselves to manufacture everything which is useful for domestic life according to their own plans. Naturally, the near future will have the task of showing whether this is realistic or just utopia.

An interesting historical precedent helps us to understand the import of what is happening. "The man who passes his whole life in carrying out a few simple tasks with results that are about the same or almost has no opportunity to exercise his intelligence or inventiveness in finding expedients which can overcome difficulties which he never encounters."[6] This is why Smith wishes for a decisive intervention by the State to impose a system of compulsory education for all as a way to counter the dulling of the faculties

---

6. See Book V of Smith, *Wealth of Nations*.

of the workers caused by that process. The coming of the First Industrial Revolution, however, saw another way of conceiving and so of making use of the division of labour. The great economist, David Ricardo, and, above all, the engineer and mathematician, Charles Babbage, were its creators. The idea from which they start is that, since individuals vary in abilities and personal gifts, each is the bearer of a specific and comparative advantage in the world of work. Now, the division of labour and the ensuing specialisation become the practical instruments enabling society to draw the maximum advantage from the existence of these different abilities among individuals. As is clear, while, for Smith, the division of labour is the "cause" of the differences in personal abilities, for Ricardo and Babbage, the opposite is true: it is these differences which render the division of labour suitable.[7]

It is easy to grasp the "pedagogic" implications of this reversal of the causal connection: where "Smith's worker" has to invest in continual education so as not to lose his own abilities (and ultimately his own identity), and therefore the division of labour is seen as the opportunity to favour and incentivise the acquisition of new knowledge with study and culture, "Babbage's worker" does not possess any motive of this kind since the division of labour serves precisely to minimise the need for learning on the part of the worker before he enters the productive process: on the contrary, the more rigid the process of the division of labour, the more restricted is the content of knowledge needed for each job, and therefore there is less to learn before beginning it. It follows that, whereas Smith's workers "grow" alongside their work, Babbage's workers are subject to a terrible threat, that of seeing themselves replaced at any moment since they are characterised by a high degree of replaceability. Now, whereas during the Fordist period, Babbage's conception was dominant—and it could not be otherwise—the post-Fordist model "vindicates" Smith: both process and product innovations demand the central importance of human resources with all that that involves.

3. ON THE ETHICAL IMPLICATIONS OF THE FOURTH INDUSTRIAL REVOLUTION

It is in the field of public ethics that the consequences of the diffusion of the convergent technologies in our society are posing the most delicate problems, first of all that of understanding how the digitalisation of our lives is

---

7. Dazzled by the ideas of W. Leibnitz, who, in the second half of the XVII century had already gone so far as to invent the calculating machine, Babbage, at the beginning of the XIX century, claimed that, in time, a superhuman calculating reason would be achieved. See Bostrom, *Superintelligenze*.

succeeding in also changing the way in which we perceive them. Yet, it is precisely on this front that we observe a kind of *"fin de non recevoir"* on the part of high culture, scientific and philosophical. I wish to say something about (only) two aspects of this problem. The first concerns the question of trust: can artificial intelligence create the trust which is necessary for the correct functioning of our market economies? The second aspect concerns the problem of responsibility, of what it means to be responsible in the era of digitalisation. Are "smart machines" moral agents and therefore responsible agents? Will it be algorithms which will rule us in all those cases where people are not able to have a full understanding of the questions on which they have to pass their judgements? I shall begin with the first aspect.

It is generally agreed that trust is one of the decisive factors to ensure the advantages of collective action and so to maintain the process of development. This is easily explained. All the exchanges which take place in the market are incorporated in contracts: explicit or implicit; spot or forward; complete or incomplete; contestable or not. Except for spot contracts, all the other types need some kind of mechanism for them to be enforced. We know that the enforcement of contracts—what to do so that the terms and obligations of the contract are honoured—depends, in different ways and to various degrees, on legal norms, on the social norms of behaviour prevalent in a particular community, and on mutual trust. So, when the first two factors are not sufficient to ensure the enforcement of contracts, trust is necessary for the market to function. This is especially true in our days, given that globalisation and the Fourth Industrial Revolution have cut off the traditional bonds (of blood, religion and tradition) which functioned in the past as more or less perfect surrogates for trust.

Notice the typical paradox of the present period of history. While trust in institutions, both political and economic, is declining for a variety of reasons, among which is the endemic increase in corruption, the global market is dominated increasingly by firms and organisations which demand unprecedented signs of trust from their clients and users. It is as if the individuals were learning the lesson of the well-known story of Puccini's Tosca: mutual distrust always produces suboptimal results.[8] As an example, consider the giving of permission to total strangers to use one's own home (Airbnb) or the sharing of car journeys with people one does not know (Uber, Blablacar). Indeed, what is happening is that the decline in institutional trust of the vertical type is being matched by an increase in personal trust, that is, horizontal trust between people. For Tim Wu, the famous jurist of Columbia University, what we are facing is a massive transfer

---

8. Leibenstein, *On some economic aspects of a fragile input: trust.*

of social trust: after the abandonment of trust in institutions, there is a move to technology. "Trust is the new currency of the world economy. It is a real multiplier of the opportunity for gain because it enables the development of underutilised goods."[9] One thinks of the phenomenon of cryptocurrencies—the best known of which, but certainly not the only one, is the bitcoin—which are digital currencies that are exchanged among peers. The transactions are not guaranteed by any central authority but validated by the participants themselves by means of an algorithm. At the same time, the strength of these cryptocurrencies enables the performance of anonymous transactions which are not subject to taxation and ensure protection from confiscation by the State. Their basic infrastructure is the blockchain which is a register of distributed properties on which are noted all the transactions without possibility of modification. Today, blockchain technology—until now used practically only in the financial sphere—already allows a vast gamut of applications, from those in the social sphere to those of a politico-administrative type. One thinks of the handling of administrative processes where the blockchain can certify a particular act, in a secure way and for ever, without the need for third-party certification. Consider also that the United Nations are planning to make use of the same technology for the handling of aid of various kinds to refugees and migrants. And so on.[10]

The heart of the contemporary paradox lies in the fact that today's market economy has more need than ever of mutual trust in order to be able to properly function. At the same time, however, the extraordinary levels of efficiency reached by our economic systems so far make us forget that it is necessary to strengthen the fiduciary links between people. This is because, while the market "consumes" trust increasingly, it does not succeed, in the present institutional situation, in producing enough of it. Hence the disturbing social dilemma: we are seeking ever greater efficiency in order to increase material well-being, wealth and security, but, in order to pursue this objective, we squander irresponsibly the patrimony of trust which we have inherited from previous generations. (Patrimony is a word which comes from "patrum munus": the gift of the fathers). Bear in mind, a command economy can fare well without trust to ensure its proper functioning; not so a market economy, as we said above. In the time of the USSR ("Trust is good, control is better," Lenin was accustomed to say) people felt no need to invest in interpersonal trust; institutional trust was enough.

How do we solve this dilemma? David Hume's proposal is well known. For the founder of philosophical empiricism (and initiator of ethical

---

9. Botsman, *Di chi possiamo fidarci*.
10. Gaggi, *Il sogno di blockchain*.

non-cognitivism), the disposition to award trust, and to repay the received trust, finds its real foundation in the personal advantages which spring from a good reputation. "We can satisfy our appetites better in an indirect and artificial way . . . It is thus that I learn to give a service to someone else without feeling a real benevolence for him. In fact, I foresee that he will render me a service, expecting another of the same type in order to preserve the same *reciprocity* of good offices with me or with others"[11] (). It is almost unbelievable that a great philosopher like Hume could fall into such a conceptual oversight as to confuse reciprocity with a sequence of self-interested exchanges. By contrast with the principle of exchange of equivalents, reciprocity is a body of gift relations, interrelated among them. It is even more strange that subsequent philosophical thought never observed the pragmatic contradiction into which Hume fell when, a few lines above the passage just quoted, he gives the example of two cultivators of grain who end up suffering loss on account of the absence of reciprocal guarantees. Again in the *Treatise*, we read: "Your grain is ripe today; mine will be tomorrow. It will be useful for both of us if I work for you today and tomorrow you give me a hand. But I am not displaying any particular sentiment of benevolence towards you and I know that neither are you doing the same for me. Therefore, I shall not work for you today because I do not have any guarantee that tomorrow you will show me any gratitude. Thus, I shall leave you to work on your own today and you will do the same tomorrow. In the meantime, however, the bad weather will intervene and so we shall both end up in losing our crops through lack of reciprocal trust and guarantee." (*Ibid*).

Nor is the solution of the Kantian categorical imperative of great help for present purposes. "Follow the rule which, if everyone followed it, you could wish for its result." This is a principle of equality of duty. However, Kant's theory suffers from an evident aporia when one seeks to put it into practice. In fact, the Kantian individual chooses the rule which he is going to apply by assuming that everyone else is also going to apply it. However, since, in general, different people have different preferences about the final result, the Kantian rules preferred by people will also be different *a priori*. The result is that each will follow his preferred rule (whence his action) assuming that others will act in a way in which, in reality, they will not act at all. That means that the Kantian principle cannot be applied to itself; it cannot validate itself: this is really a serious logical inconsistency for a moral doctrine which is intended to be universal. Only if all the individuals were identical among themselves in terms of their own preferential system would

---

11. Hume *Treatise of Human Nature*, 552–3.

the aporia in question disappear. But it is clear that if this were the case, then the Kantian principle would lose all its practical relevance.

Today, on the basis of laboratory experiments and of some results obtained from the neurosciences, behavioural economics suggests the following way of escape from the dilemma indicated above. In a miscellaneous work published in the prestigious American journal, *Science* (2006), it is reported that if one deactivates a particular zone of the cerebral cortex, by transcranial magnetic stimulation, the subjects increase their pro-social behaviour. This leads to a substantial increase in their degree of trust. In particular, by the nasal administration of a certain amount of oxytocin (a hormone produced by many mammals), it has been discovered that it deactivates the cerebral activity of a specific region of the brain (the amygdala) which serves to control the behaviour of individuals in their relations of trust.[12] Consider also the procedures aimed at cognitive development which act on capacities such as attention, memory and the tendency to mental fatigue. There are already techniques such as deep brain stimulation which envisage the planting of a microchip in the brain; and such as transcranial direct current stimulation which provides for the stimulation of the brain with doses of electric current.

Several years ago, a group of researchers from the University of Berkeley tested out on a sample of thirty-five subjects a drug "able to produce artificially feelings of kindness and generosity towards others."[13] The results obtained confirm that tolcapone, another human hormone, contributes to increasing the degree of equanimity in dealings even with strangers and so increasing the propensity to trust. (These are attempts which aim at the mood enhancement of the subjects by modifying their character and augmenting their psychological well-being, countering their disposition to melancholy and introversion). This is not the place to discuss the plausibility of such results and to judge the effectiveness, in practice, of proposals such as that of the chemical administration of molecules aimed at strengthening our morality. I limit myself to observing that the attempt to attribute the origin of the moral sense to biology—an attempt which reduces this sense to mere cerebral chemistry—if on one hand can produce desired effects with regard to the good conduct of things, on the other hand, it reduces the space for (positive) freedom and, therefore, of individual responsibility. Viewing moral thought as intrinsic to the human brain, rather than as the product of will and culture, would involve a withdrawal in relation to the already problematic and reductive figure of *homo oeconomicus*.

12. Narvaez, *Neurobiology and the Development of Human Morality*.
13. *Current Biology*.

There is no one who does not see that, beyond appearances or official declarations, methods of this kind are to be located in the sphere of that great project, at once political and philosophical, which is transhumanism and whose aim is both to fuse man with the machine to extend his potential to an indefinite extent and (above all) to demonstrate that conscience is not an exclusively human phenomenon. The objective here is not so much commercial or financial: it is political, and, in a certain way, religious, and that in the sense that the project aims at transforming—not so much at improving—our way of life as well as our basic values. Transhumanism is the apologia for a human body and brain "augmented," that is, enriched by artificial intelligence the use of which would enable the separation of the mind from the body and so the affirmation that, in order to function, our brain would not need to have a body. This would permit the development of arguments regarding the meaning of the person and its unity. It could be interesting to recall that the word "robot" derives from the Czech *"robota"* which signifies, literally, forced labour. It appears for the first time in the science-fiction novel of Karl Capek in 1920, *RUR—Rossum's Universal Robots*. The novel describes the dream of the boss of the firm *RUR* who foretells the coming of a time in which the prices of goods will fall to zero thanks to the increase in productivity ensured by robots and in which toil and poverty will have been defeated. But the dream vanishes when the robots "decide" to eliminate their creators, killing all human beings. In the era of the Fourth Revolution, the mechanical make-up of the robot—which rendered them not so versatile and so hardly much of a benefit—has been replaced by the electronic-computer one. It is thus that cognitive manufacture has been reached where the robots are placed on the human level, understanding the context in which they operate (YuMi is one of the first collaborative robots on the market which operates not only in the manufacturing but also in the service sector).

The strategy pursued by Ray Kurzweil, the man in charge of the project which Google has been implementing for some time, aims at the production of cyborgs endowed with physical features and capacities similar to those of the *homo sapiens*. It is the objective of playing God which is hidden by the desire to take control of the reins of evolution.[14]

The physicalist approach (according to which there exists only one reality—the physical—which the cognitive sciences seek to understand by explaining how consciousness is generated), welcomed by the neurosciences, raises the serious question dealing with the connection between

---

14. Kurzweil, *Come creare una mente*, 2013. For a general treatment, see Camerer, *The potential of neuro-economics*.

responsibility and freedom. We come out of a long period during which it was accepted that freedom as expression of responsibility was matched by responsibility as consensus to the application of freedom itself. What does it mean for a worker to work all day long with a collaborative robot? We know already how the advent of social networks and the use of smartphones are changing our habits and our lifestyles. But can we imagine a future in which people pass their whole working day in "dialogue"—so to speak—with a robot without falling into new and more serious forms of alienation? It may be interesting to recall the thought of Gramsci on a question of this kind. Referring to the famous phrase of F. Taylor on the "tamed gorilla," Gramsci writes: "With brutal cynicism, Taylor expresses the goal of American society: to develop in the laboratory mechanical and automatic behaviour to the highest degree, to break the old psycho-physical connection of qualified professional work which demanded a certain active participation of the intelligence, the imagination and the initiative of the worker, and to reduce productive operations solely to their physical, mechanical aspect. But, in fact, this is nothing new: it is only the most recent phase of a long process which began with the rise of industrialism itself, a phase which is only more intense than the preceding ones and manifests itself in more brutal forms, but which too will be superseded with the creation of a new psycho-physical connection of a different type from the preceding ones and undoubtedly superior."[15] The question posed introduces us to the theme of responsibility—the second aspect I mentioned at the beginning of the section—and it is quite an intriguing one. As we know, responsibility has different meanings. One can talk about responsibility to mean a freedom which has the sense of responsibility. But one can talk of responsibility in a very different sense when it carries an obligation to which one has to respond. (This is the American concept of "accountability"). In fact, one can talk of responsibility to indicate that one is guilty of an action that has been performed. In this sense, "I am responsible" means that I am guilty of something. Thus, responsibility and freedom turn out to be closely related even if, in recent times, on the wave of advances in the neurosciences, the tendency has been to loosen the connection between freedom and responsibility. Take the enhancing operations which I have mentioned above. The subject who has been empowered would be taking his decisions not on the basis of the reasons for and against but as the result of a causal influence exercised on his brain by means of biotechnological manipulation. This is tantamount to

---

15. Gramsci, *Americanismo e fordismo*. But already in Pope Leo XIII *Rerum Novarum*, these considerations had been formulated, although in a very different context.

saying that, in order to improve the performance of human beings, they are deprived of their moral autonomy, which is the greater good.[16]

While it seems relatively easy to identify the direct responsibility of agents—as when the owner of a sweatshop exploits child labour for gain—what can we say about the economic activity which is undertaken with the intention of disadvantaging no one and which yet causes negative effects for others? For example, who is responsible for unemployment, poverty, inequality, etc.? In economics, the traditional responses consist in maintaining that these are the "unintended consequences of intentional actions" (spoken of by the school of Scottish moralists in the 18th century). Therefore, the only thing to do is to assign to society the task of remedying (or alleviating) the negative consequences. Indeed, the welfare state arose and was developed precisely to make collective and impersonal the responsibility of each individual. But is it really like this? Are we sure that the mechanisms of the free market are inevitable and that their results are unintended as we are led to believe?[17]

It is worth giving a single example. In his essay, "Is business bluffing ethical?"[18] the essay always most cited in financial theory—Albert Carr writes: "Where it seeks to do to others what it does not want others to do to us (sic!), finance must be guided by a body of ethical standards different from those of common morals or of religion: the ethical standards of the game. If an action is not strictly illegal, and can yield a profit, then to carry it out is an *obligation* for the businessman." It is this way of thinking—founded on the thesis of double morality—which lies at the origin of the great financial scandals, among them those of the last twenty years. As Z. Bauman was one of the first to note, the social organisation of second modernity has been thought up and designed to neutralise the direct and indirect responsibility of the agents. The strategy adopted—one of great intellectual subtlety—was twofold: on the one hand, to lengthen the distance (spatial and temporal) between the action and its consequences, and, on the other hand, to achieve a huge concentration of economic activity without a centralisation of power. This is the specific character of the adiaphoric company, a form of company unknown in the periods before the Second World War, whose aim is that of eliminating the question of the moral responsibility of group action. Adiaphoric is "technical" responsibility which cannot be judged in moral terms of good/evil. Adiaphoric action is assessed in solely functional terms, only on the basis of the principle that everything that is possible for the agents

---

16. On this theme, see the reflection of Donati, *Globalization of markets*.
17. See chaps. 3 and 4 of Benedict XVI *Caritas in Veritate*.
18. Carr, *Is business bluffing ethical?*

is also ethically licit, without there being the necessity of making an ethical judgement of the system, as Luhmann has taught.

In recent times, adiaphoric responsibility has received a new impulse precisely from the Fourth Industrial Revolution which is producing means which are in search of "questions" or of problems to be solved. Exactly the opposite of what happened with the previous Industrial Revolutions. Indeed, in what does it consist the principle of responsibility in the society of algorithms? From the new industrial technologies to medical diagnostics, from the social networks to the flights of aircraft, from the big data to the search engines: we entrust ourselves to complex procedures to which we delegate the success of operations which human beings do not know how to perform on their own. Yet, algorithms are irresponsible, though neither neutral nor objective, as is erroneously believed. When a programme makes an error, it does not suffer the consequences because the argument is that mathematics is exterior to morality. But this is not the case: algorithms are not pure mathematics; they are human opinions enshrined in mathematical language. They therefore discriminate, like human decision-makers. For example, the process of employment is becoming increasingly automated because this is thought to render recruitment more objective, eliminating prejudices. But, rather than diminishing, discriminatory dynamics are increasing in our society.[19]

Generalising for a moment, the real problem of smart machines begins at the moment when they perform actions which involve the need to choose or decide. The soldier-robot, the car-robot, the cleaner-robot can all make choices that are fatal for non-robotic lives. Whose is the responsibility in these cases? What is the subliminal message of Bill Gates's recent challenge to tax robots, which are endowed with electronic personalities, just like corporations which are endowed with juridical personalities? As Gunther Anders[20] has clearly explained, the XXI century has inaugurated the era of human irresponsibility, immunising subjects from their relations. "Smart machines" (those endowed with artificial intelligence) are able to take autonomous decisions which have implications both social and moral.[21] How then do we ensure that the decisions taken by these objects are ethically acceptable? Given that these machines can cause all kinds of damage, how do we make sure that they are able to differentiate between decisions that are "right" and "wrong"? And where some kind of harm cannot be avoided—think of the case of the motorless vehicle which has to choose between

---

19. Zellini, *Saranno gli algoritmi a governarci?*.
20. Gunther, *L'uomo è antiquato*.
21. See the case of the driverless car, Tesla, which killed a passenger in May 2016.

colliding with another vehicle, killing all its passengers, or running over some children who are crossing the road—how do we instruct (in the sense of programming) these machines to choose the lesser evil? The examples in the literature are already abundant. All agree on the need to endow AI with some kind of ethical canon for solving ethical dilemmas of the type of the "autonomous driver."[22]

The differences arise the moment one has to choose the way (that is, the approach) with which to proceed: top-down (the ethical principles are programmed into the intelligent machine: the human being transfers to the artificial intelligence his own ethical view of the world); or bottom-up (the machine learns to make ethically sensitive decisions from observing human behaviour in real situations). Both approaches pose serious problems. These are not so much of a technical nature; rather, they concern the larger question as to whether intelligent machines can or cannot be considered moral agents (that is, moral machines). We are just at the beginnings of a cultural and scientific debate which already promises to be simultaneously fascinating and worrying. Look, for example, at the recent positions of A. Etzioni and O. Etzioni[23] who deny the possibility of attributing the status of moral agent to Artificial Intelligence and so deny all foundation to the research programme of Internet Ethics which studies the ethical aspects of Internet Communication in its various forms.

The conclusion the two Etzioni draw is that there will be no need to teach ethics to machines even if that can be done. The same opinion is not shared, for example, by the research group which operates through the Neurolink Corporation in California. For some time, it has been developing digital technologies to achieve connections between computers and the human mind and is planning a cyber-man with a microchip in his brain. On the intricate and delicate question of the possibility of attributing "electronic personality" to intelligent robots and, more generally, the opportunity of the passage from Darwinian natural selection to the deliberate choice of the process of selection by means of the shortcut of biotechnology.[24] An important reflection is that of Adriano Fabris who distinguishes between "ethics of the internet" and "ethics on the internet."

It could be useful to consider that, in the current debate, two different ways of conceptualising AI are coming into conflict. As L. Palazzani explains, the first concerns software which seeks to reason and take cognitive

---

22. I refer to the careful work of Palazzani, *Dalla bioetica alla tecno etica*.

23. Etzioni and Etzioni, *Incorporating ethics*.

24. Bostrom, *Welcome to a world of exponential change;* and Kampowski, Moltisanti, *Migliorare l'uomo?*

decisions in the same way as human beings. For such a conception, AI would be aspiring to replace man. (Turing's famous thesis has to do with this type of AI). The second way aims rather at providing smart assistance to human actors. It represents an AI which is a partner of human beings, often referred to as "Intelligence Augmentation" or else "Cognitive Augmentation." In practice, Google is moving in the former direction; the declared object being that of fusing the human with the machine in order to increase the capacities of both in an unlimited direction; IBM, with its cognitive computing, is moving in the latter direction. In 2013, IBM launched the system of Artificial Intelligence called "Thomas Watson" in homage to its first president. Watson replies to questions on any theme, presented in ordinary language. On the first page of the site devoted to Watson, it says: "Watson is a cognitive technology which can think like a human being." It will be a question of seeing whether the machine can become more intelligent than human beings. In any case, it remains true that the standardised responses which Watson (or another machine) will be able to give will never be more effective than those which can be given by people who are able to understand the problems of other people. Indeed, although intelligent, machines will never be capable of empathy because they are not endowed with moral sentiments. In any case, more wide open than ever today is the problem of knowing how and how much the development of potentive technologies will relatively affect the values of justice and social equality. To the extent that these technologies will never be able to be enjoyed by all, in that they are very costly, there arises the question of the increase in social inequalities which is already intolerably high today. The serious risk is that of forming a parallel society made up of the richest part of the population which is growing gradually further away from the poorer, unempowered part.[25]

4. INSTEAD OF A CONCLUSION: BEYOND LIBERTARIAN INDIVIDUALISM

It is when one is confronted with problems such as those we have discussed in the previous pages that one comes to understand the serious limitations of libertarian individualism as the anthropological foundation of the current prevalent cultural matrix, especially in the West. As is well known, individualism is the philosophical position according to which it is the individual who attributes value to things and to interpersonal relations. Moreover, it is always the individual alone who decides what is good and what is evil; what is licit and what is illicit. In other words, everything is good to which

---

25. Sandel, *Contro la perfezione*.

the individual attributes value. For axiological individualism, there are no objective values but only subjective values or legitimate preferences. Z. Bauman explains that "the fact of conceiving its own members as individuals [and not as people] is the distinctive mark of modern society."[26] Individualisation, Baumann continues, "consists in the transformation of the human identity from something given to a role, and in the attribution to the actors of the responsibility for the performance of this role and the consequences of their actions"[27]. Baumann's thesis, therefore, is that "individualisation guarantees an ever-increasing number of men and women an unprecedented freedom of experimentation, but also carries with it the unprecedented role of facing its consequences." Therefore, the continually increasing gap between the "right of self-affirmation," on the one hand, and the "ability to control social contexts" in which this self-realisation has to have a place "appears to be the principal contradiction of second modernity."[28]

On the other hand, libertarianism is the thesis advanced by not a few philosophers according to whom, in order to establish freedom and responsibility, it is necessary to have recourse to the idea of self-causation. For example, G. Strawson[29], among many, maintains that fully free is only the agent who is self-caused, self-created, or, in his own words, *causa sui*, as if he were God. It is now possible to understand why, from the marriage between individualism and libertarianism, that is, from libertarian individualism, there has been able to spring the watchword of this period: "volo ergo sum," that is, "I will, therefore I am." The radicalisation of individualism in libertarian terms has led to the conclusion that every individual has the "right" to extend himself as far as his power allows him. Freedom as the loosing of links is the dominant idea in cultural circles. Since it is they which limit liberty, the links are what must be loosed. Wrongly equating the concept of links with that of chains, the limitations on freedom—the chains—are being confused with the conditions—the links—of freedom.[30] Consider the following: whereas the freedom of the moderns was basically political—the possibility of being masters of the material and social conditions of one's own existence—the individualistic freedom of the post-moderns is the claim to the right of the individual to do everything that is technically possible. We enjoy an abundance of these freedoms, but no longer the freedom to affect in practice what Marx called the social and material conditions of the society in which we

26. Bauman, *Individualmente insieme*, 29.
27. Bauman, *Individualmente insieme*, 31.
28. Bauman, *Individualmente insieme*, 39.
29. See Strawson, *Free Agents*.
30. See Dumont, *Saggi sull'individualismo*.

live. Consider what is happening today with the new technologies. On the one hand, our space of freedom is expanding, thanks to the opportunities offered by the technological enhancement of our capacities for communication. On the other hand, in order to enjoy such opportunities to the full, our freedom is exercised in uncritical subordination to the structure of the net. It seems as if today's society is returning to what, in the 16th century, Etienne de la Boetie prophetically labelled "voluntary servitude."

This is an aspect which Michel Foucault has grasped with rare perspicacity when, tackling the problem of access to the truth, he asked if it is true that today we live in a time when the market has become a "place of truth," that is, where the entire life of the subjects is subsumed in economic efficiency and where it is again the market which sees to it that the government, "to be a good government," must function according to that place of veridiction: "the market must speak the truth, and must do so in relation to the practice of government. It is its role of veridiction that, from now on, and in a clearly indirect way, will bring it to command, dictate and prescribe the legal mechanisms according to the presence or absence of which the market will have to organise itself." It is interesting to note that even a leading advocate of the digital revolution like J. Taplin has written: "The libertarians who control some of the main Internet companies do not actually believe in democracy. The people who run these monopolies believe in an oligarchy in which only the most brilliant and rich succeed in determining our future."[31] It is to be borne in mind that the various transhumanist positions are all of an individualistic stamp. But there is a further serious consequence of this cultural arrangement on the recent developments in the economic theory about the Fourth Industrial Revolution. If one consults the extended and well-documented critical survey of A. Goldfart and C. Tucker[32]—a survey which considers more than four-hundred works on the subject—it will be noted that only one aspect is made the object of attention and analysis: how far the new technologies reduce the costs of production, increase productivity, enable share prices to increase, etc. But nothing is said of the impact of digitalisation on the structure of people's preferences, on their lifestyles, on their cognitive maps. Ignoring that side of the question, as if people did not care about the fact that "numerocracy," associated with today's rampant "omnimetrics" (the tendency to measure every dimension of human life), holds out no promise of good!

The question arises spontaneously: how do we trace the origin of the spread of the individualistic-libertarian culture like wildfire? In reply, it is

---

31. Taplin, *Move fast and break things*, 3.
32. Goldfart and Tucker, *Digital Economics*.

worth recalling that the term *individuum* arose in the context of medieval scholastic philosophy and is the translation of the Greek *atomos*.[33] But it is from the end of the eighteenth century, when the civil vision of the economy disappears both from scientific research and politico-cultural debate, that individualism begins to be coupled with libertarianism. The reasons for this marriage are several and different. I limit myself to indicating the two most important. On the one hand, the spread in the spheres of European high culture of the utilitarian philosophy of Jeremy Bentham, whose principal work, dating from 1789, was to take a few decades before becoming a leading part of economic discourse. It is with utilitarian morals and not earlier with the Protestant ethic—as some still maintain—that there takes foot within economic science the hyper-minimalist anthropology of the *homo oeconomicus* and with it the methodology of social atomism. The following passage from Bentham is notable for its clarity and profundity of meaning: "The community is a fictitious body, composed of individual subjects, which is considered as if they made up its members. The interests of this community are what? The sum of the interests of the several members of which it is composed."

On the other hand, the full achievement of industrial society following the First Industrial Revolution. The industrial society is one that produces goods. The machine predominates everywhere and the rhythms of life are marked in a mechanical way. To a large extent, energy replaces muscular power and is accountable for the enormous increase in productivity which, in turn, is accompanied by mass production. Energy and machine transform the nature of work: personal abilities are broken up into basic components. Hence the need for coordination and organisation. Thus steps forward a world in which men are visualised as "things" because it is easier to coordinate "things" than people, and in which the person is separated from the role she performs. Organisations, *in primis* businesses, are concerned with roles, not so much with people. Moreover, that happens not only within the factory but within society as a whole. This is the deep meaning of Ford-Taylorism as a (successful) attempt to theorise and to translate into practice this model of social order. The claim of the "assembly line" finds its correlation in the spread of consumerism. Hence the schizophrenia typical of "modern times": on the one hand, there is an intensification in the loss of the meaning of work (the alienation owing to the depersonalisation of the figure of the worker); on the other hand, by way of compensation, consumption becomes opulent. In the course of the twentieth century, Marxist thought and its

---

33. It is Severino Boezio who defines the person as "naturae relationalis individua substantia."

political ramifications were to be adopted, with varying but modest success, to offer ways of escape from this model of society.[34]

Very different from each other in their philosophical assumptions and their political consequences, these two reasons ended up by generating on the economic level a result that was perhaps unexpected: the affirmation of an idea of the market antithetical to that of the tradition of thought of civil economy. An idea which sees the market as an institution founded on a double norm: the *impersonality* of the relations of exchange (the less I know my counterparts, the greater will be my advantage because it is better to do business with strangers!); and the *exclusively self-interested* motivation of those who take part so that "moral feelings" such as sympathy, reciprocity, fraternity etc. do not play any significant role in the arena of the market. Thus it has happened that the gradual and majestic expansion of the relations of the market in the course of the last century and a half have ended up in reinforcing that pessimistic character of human beings which was already theorised by Hobbes and Mandeville according to whom only the harsh laws of the market would succeed in taming their perverse impulses and forces of an anarchic type. The caricature of human nature which thus stands out has contributed to endorsing a twofold error: that the sphere of the market coincides with that of egoism, with the place where each one pursues, as best he can, his own individual interests, and, symmetrically, that the sphere of the State coincides with that of solidarity, of the pursuit of collective interests. This is the foundation of the well-known dichotomous model of social order based on the State and market: a model in which the State is identified with the public sphere and the market with the private one.[35]

Which component of our conceptual infrastructure has to change if we are to be able to go beyond the individualistic-libertarian thought which is rampant today? Firstly, we must abandon that anthropological pessimism which goes back to Guicciardini and Machiavelli, passes through Hobbes and Mandeville and ends up with the modern systematisation of economic mainstream. It is the assumption that human beings are individuals who are too opportunistic and self-interested to think that, in their actions, they can take account of categories such as moral feelings, reciprocity, the common good etc. In his famous *Fable of the Bees. Private Vices, Public Benefits*, B. Mandeville wrote: "I think I have shown that neither the friendly qualities and the kind feelings which are natural in man nor the virtues which he is able to acquire... are the foundations of society. The latter are what we call the evil in the world. This is the great principle which makes us social

---

34. On this point, I refer to Pope Francis, *Evangelii Gaudium*.
35. In this connection, see the reflection of Habermas, *Morale, diritto, politica*.

creatures, the solid base, the life and the support of all trade and business without exceptions."[36]

It is on this anthropological cynicism—founded, bear in mind, on an assumption and not on evidence drawn from the real world—that there has been constructed that imposing edifice of self-interest which is still the dominant paradigm in economics. It is clear, or ought to be on careful reflection, that within the horizon of the *homo oeconomicus* there cannot be any room for solving the ethical dilemmas stemming from convergent technologies. In fact, from this perspective, the human is a one-dimensional being, able to act only to attain a single aim. The other dimensions, from the political to the social, emotional and religious must be held strictly apart, or, at most, can contribute to making up the system of chains within which the objective function of the agents is to be maximised. The category of the "common" knows two dimensions: being in common and what is owned in common. So then, there is no one who does not see that, in order to solve the problem of what is owned in common, it is necessary that the subjects involved recognise their being-in-common. This is hammered home in Pope Francis's *Laudato Sì* with a wealth of details.

Clearly, a conception of this kind would make sense if it were true that all (or the majority) of individuals were self-interested and asocial subjects. But the factual evidence, which is now quite abundant and based both on experiments in the laboratory and on empirical research, informs us that this is not the case because the majority consists of those who, in reality, exhibit pro-social behaviour (for example, sacrificing themselves for collective aims) and are not self-interested (for example, they practice charitable giving systematically). This is why Lynn Stout[37] advances forcefully the proposal to take seriously, in the theory of law, the idea of conscience, that interior force which inspires pro-social and non-egoistical behaviour. Conceptualising the law as a kind of system of prices which have to be paid as compensation for various kinds of negligence and disregard for contractual terms has as its, certainly negative, result that of increasing the "cost of conscience." Teaching egoism is a self-fulfilling prophecy.

We know that the behavioural traits which are observed in reality (prosocial, asocial, antisocial) are present everywhere in society. What changes from one society to another is their combination: in some historical periods antisocial and/or a social behaviour is prevalent; in others, prosocial behaviour, with effects on the economic plane and on civil progress which it is easy to imagine. This raises the question: what is the deciding factor that,

---

36. Mandeville, *Fable of the Bees*.
37. See Stout *Cultivating Conscience*.

in a given society, in a particular historical period, the organic composition of behavioural traits sees the prevalence of one type or the other? Well, a decisive, if not the only, factor is the way in which it structures its legislative system. If, in adopting a Hobbesian anthropology, the legislator makes laws which lay on the shoulders of all the citizens heavy sanctions and punishments intended to prevent illegal acts on the part of the antisocial, it is evident that the prosocial (or social) citizens, who would certainly have no need of those deterrents, will not be able to bear the cost and so, be it even *obtorto collo*, modify their own motivational system in a home-grown way. As Stout writes (2011), if you want to increase the number of good people, you must not tempt them to be wicked. Today, more relevant than ever, this question turns on the thought and warning of the great Neapolitan figure of the Italian Enlightenment, Giacinto Dragonetti. Publishing in 1766 his *Delle virtù e dei premi*, in respectful but firm criticism of the celebrated *Dei delitti e delle pene* (1764) of Cesare Beccaria, Dragonetti takes seriously the claim of the Scholastics according to whom virtue is more contagious than vice, on condition that it is made known. That is why the legal apparatus must, *in primis*, provide rewards (not incentives) to the virtuous, and, *in secundis*, threaten wrong-doers with punishments. Dragonetti's work, translated at the time into four foreign languages, was to be quoted by Thomas Payne in the *Declaration of Independence* of the United States in 1776.

This is the so-called mechanism of *crowding out*: laws of a Hobbesian stamp tend to increase the percentage of external motivations and, therefore, to augment the spread of behaviour of an antisocial type. Precisely because antisocial types are not much disturbed by the cost of law enforcement since they are always seeking to avoid the law in various ways. (See what happens with tax evasion and tax avoidance). In the light of the preceding, we are now able to understand how and where to intervene if we wish to increase the occasions to advance practices which hinder the spread of individualistic behaviour. As long as we think of economic activity as a type of acting whose logic can only be that of the *homo oeconomicus*, it is clear that we shall never arrive at the admission that there can be a civil way of managing the economy. But that depends on the theory, the spectacles through which we observe reality, and not directly on reality itself. It is to the paradigm of the civil economy and its categories of thought that we must turn if we wish the present, second great transformation—the first was that investigated by Karl Polanyi (1944)—to constitute real progress for the peoples, to aim, that is, at integral human development.[38]

---

38. Bruni and Zamagni, *Civil Economy*.

The second strategy to put in place to contain individualism within reasonable limits is that of returning to put at the centre of public discourse the principle of fraternity—a word which already appeared on the flag of the French Revolution of 1789. It is the great merit of European culture to have known how to shape the principle of fraternity in both institutional and economic terms, making it become a load-bearer of the social order. It was the Franciscan school of thought that gave the term the meaning which it has preserved over time. There are pages of the "Rule of Francis" which are a good help in understanding the real meaning of the principle of fraternity which is that of achieving, simultaneously, the fulfilling and the exceeding of the principle of solidarity. In fact, whereas solidarity is the principle of social organisation which allows the unequal to become equal, the principle of fraternity is that principle of social organisation which allows the equal to be diverse, not different. Fraternity allows people who are equal in their dignity and fundamental rights to give a diverse expression to their life-plan, or their charisma. The times which we have left behind, the 1800's and, above all, the 1900's, were characterised by great battles, both cultural and political, in the name of solidarity, and this was a good thing; think of the history of the trade union movement and the struggle to acquire civil rights. The point is that the good society cannot be content with the horizon of solidarity because a society which is only solidaristic and not also fraternal would be a society from which each one would seek to distance himself. The fact is that, whereas the fraternal society is also a solidaristic society, the *vice versa* is not true.

Not only that, but where there is no gratuitousness, there cannot be any hope. In fact, gratuitousness is not an ethical virtue like justice. It concerns the super-ethical dimension of human action; its logic is that of superabundance whereas the logic of justice is that of equivalence, as indeed Aristotle taught. Thus we understand why hope cannot be anchored in justice. In a society that was only, hypothetically, perfectly just, there would be no room for hope. What could its citizens ever hope for? This is not the case in a society where the principle of fraternity has succeeded in putting down deep roots, precisely because hope is nourished on superabundance.

Having forgotten the fact that it is unsustainable to have a human society in which the sense of fraternity is extinguished and in which everything is reduced, on the one hand, to improving transactions based on the exchange of equivalents, and, on the other hand, to increasing the transfers effected by organisations of the welfare state, this explains why, despite the quality of the intellectual powers in play, a solution to that trade-off has not yet been reached. The society in which the principle of fraternity is dissolved has no future; that is, the society in which there exists only "giving to have" or "giving through duty" is not able to advance. That is why, neither the liberal-individualist vision of the world in which everything (or almost everything) is exchange nor the statist vision of society in which everything (or almost everything) is compulsory are safe guides to bring us out of the shallows in which the Fourth Industrial Revolution is putting our model of civilisation to a harsh test—as the most recent Social Doctrine of the Church does not cease to emphasise.

BIBLIOGRAPHY

Anders G. *L'uomo è antiquato*. Turin: Bollati Boringhieri, 2002.
Bauman, Z. *Individualmente insieme*. Rome: Diabasis, 2008.
Bostrom N. *Superintelligenza: Tendenze, pericoli, strategie*. Turin: Bollati Boringhieri 2017.
———. "Welcome to a World of Exponential Change." In *Better Humans? The Politics of Human Enhancement and Life Extension*, edited by P. Miller and J. Wilsdon. London: Demos, 2006.
Bruni, L., and S. Zamagni. *Civil Economy*. London: Agenda, 2016.
Carr, A. Z. "Is Business Bluffing Ethical?" *Harvard Business Review* 2 (1968). https://hbr.org/1968/01/is-business-bluffing-ethical.
Camerer, C. F. "The Potential of Neuro-Economics." *Economics and Philosophy* 24 (2008) 369–79.
Donati, P. "Globalization of Markets, Distant Harms and a Need for a Relational Ethics." *Rivista Internazionale di Scienze Sociali* 125 (2017) 13–42.
Dumont, L. *Saggi sull'individualismo*. Milan: Adelphi, 2013.
Etzioni A., and O. Etzioni. "Incorporating Ethics and Artificial Intelligence." *Journal of Ethics* 21 (2017) 403–18.
Goggi, M. "Il sogno di blockchain." Lecture, February 4, 2018.
Goldfort, C. Tucker. "Digital Economics." NBER, 23684, August 2017.
Gramsci, A. "Americanismo e Fordismo." in *Quaderni dal Carcere*. Turin: Einaudi, 1948–51.
Habermas, J. *Morale, diritto, politica*. Turin: Comunità, 2001.
Hume, D. *Treatise of Human Nature*. 1740. Reprint, Oxford: Clarendon, 1971.
Kampowski, S. M., and D. Moltisanti, eds. *Migliorare l'uomo? La sfida dell'enhancement*. Siena: Cantagalli, 2011.
Kurzweil, R. *Come creare una mente*. Milan: Mondadori, 2013.
Leibenstein, H. "On Some Economic Aspects of a Fragile Input: Trust." In *Essays in Honour of Kenneth Arrow*, edited by A. Feiwel, 600–612. Cambridge, MA: MIT Press, 1987.
Magone A. "Tecnologia e fattore umano nella fabbrica digitale." *Industria* 3 (2016) 407–26.
Mandeville, B. *The Fable of the Bees, or Private Vices, Public Benefits*. 1713. Reprint, Indianapolis: Liberty Fund, 1988.
Narvaez, D. *Neurobiology and the Development of Human Morality*. New York: Norton, 2014.
Paine, T. *Common Sense*. 1776. Reprint, Los Angeles: Enhanced Media, 2016.

Palazzani, L. *Il potenziamento umano: Tecnocrazia, etica e diritto.* Turin: Giappichelli, 2015.
Palazzani, L. *Dalla bioetica alla tecnoetica.* Turin: Giappichelli, 2017.
Sandel, M. *Contro la perfezione: L'etica nell'età dell'ingegneria genetica.* Milan: Vita e Pensiero, 2008.
Smith A. *An Inquiry into the Nature and Causes of the Wealth of Nations.* 1776. Reprint, Indianapolis: Liberty Fund, 1981.
Stout, L. *Cultivating Conscience: How Good Laws Make Good People.* Princeton: Princeton University Press, 2011.
Strawson, G. "Free Agents." *Philosophical Topics* 32 (2004) 371–403.
Taplin, J. *Move Fast and Break Things.* London: Macmillan, 2017.
Twenge, J. *iGen.* New York: Norton, 2017.
Venier, F. "La forza lavoro digitale e il futuro dell'organizzazione." *Sviluppo e Organizzazione* 3 (2017) 74–84.
Zellini, P. "Saranno gli algoritmi a governarci." *La Repubblica*, March 12, 2017.

9

Cultural Diversity and Political Culture in India
ANTHONY DIAS, SJ

ABSTRACT

This paper has five sections: The first explores very briefly the diversity that India is known for in many domains. The second one attempts to look at the way culture has been defined and its role in the lives of people. It then goes on to outline the current threats to cultural diversity that come from several actors, both state and non-state. In the third section, the paper begins by exploring the complex political culture in India and presents a brief historical perspective. It then deals with some of the specific features of this culture and their implications. It argues that both—the threats to diversity and the prevalent political culture—combine to undermine sustainability and democracy, affecting adversely sustainable and integral human development. The fourth section looks for ways and means to strengthen democracy and sustainability to make integral human development not only a realizable goal but an end-in-itself. The fifth and final section makes some concluding observations.

1. INTRODUCTION

India's diversity spans many domains making it one of the world's most complex, perplexing, perhaps even intriguing countries. In the world of nature, it is known not only for its spellbinding beauty but also its rich biological diversity. It harbors some of the most precious and sought-after bio-diversity hotspots that are still being explored for new species of flora and fauna.¹ It has climatic conditions that differ widely and has weather conditions that range from very cold to the very hot and humid. With respect to its population, it is not only one of the most populous countries in the world but veritably the most complex, in terms of physical features of its people, customs and traditions, languages and so on. In the area of politics, there is diversity in terms of ideology, structure of political parties and styles of functioning of political leaders. Its political culture is not only complex but also befuddling. There is a wide variety in the way political and social protests are done. Culturally, its diversity is remarkable.

2. CULTURE, DIVERSITY AND DEVELOPMENT

According to Jain, the word "culture" is derived from the Latin word *cultura*, which originally meant the cultivation or tending of something, such as crops or animals. It has evolved from the early sixteenth century from the sphere of husbandry to the process of human development and from the cultivation of crops to the cultivation of the mind.² Zimmerman describes culture in terms of characteristics, practices, and knowledge of a particular group or groups of people, encompassing language, religion, cuisine, social habits, music, song, and dance, and includes the arts³ and goes on to cite other sources that define it as a shared pattern of norms and behavior, cognitive constructs, and understanding learnt through socialization. Culture includes a whole lot of things such as clothing, language, marriage customs, beliefs, about what is right and what is wrong, about how we sit at table, how we greet visitors and how we behave with loved ones. The word "culture" shares it etymology with a number of other words related to actively enhancing growth. Hence culture is therefore dynamic and live and grows with interactions.⁴ India's culture has been enriched by trade and commerce with other nations and also by waves of migration and/or occupation by those who made India their home.

The Anthropological Survey of India indicates that India has 4,635 communities that are diverse in biological traits, dress, languages and forms of worship, occupation, food habits and kinship patterns.⁵ The Linguistic

1. Ians, *300 Plant Species Discovered in 2016: BSI.*
Shiv Sahay Singh, *India's biodiversity riches grow by 499 species.*
2. Sheena Jain, *Structure and Transformation—Theory and Society*, 1–16.
3. Kim Ann Zimmermann, *What Is Culture? Definition of Culture.*
4. Kim Ann Zimmermann, *What Is Culture? Definition of Culture.*
5. Anthropological Survey of India, Ministry of Culture—Government of India, *People of India*; Hamid Ansari, *India's Plural and Diverse Identity Is Under Threat.*

Survey of India indicates that apart from the 22 languages in the *Eighth Schedule of the constitution*, there are 100 other languages and thousands of dialects in the country.[6] The *Bhasha* research centre's study states that "India has a fascinating diversity of languages unlike anywhere else in the world, with 780 languages reported in our volumes and another 100 or so which we were not able to report. So it is like having about 900 living languages in a country. Each language presents its own worldview."[7] The identity of India is plural and diverse, a consequence of coming together of people with varying social and cultural traits. It is this plurality that constitutes Indian identity.

People are born into a culture which helps them grow and develop their full potential as human beings and as citizens of their respective countries or nations. National constitutions generally guarantee to people their right to follow their cultural practices and religious rituals, norms and festivals. In a democracy, the rights of minorities are specially taken care of by national constitutions.[8] Tribal communities in various regions of India have their unique cultures that are different from mainstream societies. These peoples find their individual and communitarian development in and through their cultures. India's first Prime Minister recognized this and hence his *Panchsheel* states that these communities should be allowed to "develop according to their own genius."[9] The nomadic and de-notified tribes are very unique communities and have a world view and way of life that is quite at variance with sedentary societies.[10]

---

6. Census of India, http://censusindia.gov.in/2011-documents/lsi/ling_survey_india.html; Hamid Ansari, *India's Plural and Diverse Identity Is Under Threat*.

7. Lalmalsawma, *India speaks 780 languages, 220 lost in last 50 years—survey*.

8. Bakshi, *The Constitution of India*, 13–111.

India's Constitution is secular in the sense that it accepts the rights of all peoples to profess and practice their respective faiths or religions. It is democratic and guarantees to people their basic and fundamental rights.

9. Tribal Cultural Heritage in India Foundation, *Jawaharlal's five principles for the policy to be pursued vis-a-vis the tribals*.

Nehru, India's first Prime Minister, understood and recognized the unique ways of living and the vulnerability of tribal peoples and so wanted them and their culture protected. India's Constitution contains two special schedules (V and VI) for their special protection, as also several other provisions in the Constitution to protect and promote them. To safeguard them from forces inimical to their cultures, Parliament enacted a special law in 1996 known as *Panchayats* (Extension to Scheduled Areas) Act, 1966.

10. Nomadic tribes are found in many parts of the world. However, de-notified tribes are unique to India. These are also pejoratives referred to as "ex-criminal" or "former criminal" tribes. There are hundreds of these unique communities who are not in the mainstream and who practice their own ways of living quite at variance with mainstream communities. Although they number over a hundred million, they are large "invisible" because they are largely "undocumented" due to their way of life and world view.

India is a multi-religious' culture and some of these major religions such as Hinduism and Buddhism, and Jainism and Sikhism, were born in India. Tribal communities have their distinctive religio-cultural practices that are unique. India continues to remain a sort of a meeting ground of all religions. Despite clashes and conflicts among and between some religious groups before and after independence, there has generally been peaceful co-existence. India's composite culture facilitates *integral human development*. This has now changed due to threats, direct and imminent, to cultural diversity.

As a concept, "Integral Human Development" (IHD) promotes the good of the whole person and has several dimensions such as cultural, economic, political, social and spiritual. In 1967 Pope Paul VI in his encyclical *Populorum Progressio* introduced the concept of IHD which clarified that development cannot be limited to *mere economic growth* (emphasis added). In 1987 Pope John Paul II in *Sollicitudo Rei Socialis* brought in the dimension of inter-faith dialogue and collaboration in a universal perspective. It stated unambiguously that in the pursuit of IHD we can do much with the members of other religions; that collaboration in the development of the whole person and of every human being is in fact a duty of all towards all, and must be shared with the whole world.[11]

Organizations such as the Catholic Relief Services (CRS) bring in other dimensions to enrich IHD, such a wholesome environment. True IHD is a long-term, dynamic process based on human dignity and right relations: i.e., each person's relations with God, self, others and all of creation. Advancing IHD means working with a variety of actors to transform the way that societies live. Progress toward IHD is achieved through engagement with others in society that respects the sanctity of life and the dignity of every human person.[12] On the 50th anniversary of *Populorum Progressio*, Pope Francis emphasized other dimension such as inclusiveness, solidarity and sharing. The Pope also said that "integrating involves offering effective models of social integration." He also talked about the need to integrate the individual and communitarian dimensions of IHD.[13] The praxis of IHD mandates a big role for culture. Hence threats to culture are threats to *democracy* and to *sustainable development* as a whole and to *human* development in particular.

---

11. Geoff et al., *A User's Guide to Integral Human Development*.
12. Geoff et al., *A User's Guide to Integral Human Development*.
13. Senèze, *Pope Francis Explains*.

2.1. Threats to Cultural Diversity

There are several threats to diversity. The following three are imminent and pervasive demanding action at the local and international levels to promote genuine development:*Religious fundamentalism*: Religious fundamentalism poses a grave and continuing threat to cultural diversity all over the world. It refers to the belief of an individual or a group of individuals in the absolute authority of a sacred religious text or teachings of a particular religious leader, or a prophet. These fundamentalists believe that their religion is beyond criticism and that it should be forced upon others. Logic and science are disregarded if they go against their bigoted beliefs. For them, religion dictates every sphere of their lives. They also attempt to involve the entire society into their own belief system, often by the use of force,[14] harming cultures not their own. Most religions of the world have fundamentalist elements. Christian fundamentalists, who have absolute beliefs in the words of the Holy Bible, are found everywhere in the Christian world. In the earlier part of the twentieth century, Christian fundamentalists in the United States protested against Darwin's Theory of Evolution.[15] Islamic fundamentalists believe in the literal interpretation of the Holy Quran and Hadiths and attempt to enforce the Sharia law into every aspect of Islamic life. Ibn Taymiyyah was one of the early Islamic fundamentalists who initiated a reform movement in the thirteenth century against the Islamic scholarship, criticized the Shi'a in Lebanon as the Rifa'i Sufi order.[16] Many Islamic terrorist organizations, such as al-Qaeda, Boko Haram, and ISIS,

---

14. Nag, *What Is Religious Fundamentalism?* Modern religious fundamentalism as a concept was introduced with the publication of the *The Fundamentals*, between 1909 and 1920 appealing to Christians to believe in certain religious doctrines of Christianity. The term "fundamentalist" was soon used to describe a section of Protestant Christians who were skeptical of modernity. Later the term was used to relate to the most extreme believers of every religion in the world. Ibid. [AQ: repeated in next 5 footnotes]

15. Oishimaya Sen Nag, *What is Religious Fundamentalism?* Modern religious fundamentalism as a concept was introduced with the publication of the *The Fundamentals*, between 1909 and 1920 appealing to Christians to believe in certain religious doctrines of Christianity. The term "fundamentalist" was soon used to describe a section of Protestant Christians who were skeptical of modernity. Later the term was used to relate to the most extreme believers of every religion in the world. Ibid.

16. Oishimaya Sen Nag, *What is Religious Fundamentalism?* Modern religious fundamentalism as a concept was introduced with the publication of the *The Fundamentals*, between 1909 and 1920 appealing to Christians to believe in certain religious doctrines of Christianity. The term 'fundamentalist' was soon used to describe a section of Protestant Christians who were skeptical of modernity. Later the term was used to relate to the most extreme believers of every religion in the world. Ibid.

hold fundamentalist attitudes and regard Western civilization as the symbol of the secular modernization that is a threat to traditional Islamic values.

Hinduism is a complex sets of beliefs contained in some holy texts such as the *Vedas*, the *Bhagavad Gita*, the *Upanishads*, and the *Brahmanas*.[17] Hindu fundamentalism is growing on account of it being politicized by rightist political forces, better known as *Hindutvavadis* or cultural nationalists. Believers of Buddhism and Jainism exhibit relatively less fundamentalism. However, the Soka Gakkai sect of Nichiren Buddhism in Japan, which denies the credibility of all other forms of Buddhism, is sometimes labeled as being fundamentalist.[18] Fundamentalism of the extreme kind in today's world is responsible for much violence and suffering. A society with fundamentalist beliefs breeds a closed attitude towards life to the degree of paranoia and resorts to aggression.[19]

Cultural Nationalism

The biggest threat today to India's composite culture comes from the "cultural nationalism," an ideology which uses religion to gain political power. It is propagated by the rightist Hindutva forces whose roots are in the Rashtriya Swayam Sevak Sangh (the RSS) which projects itself as a "cultural organization." Hindutva is a political ideology that believes in the supremacy of the Hindus. It is also known as religious communalism[20] which considers

---

17. Oishimaya Sen Nag, *What is Religious Fundamentalism?*
Modern religious fundamentalism as a concept was introduced with the publication of the *The Fundamentals,* between 1909 and 1920 appealing to Christians to believe in certain religious doctrines of Christianity. The term 'fundamentalist' was soon used to describe a section of Protestant Christians who were skeptical of modernity. Later the term was used to relate to the most extreme believers of every religion in the world. Ibid.

18. Oishimaya Sen Nag, *What is Religious Fundamentalism?*
Modern religious fundamentalism as a concept was introduced with the publication of the *The Fundamentals,* between 1909 and 1920 appealing to Christians to believe in certain religious doctrines of Christianity. The term 'fundamentalist' was soon used to describe a section of Protestant Christians who were skeptical of modernity. Later the term was used to relate to the most extreme believers of every religion in the world. Ibid.

19. Oishimaya Sen Nag, *What is Religious Fundamentalism?*
Modern religious fundamentalism as a concept was introduced with the publication of the *The Fundamentals,* between 1909 and 1920 appealing to Christians to believe in certain religious doctrines of Christianity. The term 'fundamentalist' was soon used to describe a section of Protestant Christians who were skeptical of modernity. Later the term was used to relate to the most extreme believers of every religion in the world. Ibid.

20 Anthony Dias, "Reconciliation and the Religious Communalism In India," *Promotio Iustitiae, Agents of Reconciliation in a Broken World,* no 124, (2017/2): 54–57; Irfan Engineer, *Issues of Communal Violence: Causes and Respons,* 1–5.

non-Hindus as the "other" who are projected as threats to the Hindus. It has nothing in common with the tenets and tradition of Hindu religion, which despite fault lines has significant positive features. *Hindutva* is political Hinduism and believes in forcibly converting others.

The danger to tribal culture is from *Hindutva* that manifests itself in different forms. It tries to homogenize all cultures of India into one single monolithic Hindu culture. The process of Hindu-isation can be direct or subtle and is for political purposes.[21] One of the biggest exercises of religious conversion in India is done by various Hindu organizations who seek to convert more and simple *dalits* and tribals to Hinduism through force or fraud. In many places, tribals who had earlier converted to Christianity were forced to "reconvert" to Hinduism in the often widely publicized *ghar wapsi* (home-coming) programs. The same was the case with others who had converted to Islam. These forced conversions offend the dignity of the tribals and others, because it involves coercion and public humiliation.

When these forces gain political power they do harm to society, to the rule of law, to the people, to democratic institutions and to sustainability. They pose a direct threat to the secular constitution. After their victory in the general elections in 2014, these forces have done a lot of damage. Democracy has been throttled as voices that protest and dissent are silenced,[22] often through negative propaganda and harassment, even murder. The sensational daylight murders of thinkers and rationalists who spoke up against oppressive religious and cultural mores and prescriptions and against obscurantism are a case in point. The fact that investigating agencies have not been able to apprehend the criminals is indicative of the clout and power of both state and non-state actors who shield them. Secular democracy and the rule of law are challenged.

After the landslide victory the BJP, the "fringe" became the mainstream and cultural nationalism got a boost. There were attacks on churches and Christians. Muslims were attacked in many places merely because they were suspected of storing and/or eating beef which is banned in many states because of "cow politics." The cow is a sacred animal for many Hindus but it is eaten by the Muslims, dalits, Christians and many other communities for whom it is a part of their diet and a source of nutrition. For Muslim traders it is also a source of livelihood[23] From majoritarianism there is a shift to-

21. Jaffrelot, *Critical Issus in Indian Politics*, 1–22.
22. Hasan, *Restricting Protests, Stifling Dissent*.
23. Jaffrelot, *The Hindu Nationalist Movement and Indian Politics*, 202–10. Muslims in many parts of the country have been lynched for allegedly trading and/or possessing or eating beef, which is part of the diet of many Muslims and *dalits* in India. In the name of "cow protection."

ward authoritarianism, and to terrorism known as "saffron terror." Cultural nationalism breeds a culture of violence that goes against democracy, the rule of law and violates the values and spirit of the Constitution of India.[24] Threats to cultural diversity are a threat to societal and human development.

Development Paradigms and Projects

The neo-liberal paradigm of development India espoused in the 1990s was meant to speed up economic growth. The focus was on economics-driven Gross Domestic Product (GDP) rather than on holistic or sustainable development that would protect nature and humans and thereby promote all-round human development. As a result, although the country has done well in terms of generating more industrial and grain production resulting in increased GDP, human development indicators fared poorly. Poverty and deprivation, hunger and starvation, disease and illiteracy continued to haunt the country. Development projects not only damaged nature and ecological treasure troves and bio-diversity, but they also harmed people and their culture.[25]

These projects uprooted forest dwelling and rural communities. The displaced[26] were hardly rehabilitated and wherever these attempts were made, scant regard was paid to the culture of the people. Hence neither development nor resettlement policies cared about the culture of the uprooted people. The state resorted to the power of eminent domain[27] under which it could expropriate any private land for public purpose after giving compensation to the land losers. However, in practice the state engaged in land grab and assisted private players to get land at throwaway prices. Compensation and rehabilitation were never taken seriously. All this resulted in impoverishment of the tribals who were crushed under the development juggernaut.[28]

---

24. Mehta, "'Illegal' Bangladeshis in *Akhand Bharat*: Inscriptions of Race and Religion on Citizenship." *Economic and Political Weekly*. 62–68, Vol LIII no 7 (2018): 62–66.

25. Anand Teltumde, "Development of a few, misery for the masses," *Economic and Political Weekly* 52.36 (2017) 10–11.

26. The word "deracinate" better represents the situation than the word "displaced" because of the violence and violations of rights and dignity that occurs when people are evicted from their traditional habitats in the name of "development."

27. Anthony Dias, "Eminent Domain, Displacement and Resettlement," 183–98. The paper discusses the origin and use of state power of eminent domain and impoverishment of tribal and indigenous peoples caused by development projects.

28. The injustices meted out to the tribals resulted in tribal resistance and the growth of Maoism and *Naxalism*, a form of extreme and violent left wing ideology.

This is state-sponsored impoverishment.[29] Instead of democracy and people's participation in development, there is the overbearing state, in cahoots with big companies, imposing its will on the people, using threats and violence against those who resisted the takeover of their land, cultural heritage and natural assets. Instead of sustainable development we have environmental degradation in the form of deforestation and pollution of land, air, rivers and other water bodies. Inequality was more accentuated with the gap between the rich and the poor increasing exponentially. The recent Oxfam survey reveals startling facts of this inequality.[30]

As can be seen from the above discussion, culture and the celebration of diversity is necessary for holistic development. However, cultures are facing threats from inimical forces such as global capital and the nexus between transnational corporations and governments. These forces are also a direct threat to: a) sustainability vis-à-vis human beings and nature, and b) to democracy, in terms of good governance, rule of law and special protection of the minorities and weaker sections of society. How can cultural diversity be protected in order t better protect human societies and sustainability? What kind of governance or politics are needed to do this? The next section explores these questions.

3. POLITICAL CULTURE IN INDIA

The political culture in India has distinctive features. But before we explore that a brief historical perspective would be appropriate. The Constitution of India, the foundational document of a nascent Republic, was inspired by the values of the Freedom Movement (FM), and declares India as a

---

29. Anthony Dias, *Development and Its Human Cost: Displacement, Resettlement and Rehabilitation of Tribals in India*, 114–44. The book discusses the costs the poor, especially the tribals and other subalterns, pay for development projects that benefit the better-off classes.

30. The Oxfam survey 2017 notes: The richest 1 percent in India cornered 73 percent of the wealth generated in the country. In 2016 the same survey found that the richest 1 percent held 58 percent of the country's total wealth, indicating increase in inequality. The wealth of India's richest 1 percent increased by over Rs 20.9 lakh crore during 2017—an amount equivalent to the total budget of the central government in 2017–18. In India it will take 941 years for a minimum wage worker in rural India to earn what the top paid executive at a leading Indian garment firm earns in a year. The benefits of growth continues to be concentrated in fewer hands. The billionaire boom is not a sign of hope. On the contrary it is a sign of failing economic system. Those toiling, growing food for the country, building infrastructure, working in factories are struggling to educate their children, buy medicines for the family and manage two meals a day.

Poulose Mangai. "Showcasing the Republic." *Vidya Jyothi Journal of Theological Reflection*.82, no. 2 (2018):84–85.

Democratic, Secular, Socialist, Republic. The FM did deliver political freedom. It gave Indians, as Dr B. R. Ambedkar[31] said, political democracy in a technical sense, on the principle of "one-person-one-vote." The Preamble to the Indian Constitutions expresses some of these basics eloquently. The Fundamental Rights guarantee a range of rights and freedoms. The section on Directive Principles of State Policy (DPSPs) enjoins the state to include a whole gamut of socio-economic and cultural rights. Special attention is paid to the specific needs of the downtrodden (*dalits*) and vulnerable communities such as the tribal and indigenous people. The minorities are given special protection so that they can develop their individual and communitarian potential fully.

The FM was a unique struggle and was led by some extraordinary persons. Its tallest leader who motivated and galvanized an entire nation to fight against the British occupation and the oppression and subjugation of the people was Mohandas Gandhi. His politics saw an effortless blending of the ethical and secular with the spiritual and religious. During the FM, he articulated values, concepts and methods that were innovative as they were effective. Truth (*Satya*) became equated with God (*Ishwar*), and God with Truth. Under his leadership, non-violence in word and deed became the defining praxis of the freedom struggle. The struggle had to be founded on *ahimsa* (non-violence). Hence, *Satyagraha*[32] became the cornerstone of his political movement. The concept caught the imagination of a people fighting to shake off the yoke of foreign rule. Although he was rooted in his own religious tradition, he was open to other religions and embraced their teachings. Although he was against conversion to Christianity he revered Jesus Christ and was inspired by the Sermon on the Mount. No one ever accused Gandhi of engaging in divisive "communal politics."[33]

Another leader was Gandhi's confidant, Pandit Jawaharlal Nehru, who became India's first Prime Minister. He inherited Gandhi's legacy despite differences with him. Nehru practiced secular politics and he was more concerned about the seemingly intractable problems that the new nation was bedeviled with. The political economy of development he espoused

---

31. Dr. B. R. Ambedkar, was a *dalit* (literally trodden beneath the feet; a person who is the member of the lowest among the castes), is considered the architect of the Indian Constitution. Despite being severely disadvantaged socially and economically, he rose to great heights due to sheer hard work and commitment. He was able to see the deep fault lines in Indian society and culture and felt that these if not corrected would result in the deterioration of Indian society.

32. *Satyagraha*, which means (persistent commitment for truth), became a non-violent method of protest against the oppressive rule of the British. These methods inspired persons such as Nelson Mandela and others.

33 Sharma, *Modern Hindu Thought*, 249–70.

was radically different from Gandhi. The "Nehruvian model" of development believed in fast-tracking India's economic growth. In his model, he invited the private sector to join hands with state enterprises. It was a mixed economy, borrowed from the erstwhile Soviet Union. Sustainability was not part of the agenda of development that saw the building of large dams and industries for which huge tracts of land was acquired and forests felled. Along with environmental destruction there was huge population displacement. Indigenous people suffered disproportionately.[34]

The emergence of Prime Minister Indira Gandhi, Nehru's daughter, changed the course of Indian Politics forever. The cult of personality over principles and policy became entrenched. She became powerful and authoritarian. Only a small coterie of politicians and bureaucrats had access to her. Sycophancy plumbed its lowest depth. "India is Indira and Indira is India" was what a Congress politician chanted. However, things changed dramatically when she lost her case in one of the higher courts in India. She did something that changed dramatic and drastic. After she was unseated by a court of law, she declared a state of Emergency, the biggest blow to democracy and the rule of law.

All the fundamental rights were suspended. Dissenting voices were silenced and political opponents were either tortured and/or put behind bars.[35] The Indira era ended after her shocking assassination by her Sikh bodyguards in revenge for "Operation Bluestar."[36] Her son, riding the "sympathy wave" (a feature of Indian politics), won the elections with a massive majority. A suicide bomber of Sri Lanka's LTTE ended his career abruptly. The Congress party then pleaded with Rajiv's wife, an Italian, to lead the party.

The demolition of this Babri mosque marked a dramatic change and a significant point of departure in Indian politics. It signaled the rise of the BJP, which tried to manipulate sentiments of the majority by playing the card of "Muslim appeasement." It claimed that minority appeasement was at the cost of the majority who were constantly asked to make unreasonable and unwarranted sacrifices. The BJP's strategies paid rich dividends and the party first ran a coalition government and then won a landslide majority on its own in the 2014 general elections, which marks a significant point of departure for Indian politics. The PM of the new dispensation talked about "development"

---

34. McCully, *Silenced Rivers: The Ecology and Politics of Large Dams*, 65–72.

35. Mankekar and Mankekar, *Decline and Fall of Indira Gandhi—19 months of Emergency*, 1–30. In their book, the Mankekars recount the horrors of the Emergency in vivid detail.

36. The Indian army's entry into the Golden Temple to eliminate the leader and fighters of the Khalistan resistance movement of the Sikhs was considered a serious act of desecration by the Sikhs, which finally resulted in her assassination.

which actually did harm to the poor and the environment. It benefited big industrialists and business houses at the cost of the poor and ecology. The new government also started dividing the people on the basis of religion in the process harming the growth and development of the minorities and other poor.

3.1 Feature of Political Culture and Their Implication

The values that guided FM and which were enshrined in the Constitution of India began to erode after the demise of the great leaders of the movement. Politics began to be personality centered and saw the rise of authoritarian, sectarian and/or communal leaders. Some of the features of this politics, and its implications, are worth noting:

Dynasty

Indian politics is marked by what analysts call "dynastic rule." The Nehru family is cited as a classic example of this. After Nehru passed away, it was his daughter who became PM. She was succeeded by her son, a commercial pilot by profession. His wife Sonia Gandhi who took over the reins of the party became "kingmaker."[37] Although the family connection is the key to becoming the PM, the process seems democratic in nature. Had there been no elections, then it would indeed be dynastic politics. Some of the other political parties also have this dynastic dimension. Democracy is not compromised in a situation where there is intra-party democracy as well as the national democratic processes. However, there are others who say that the supreme leader influences everything and so conditions for democracy do not exist.

The Cult of Personality

When a politician becomes powerful, a coterie begins to be formed around her. This was the case with Indira Gandhi. Only those in the coterie had access to her and they would be ones to feed her with information. When this happens, intra-party democracy suffers and decisions regarding the country are based not on policies, democratic processes and consensus but on the orders of the Supremo. Governance is personality- rather than policy-driven. All democratic institutions then run the risk of being interfered

---

37. Sonia is now grooming her son, Rahul Gandhi, a potential PM-in-waiting, even as her charismatic daughter Priyanka waits on the sidelines with everyone watching her every move.

with, even harmed and destroyed, by the untrammeled power the Supremo possesses. This is the case now with the present PM of the country. Sustainability is either given a fillip or is harmed by the personal preferences and predilections of the Supremo. Both sustainability and democracy can be undermined in such a situation.

The Politics of Appeasement

This was the main allegation leveled against the Congress by the BJP. It claimed that the Congress simply wanted to please the Muslims to win their votes and was not interested in the genuine development of the community. This argument has generally come to be accepted by the majority community. It has proven to be true on the ground. The Sachar Committee Report describes in much detail the backwardness of the Muslim community. Appeasement politics is also played by BJP to please their constituency. It is also done by other regional parties. These come to the fore when state or federal elections are round the corner. Appeasement policies, while they might help win elections are harmful to human development and sustainability.

Jumla and the Politics of False Promises

Jumla is a rather new word in the political lectionary of the country but its practice is now very well entrenched. Simply stated, it refers to the promises made by politicians during elections knowing these cannot, or will not, be kept. However, voters do get swayed by these promises. Popular politicians are adept at winning people's votes by using *Jumlas*. A BJP strategist and leader openly said that during elections a lot of extra-ordinary promises have to be made which obviously cannot be fulfilled! There is deceit involved in this unethical practice.

Win-ability

Political parties offer tickets to those who can win elections for them, even when those candidates have criminal cases lodged against them. At one point in time, the Election Commission warned political parties against this practice. The Judiciary also was on record saying candidates who have made promises should be held to account if they fail to fulfill their election promises. The principle of winability is inimical to democracy and sustainability. It is well known that politicians tell the people that if elected, they will prevail upon the government to bring in "development projects" to their constituency. Studies have shown that these projects have limited benefits but huge social and environmental costs.[38]

Scam after Scam

The word "scam" is frequently associated with politicians and political parties in India. Although all sections and sectors of society have been affected by the taint of corruption, politicians have the dubious distinction of being the most corrupt. Corruption has become a way of life. It has seeped so much into the system that hardly any institution is untouched by it. Corruption has direct and negative implications for both democracy and sustainability. It affects human rights and the lives of the poor because money meant for them is siphoned off. Rajiv Gandhi's comment on the issue of corruption is telling and oft-quoted.[39]

Vote-Bank Politics

The political parties constantly engage themselves in creating vote-banks on the basis of caste and/or religion or on the basis of a particular social category such as migrants. It diminishes democracy by harming democratic processes by holding people hostage to the clever designs and devices of wily politicians and their parties who are not genuinely interested in uplifting the people. It is unethical as it does not help people who have been converted into mere "banks" and who have no choice but to vote for their leader or their party. The means adopted to create vote bank are unethical because very often false our outlandish promises are made. At other times threats and intimidation are used.

Horse Trading and the Politics of the Last "Resort"

This is a process where moneybags are used to entice and buy politicians from other parties, or who are independent candidates. There have been several instances of this in Indian politics. It is defeats democracy because it interferes with the will and mandate of the people. It harms democratic processes and the people feel cheated and lose whatever faith they have in the

---

38. Patrick McCully, *Silenced Rivers: The Ecology and Politics of Large Dams*, 236–80.

39. Former PM Rajiv Gandhi had in 1985 famously remarked that only 15 out of the 100 *paise* (one rupee) reaches the poor. The rest is siphoned off by intermediaries.

system. Politicians will do anything for power and money. A recent example of this is the elections in Goa where the single largest party (Congress) could not form the government because the BJP allegedly bribed the independent candidates. The Congress vice-President accused the BJP of "stealing the people's mandate."[40] Not unrelated to the above, political parties which fear "poaching" and "horse trading" herd their flock of politicians to distant and safer havens, such as hotels and holiday resorts to protect them from being poached. Such is the insecurity among even established parties and such is the vulnerability of politicians to allurement, threats and intimidation.

The Toxic Politics of Communal Polarization

Indian politicians have engaged in very same cynical politics which they accuse the British of: "divide and rule." Almost all the major and minor political entities have played this game at some time or other. However, it is the BJP which has stolen a march over the other parties in playing it, ignoring ethics and human rights. It uses any and every trick in the book, or invents some when the books do not offer anything new, to divide people and then reap rich electoral harvest. "Communalism" has been a strong factor in Indian politics from the beginning. All political parties have flirted with it for which the country and her people have had to pay a huge price. With the rise of the far right, communalism is going to be a regular feature of Indian politics for years to come. Communalism has resulted in violence leading to loss of not only livelihood but also property and lives of people. It has taken a toll on human development. It creates a kind of fear psychosis among both communities and by extension among all. Societal peace and economic growth takes a hit and all suffer in the process.

Communal polarization is one of the strategies to win votes and thereby political power with the ultimate purpose of creating a hegemonic theocratic state (Hindu *Rashtra*) with larger militarist-imperialist intentions. The culture of the majority is sought to be imposed on the minorities—Muslims, Christians, *Dalits*, Tribals and others. This has taken various forms: from the banning of beef to prohibition of the sale of cattle to imposing the idea of nationalism. Any opposing or different view is not tolerated and those holding these views are branded "anti-nationals." Most recently, the cow has become the most preferred and revered symbol of Hindu culture. The chief

---

40. Rahul Gandhi, the President of the Congress party, accused the rival BJP of engaging in unethical practice of defeating democracy by not respecting the people's mandate. His party was the largest single party in the state of Goa, but the government was formed by the BJP. The same has happened in other states of India.

minister of Uttar Pradesh, India's most populous state, a saffron-clad self-styled Yogi has just declared that without the cow, Hindus would have no identity, which would result in the death of Hindu culture. Gangs of *Gau Rakshaks* (cow protectors—a vigilante group), who enjoy state patronage, have run amok killing innocent Muslims and *Dalits*. These have rightly been described as acts of terrorism.

A political culture marked by the above features is harmful to sustainability and democracy. This in turn threatens integral human development. How then can IHD be promoted.

4. PROMOTING INTEGRAL HUMAN DEVELOPMENT

As seen above, the threats to cultural diversity coupled with the prevalent political culture in India today threaten humans, their environment and good governance. In other words, these limit, or eliminate, the possibility of the holistic development of human beings and their natural environment. Integral human development takes place when enabling conditions for it exist. Enjoyment of the various basic freedoms and rights and justice are a necessary pre-condition for human development. In the Indian context, most of these are guaranteed by the Constitution of India. However, this is easily stated than achieved because the Constitution is under grave threat of being not only violated but even desecrated. Hence there is a need to protect the Constitution and strengthen the values enshrined in it, which will protect not only the people but the nation as a whole.

The liberties are threatened like never before. The Constitution can only be protected by secular, socialist and democratic forces within and outside the country. The need to build and strengthen democratic institutions and a culture of democracy is paramount and urgent. The words of US Supreme Court Justice Felix Frankfurter needs to be remembered:

> Democracy involves hardship—the hardship of the unceasing responsibility of every citizen. Where the entire people do not take a continuous and considered part in public life, there can be no democracy in any meaningful sense. Democracy is always a beckoning goal, not a safe harbor. For freedom is an unremitting endeavor, never a final achievement. That is why no office in the land is more important than that of being a citizen.[41]

---

41. Chhokar, "Black Money and Politics in India," 91–98.

The Role of the Media

In a democracy, the media has a crucial role to play as watchdogs and conscience-keepers. They have to keep a watch on the government and its agencies and report human rights violations fairly and fearlessly. They have to offer space to activist and thinkers "to speak truth to power." An alert and watchful media can help civil society and other organs of the state (such as the Judiciary) to protect the constitution and the rights and entitlements of the people.

Judiciary and the power of Judicial review

The role of the Judiciary to protect the Constitution and Democracy and to promote human and environmental rights and ecology can never be overstated. Judicial Review is its most important and sacrosanct power. In India some bold, creative and enlightened judges have promoted a rich jurisprudence of human rights. They have advanced and enhanced human freedoms and affirmed human dignity by protecting the rights of not only individuals but also communities. Their interpretations of certain articles of the Constitution, especially Art 21 has advanced human and environmental rights and the dignity of human person and integrity of creation. Defending the right to life under Art 21,[42] the courts have said that this right envisages right to life with *human dignity*.

The Role of Universities and Intellectuals

Universities are sites where informed debate on matters that affect humans and the planet are conducted. Documentation, research and publications form a crucial part of this process. The University should not stop at that. It should perform its social responsibility by offering and providing its knowledge and expertise to students, society and grassroots activists.[43] For instance, the Jesuit professors of UCA in San Salvador conscientized the students at the University and the general public through their writings and publications. They believed in what Chomsky's well-known position that the role of the intellectual was to expose lies and to speak the truth. The role of Universities in advocacy work has been good and it needs to expand more. The University must produce and encourage public intellectuals.[44]

---

42. Article 21 of the Constitution of India states, "No one shall be deprived of his life or personal liberty except through procedure established by law."
43. Virmani, "Social Responsibility of the Historian," 46–50.
44. Romila Thapar, *Searching for the Public Intellectual*.

Election Commission

These are constitutional bodies and hence the central and state Election Commissions have a crucial role to play before and during elections to make sure that the exercise of the political right to vote is free and fair. Elections in India are not only a logistical nightmare but are also fraught with risks of booth capturing, rigging, criminal elements entering the electoral contest, political interference and violations of the model code of conduct brought into effect by the Commissions. By and large, these bodies have played a commendable role and some fearless Commissioners have made the EC true guardians of democracy. However, in some cases they have failed to live up to the expectations.[45]

Networks and Alliances

CSOs do credible work individually. Some of them do collaborate and network with other groups and organizations. However, this is happening on a very limited scale. More networking and alliance building among and between CSOs is needed to build solidarity. A collective or a broad alliance has great power to negotiate with the government on behalf of the people. History has demonstrated this power.[46]

The Role of Civil Society Organizations (CSOs)

India already has a large number of NGOs, CBOs and Social or People's movement. These have done a big service to humanity, especially the poor. Some of these have worked for the integrity of creation by fostering ecological consciousness and by actually engaging in grassroots work. The protests led by civil society movements have had mixed success.[47]

---

45. Although there have been commissioners who were outstanding and with impeccable credentials, there have also been times, as for instance in the present day scenario, where the credibility of this institution has been undermined.

46. 'The Coalition Against Genocide' (CAG) is an international body that was successful in lobbying with the US government to deny a visa to the then chief minister of Gujarat, and currently the Prime Minister of India, on grounds of alleged grave human rights violations and genocidal violence against the Muslim community. Another example is the successful scraping of the *Silent Valley* project in India's Kerala state—a direct result of pressure from international environmental organizations, including "International Rivers Network."

47. Tribal people's movements in some parts of India are a good example of how affected people have resisted and stalled harmful projects. The *Koel Karo* river valley project in the tribal-dominated northern state of Jharkhand is a good example. Another

5. CONCLUDING OBSERVATIONS

The composite culture of India, with its diversity held the country together and fostered human development, despite limitations and imperfections. Today this diversity is threatened. Economic growth, production of wealth, a narrow and flawed understanding of culture and nationalism are privileged over sustainable and holistic human development and a celebration of diversity. The GDP, and not sustainable development with its intra- and inter-generational equity, is the focus. The human person is no longer at the center of development. This has already harmed nature and the minorities and other vulnerable groups in many ways, affecting their full human development.

There are also threats from a culture of politics that has deteriorated from what it was. This is a threat not only to cultural diversity but also to sustainability, both of which are needed for integral human development. These dangers can be overcome by having more and better democracy in which there is full people's participation. At the same time institutions of democracy will have to be strengthened for which active engagement of civil society, the Judiciary, the media and other actors is needed. More democracy should be in the form of more political participation of the people in non-party political movements led by self-less men and women who will empower the people even as they keep interrogating the state and its agencies. These movements will have to work harder to protect the Constitution which today is under grave threat of being disregarded.

BIBLIOGRAPHY

Ansari, Hamid (Vice President of India). "India's Plural and Diverse Identity Is under Threat." Wire, October 31, 2017. https://thewire.in/culture/indias-plural-diverse-identity-threat.

Anthropological Survey of India, Ministry of Culture—Government of India. *People of India.*

Bakshi, P. M. *The Constitution of India.* New Delhi: Universal Law Publishing, 2015.

Chhokar, Jagdeep S. "Black Money and Politics in India." *Economic and Political Weekly,* 52.7 (2017) 91–98.

Dias, Anthony. *Development and Its Human Cost: Displacement, Resettlement and Rehabilitation of Tribals in India.* Jaipur: Rawat, 2013.

---

important social movement is the *Narmada Bachao Andolan* (NBA, meaning "Save River Narmada campaign"), which, despite losing its case in the supreme court of India, nonetheless succeeded in promoting thinking on alternative, holistic models of development and in placing firmly on the agenda of government and project authorities the need for rehabilitation with due sensitivity to the cultures of indigenous peoples

———. "Eminent Domain, Displacement and Resettlement." In *Beyond Relocation: The Imperative of Sustainable Relocation*, edited by Renu Modi, 183–98. New Delhi: Sage, 2009.

Dias, Anthony. "Reconciliation and Religious Communalism In India." *Iustitae Promotio* 124 (2017) 54–57.

Engineer, Irfan. *Issues of Communal Violence: Causes and Response, Institute of Peace Studies and Conflict Resolution*. Mumbai: Institute for Peace Studies and Conflict Resolution, 2013.

Engineer, Irfan, and Neha, Dabhade. "2017—A Year of Hatred, Impunity and Heightened Identity Politics." *Secular Perspective* 21.1 (2018) 1–15.

Geoff, Heinrich et al. *A User's Guide to Integral Human Development—A Practical Guide for CRS Staff and Partners*. Baltimore: Catholic Relief Services, 2008.

Ians. "300 Plant Species Discovered in 2016: BSI." *Business Standard*, June 6, 2017.

Ilaiah, Kancha. *Why I Am not a Hindu—A Sudra Critique of Hindutva Philosophy, Culture and Political Economy*. Kolkatta: SAMYA, 1996.

Jaffrelot, Christophe. *The Hindu Nationalist Movement and Indian Politics—Strategies of Identity-Building, Implantation and Mobilization*. New Delhi: Penguin Books India, 1996.

Jaffrelot, Christophe. *The Sangh Parivar: A Reader*. Critical Issues in Indian Politics. New Delhi: Oxford University Press, 2005.

Jain, Sheena. "Structure and Culture: The Debates." In *Structure and Transformation—Theory and Society*, edited by Susan Vishwanathan, 1–32. New Delhi: Oxford University Press, 2001.

Lalmalsawma, David. "India Speaks 780 Languages, 220 Lost in Last 50 Years—Survey." *Reuters*, September 7, 2013.

Mangai, Paulose. "Showcasing the Republic." *Vidya Jyothi Journal of Theological Reflection* 82.2 (2018) 81–85.

Mankekar, D R and Mankekar, Kamala. *Decline and Fall of Indira Gandhi—19 Months of Emergency*. New Delhi: Orient Longman, 1977.

McCully, Patrick. *Silenced Rivers: The Ecology and Politics of Large Dams*. London: Zed, 2001.

Mehta, Rimple. "'Illegal' Bangladeshis in *Akhand Bharat*: Inscriptions of Race and Religion on Citizenship." *Economic and Political Weekly* 53.7 (2018) 62–68.

Oishimaya, Sen Nag. "What Is Religious Fundamentalism?" In *World Atlas*, April 2017.

Senèze, Nicolas. "Pope Francis Explains 'Integral Human Development.'" *La Croix International*, April 5, 2017.

Sharma, Arvind. *Modern Hindu Thought: The Essential Texts*. New Delhi: Oxford University Press, 2002.

Singh, Shiv Sahay. "India's Biodiversity Riches Grow by 499 Species." *The Hindu*, June 5, 2017.

Teltumbe, Anand. "Development of a Few, Misery for the Masses." *Economic and Political Weekly* 52.36 (2017) 10–11.

Tribal Cultural Heritage in India Foundation, March 2015. *Jawaharlal's Five Principles for the Policy to be Pursued vis-a-vis the Tribals*.

Virmani, Arundhati. "Social Responsibility of the Historian—The *Annales*' Agenda in Perspective." *Economic and Political Weekly* 52.36 (2017) 46–53.

Zimmermann, Kim Ann. "What Is Culture? Definition of Culture." Live Science, July 2017. https://www.livescience.com/21478-what-is-culture-definition-of-culture.html/.9

10

Weaving Voices for Our Common House
Closing Ceremony

David Fernandez, SJ

Today, we live an eschatological crisis, a crisis of purposes, direction and utopia. This is how José Laguna refers to the lack of clarity regarding the course our society is following.[1] This is the issue we have discussed throughout the meeting we close today.

The postmodern collapse of the great stories of sense has left a society with no clarity on the horizon towards which it directs its steps. Society, however, continues moving forward. This Spanish theologian asks himself: Where to? Who directs it? What for? The popular group assures that "another world is possible." However, the political outline of this proposal is not clear yet. More than ever, when rage, resistance and indignation connect politically, it is urgent to provide them with new horizons and a possible utopia. We need to create this "new world."

As a conclusion to this extraordinary colloquium, it is clear that this world in crisis, looking for its way, needs at least the following elements.

1. HERMENEUTIC: Construing history from the point of its reverse, of the victims of history, the poor and the excluded.
2. ETHICS: Above any other social understanding, compassion is the main imperative and beginning of any human relation.

---

1. Laguna, "*Pisar la Luna. Escatología y política.*"

3. UTOPIA: This, or at least a theoretical idea of where we want to go, as a project of a world transformed in favor of those who suffer. Today, we pursue some clear guidelines: "sustainability," "decline" and "equality." These names being greater than their parts.

The greatest peril in the world today is not the terrible inequality, nor the terrible poverty suffered by human beings, not even the extreme corruption of the political and ruling class, or its submission to the dictates of a blind and ruthless market. No. The worst part is running out of mobilizing dreams; we have no utopias that produce the effect we want and no projects to generate transforming activities. Today, for example, voting for a left or right wing party seems to be the same; whoever wins will have no choice but to enforce the global technocratic policies at the service of the great transnational capital and its regulating organisms. The traditional left wing is no longer the bearer of emancipating policies. In their own words, modernization and reforms have substituted revolution. The left wing offers only individualistic consumerism and welfare projects that leave out the majorities. A more social, popular and critical left wing shows critical and eventful gestures, but not a thorough comprehension of today´s world. Therefore, they lack a coherent action program.

Thus, the only possible future horizon is an absolute free market. The only horizon proposed by techno-liberal utopia is its consumer recipe and the idea that societies that nurture greed and lack of solidarity among its members generate greater benefits than those that give preference to individual desires over collective needs. This is the culmination of the depoliticizing desire of the dominant ideology; it has deprived politics of its transforming, alternative, innovative and historical character. Politics today only administer the immovable. And, water that stagnates, rots.

Man, regardless of his religious or political affiliation, has always dreamed of a better world. Utopianism itself relates to our psychological structures. We are constitutionally hopeful. Mobilizing dreams are not the superfluous luxury of idle societies, but people´s political necessity. That is why European anti-globalists made it clear to the powerful that "if you don´t let us dream, we won´t let you sleep," and the boys of the *"I am 132"* group said "our dreams do not fit in your ballot boxes." Facing the theories of "end of story" and the fate of the neo-liberal model, the basic movements continue to propose the discourse of utopia of the desirable and possible, and recover from power the language that the latter has unduly appropriated.

Considering the above mentioned hermeneutic element in all seriousness, that is, defending the project for a common house from the point of view of those who suffer reality, we should ask ourselves the following questions—just as José Laguna does in his enlightening essay, developed from a theological perspective: What suffering does the globalization dream take into account? What evils does the political party in power remedy? Do the dreams of the current government benefit the poor? Due to the ethical, theoretical, economic viability and social sustainability options that have brought us together, we understand that any policy that does not relieve suffering and fulfills the dreams of the weakest is as ineffective as any philosophy that does not remedy a malady, as Epicurus sustained. The current formal democracy disappoints us because the poor and marginalized are not the center of their projects. It disappoints us because it does not understand human rights as the rights of the poor, because it is not only a question of helping the poor but of placing them as actors in the center of reality, because in preaching the goodness of the search for the common good, it forgets people´s concrete suffering.

We cannot think of a good life, liberation, or Christians´ heaven if our backs are turned against concrete suffering, injustice and margination. Consequently, a proposal for mere tolerance, respect for differences and peace at all costs that leaves untouched the most important problems of selfishness of the powerful, of injustice, of lies and structural violence is a partial and incomplete proposal. Perhaps, it is an ideological operation, a mystification that collaborates with the disappearance of the fundamental forms that are the origin of social suffering. According to Žižek, "It is deeply symptomatic that Western societies, so sensitive to different forms of persecution, are also capable of launching numberless mechanisms destined to make us numb to the most brutal forms of violence and, paradoxically, in the same way they arouse sympathy for the victims."[2]

Our thinking is not impartial. It aims to be objective, not impartial. Therefore, another characteristic of the project we need, takes sides for the lowest classes: it demands the construction of social coexistence, urgent attention to the needs and demands of those who have less, of those most vulnerable, of those who are "nothing" or "nobody." Food, health, education, housing, (roof, work and land. says Pope Francis) are a logical and necessary *prius* in front of the claims made in more developed worlds where, supposedly, man´s basic rights have been secured. The presence of poor people and oppressed nationalities barred from welfare is the major scandal that challenges and confronts the entire social model.

One more characteristic of this project is to force a "yes answer" and a change. In other words, the project breaks the logic we use to advance, and disrupts the idea of progress sustained by society. Here I turn to the

---

2. Žižek, *Sobre la Violencia*, 244.

"philosophy of historical reality," developed by Ignacio Ellacuría, Jesuit brother, Rector of the Central American University, murdered by the death squadrons during the civil war in El Salvador in 1989. He spoke of praxis as a constitutive part of reality.

So far, history has been recorded in terms of "progress and development" within which human beings evolve from low to high levels, in ascending order, towards a better future for humanity. Well regarded, this is a mythical conception—that it to say, ideological—that history itself has destroyed. However, we still view the passing of time in this way: our children should live better than we do, in the same logic of "linear progress," with more wealth, better jobs and more resources. It is, in fact, Aristotle´s paradigm: potency becomes act. According to Zubiri, this is how modernity conceived history: the development of potencies that man possesses since the beginning of time. This determinist conception sets forth that history is the prisoner of that which nature, matter or spirit—depending on the philosophical point of view—potentially had at the beginning of time, and simply restricted itself to become act during the historical processes.[3] Thus, a human being had to become what he was called to be.

Considering this determinist and cumulative evolution of history, Ignacio Ellacuría proposes an evolution conceived not only as the *factum* of what exists already—a fatal fact—but rather as a *faciendum* that, from the praxis, creates a new reality.

The truth of reality is not only what has already been done. That is only part of reality. To understand the historical praxis in the process of transforming reality, we also have to consider what is being done, and become aware of what is about to happen. "We should not understand history as a continuous progress whose objective is an ideal final *topos*, since this would mean examining history outside history itself. History is not predicted, nor is it fatally directed towards a determined direction. Human activity of transformation produces history. Due to this, Ellacuria, and also Zubiri, criticizes the conceptions of history understood as unveiling or maturity processes.[4]

What is real is not identical to what is current. Possibilities can be updated. Real engulfs current and possible. The history of humanity is nothing but the successive creation of new possibilities together with the obstruction or discrimination of others. Therefore, human freedom derives from the appropriation of possibilities. and history advances practicing freedom. At the end, when real possibilities disappear, we will truly know what human reality is. This, only in fact, because as we go along, we will have inevitably

---

3 Zubiri, *Naturaleza, Historia, Dios*. 362–82.
4 Samour, *Voluntad de liberación*, 172.

abandoned other possibilities. History cannot be predicted; it is produced. Human beings´ freedom creates it.

THEN, WHAT SHOULD WE DO TO IMPROVE?

I will now describe the central paradigms of what we can define, not as an alternative program, but as (something more profound) an alternative way to do politics. The difference lies not only in the "what," but mainly in the "how." This, of course, is most difficult to formulate at the end of a presidential period, like the one we are going through today.

Slavoj Žižek, always controversial and intriguing, proposes doing nothing. Indeed, this Slovak philosopher defends Bartleby´s strategy: Melville´s character, an extremely passive clerk who answered all his boss´s requests saying "I´d rather not do it." To exemplify his strategy, Žižek explains the plot of José Saramago´s novel *Essay on Lucidity*. This is the story of the strange events that happened in the nameless capital of an unidentified democratic country when the majority of the population casts blank ballots. The government and the political parties panic Is it a conspiracy organized to overthrow the government in power and the democratic system? In this case, who is behind and how could they organize the subversion of hundreds of thousands of people without being discovered? The government stigmatizes the movement as "pure terrorism and not adulterated," declares a state of emergency and cancels all constitutional guarantees. Then, the government kidnaps, arrests, tortures, disappears hundreds of citizens, creates chaos in the city, and the government itself assaults the local governments. However, these actions do not work. The population resists the government's attacks with an astonishing unity and a Gandhian non-violent resistance level.

For Žižek, voters´ abstention goes beyond the intra-political negation, the no-trust vote that rejects the same framework of decision. In psychoanalytic terms—he says—voters´ abstention is, in a certain way, like *Verwerfung* (foreclosure), which is more radical than repression (*Verdrängung*). Then, he remembers Badiou´s provocative thesis: "It is better to do nothing than contribute to the invention of new forms to make visible what the empire already recognizes as existent."[5] Žižek says that it is better to do nothing than to get involved in localized acts whose ultimate function is to run the system more smoothly (acts such as providing space for new subjectivity multitudes). According to him, today the threat is not passivity but pseudo-activity, the need "to be active," to "participate," to cover up the vacuum of what is happening. People intervene all the time, they are always "doing something," professors

---

5. Badiou, *Fifteen Theses on Contemporary Art*, 119.

participate in senseless debates, etcetera. The most difficult thing is to step back, to withdraw. Rulers prefer even a "critical" participation or dialog to silence. They try to get us involved in the "dialog" to make sure our threatening passivity is broken. Therefore, abstention is an authentic political act since it confronts us with the vacuum of current democracies. Sometimes, he concludes, doing nothing is the worst and most violent thing we can do.[6]

Opposite to the "active abstention" suggested by Badiou and Žižek, Boaventura de Souza proposes three types of actions to resist domination. These actions, that can be performed at any time and in any place, are: democratize, de-colonize and de-commercialize reality. This is a brief description.

Democratize means democratize democracy: reject the idea that liberal, representative democracy is the only valid form of democracy, and legalize other forms of democratic deliberation. For example, de Sousa speaks of participative democracy or community democracy.

In a private conversation, Ilan Semo declares that he could not grant the notion of "democracy" to "liberal democracy" anymore. It is rather a system of oligarchic variations in different places. In fact, we have a parliamentary oligarchy—just like the existing parliamentary monarchies. Aristotle, Locke and Kant make a clear distinction between an oligarchic system and democracy. Technocracy must not be allowed to kidnap the idea of democracy that today, once again, is in danger—as an idea in itself.

The distinction between revolution and democracy must be ended. This is one of the conceptual frauds of the left wing who uses the concept of democracy to take right wing positions.

Back to the principles of democracy (in their community, capillary and multiform versions) can only be the result of the socialization of the forms to do politics, something very distant from the parliamentary system of current viewers.

De-colonize means trying to eliminate oppression based on the supposedly natural, racial or ethnic-cultural inferiority of the oppressed. Among many other colonial relations, we find racism present in history books, news programs, policy repression, semantic pre-conceptions, devaluation or repression of cultural diversity, public transportation and daily interpersonal relations.

It can also be found in international relations, mostly in relations between colonizing powers and new independent countries. Here colonialism combines with imperialism. The Portuguese sociologist maintains that refusing to assess the historical colonialism and disclose what

---

6. Žižek, *Sobre la Violencia*, 256

happened and how it happened is another example of a particularly lacerating present-day colonialism.

In the epistemological field—Boaventura continues—colonialism is revealed by giving it the monopoly of knowledge valid to modern science and Western philosophy. Thus, the devaluation of other popular, traditional, urban and rural knowledge that regulates the daily life of a large majority of the world's population comes about. By underestimating this knowledge, the social groups that possess this knowledge are also devalued.

Internal colonialism appears in various forms, adds the sociologist. For example, the privatization of smallholdings that were social property originally. Also, the authoritarianism of public administration exercised over citizens, the repression of cultural diversity and the lack of recognition for the authorities that existed before colonization. Another internal colonialism is found in the lack of recognition for the languages and cultures of ethnical minorities and the denial to recognize their right to autonomy and self-government.

Finally, de-commercialize means to question some common places or collective evidence about the economic operation of society. Some of the evidences mentioned by De Sousa are:

1. To conceive development as an endless development based on an intense appropriation of nature. This conception leads to disaster, as has been recognized, even by Pope Francis.[7]
2. To reduce welfare to material well-being. This cliché ignores the multidimensions of life, essential for full human development.

Therefore, it is necessary to understand that, just like any other historical phenomenon, if capitalism had a beginning, it will certainly have an end. Besides—he adds—the ecological problem has already changed the terms of the debate: the problem is not knowing if capitalism will survive, but whether the planet will survive capitalism.

De-commercialize also means to understand the many logics of economic relationships that did not go through the accumulation of wealth or the earning of profits at any price. Some of these logics existed before capitalism and still survive; some others emerged with capitalism to oppose it. The natives' concept of "good life" is the expression of a non-capitalistic system that still survives.

So, de-commercialize means to prevent market economy from extending its scope of action to such an extent that it transforms society into a

---

7. Papa Francisco, *Laudato Si'*, *Carta Encíclica sobre el cuidado de la casa común*.

market society where everything can be bought or sold, even ethical values and political options.

According to this author, the imperative need to de-commercialize personal, social, political and cultural life means

1. To promote forms of fair social economy.
2. To subject the use and management of essential and strategic resources and services to democratic public control.
3. To de-commercialize nature as far as possible, for example, water.
4. To define a new generation of fundamental rights: nature´s rights, humans´ right to water, land, biodiversity and the ensuing consecration of new common goods.
5. To prohibit financial land and food speculation.
6. To transform food sovereignty at the heart of agrarian policies so that countries cease to be dependent on food imports as far as possible
7. To regulate agro-fuels strictly because of the impact they have on security and food sovereignty.
8. To increase taxes on some food products that travel more than a thousand kilometers between producer and consumer in order to boost local economy.
9. To include the decrease of working time in the job promotion policies.
10. To prohibit patents for traditional knowledge and drastically reduce the validity of intellectual property rights of pharmaceutical products.
11. To take advantage of the digital revolution to promote a culture that collectively rewards creativity: *Open Source Software* and *Wikipedia*, for example.[8]

From my own point of view, and looking at the horizon from a different perspective—that of the European neo-communist left wing—the transforming strategy of the reality we need must find its way between the impulse of "minor" reforms that end up leading to a total collapse, (here we must remember Mao who distrusted even a minimal concession to market economy, a well-founded position as we have witnessed) and the "radical" reforms that strengthen the system in the long run (Roosevelt´s *New Deal* among others). This brings up the permanent necessity to distinguish important reforms, regardless of scope and size. It also brings up questions about the "radicalness" of different forms of resistance: quite often, a minimal legal

8. De Sousa Santos, *La Democracia al borde el Caos*, 169–76.

reform aimed at bringing the system into line with the ideological objectives it professes may be more subversive than the evident questioning of the basic assumptions of the system. This allows to situate the organization of groups and movements within a policy of "minimum rights" (Badiou): knowing how to identify and focus on a minimal measure (ideological, legislative, etc.) that, *prima facie*, not only questions the premises of the system but even seems to apply its own principles to its real functioning, and thus, become more self-coherent. However, a "vision of critical-ideological parallax" leads us to conjecture that this minimal measure, although it does not disturb the explicit mode of operation of the system in any way, actually "moves through the subsoil" and introduces a crack in its basis.

In addition, the true transforming act is an intervention that acts not only within a given background, but rather alters its coordinates and, therefore, makes it visible as a background, Thus, in contemporary politics, an act must alter the category of background of the economy making its political dimension tangible. Remember Wendy Brown´s caustic question: "If Marxism had anything of value for political theory, was it not the insistence that the problem of freedom was contained in the social relations implicitly declared "apolitical"—that is to say naturalized—in the liberal discourse?"[9] With our organization of native villages, workers, women, and migrants, the idea is to make it understood that the rules of the economic game in which we develop are inclined in favor of transnational corporations and financial capital. This must be made visible. There is no economic neutrality or free market because economy is dominated by the powerful; it is highly political.

Bur we must also change culture. Every revolution comprises two different aspects: the factual revolution and the spiritual reform. That is to say, the real struggle for state power and the virtual struggle for the transformation of customs: the essence of daily life. In the latter case, people´s organizations play a fundamental role while the conditions for achieving the first are being generated.

Postmodern left wing blames traditional Marxists Leninists for focusing on seizing state power. However, the successes obtained in seizing that power failed in the achievement of its objectives. As a result, they maintain that the left wing movements should adopt a different strategy, apparently more modest, but in fact, much more radical: withdraw from the power of the State and focus on the direct transformation of the social life network and everyday uses that underpin the social structure (John Holloway). That is why homosexual rights, human rights, and other movements are important. The problem is that these movements rely on state organizations, just like social

---

9. Brown, *States of Injury*, 14.

economy and solidarity organizations, which not only serve their needs but also provide the framework for their activity (stable civilian life). That is the reason why there can be no government without social movements, as Tom Negri said, but there can be no social movements without government either, that is, without a state power that supports their space and allows them to develop. That is why we cannot ignore the struggle for electoral or revolutionary state power. For this to be possible, the creation, development and strengthening of social movements and revolutionary patience is required.

Perhaps here it would be necessary to define what a social movement is because there is much speculation. Every political system is characterized by defining what is possible—that which does nor modify its essence—and what is impossible—that which modifies its essence. The problem originates when possible becomes impossible. Social movements begin when the options offered by the system (a certain degree of education, income distribution, socialization of power) are transformed into something impossible to achieve through the rules of the system. In contrast, political parties always want to do what is feasible: something impossible.

The "minimal differences" policy mentioned above and the creation of an alternative culture should complement each other. in addition to the active, not passive, patience that analyzes the details of the situation, the states and the world that tries to discover weaknesses hidden by the ideology in the structural architecture of the state system (Johnston), where transformation can arise. That is to say, the promotion of popular economic and political organization must be completed with the preparation and capacity to determine the moment when the possibility of real change is near and, at that moment, modify the strategy, take the risk and participate in the total fight. The great repercussions do not come by themselves. We must prepare the ground patiently, but we should not miss the moment when this Great Change is possible.

The required patience is not only that which awaits, but also that which loses battles to win the war. The right time for a revolution will never arrive, a situation is never "mature enough" for a revolution. It is always "premature," by definition. And maturation does not wait for "objective" circumstances to reach maturity, but rather for the accumulation of defeats. Nothing that has been said is possible if we do not have a conscious policy to avoid the control of the state. As we have seen, we cannot have a revolutionary policy either outside or within the framework of the State. Alain Baidou maintains that we should do it "at some distance" from the State, outside, not destroying but rather questioning the State; not destroying the State but rather improving it or moderating its evil character. The form adopted by state power is not secondary; it is crucial.

A "certain distance from the state" means with independence and autonomy. This means, among other things, that the policy itself is not structured or polarized around an agenda or calendar, or subject to deadlines set by the State. Instead, it runs between the abandonment of pure democracy, deprived of revolutionary potential, and a purely destructive denial ("terrorist"). The abandonment, the distance, must create a new space. And, this takes place when it undermines the coordinates of the very system and strikes its structural support. It is necessary to abandon the hegemonic field that intervenes energetically in it and, simultaneously, reduces it to its hidden minimal difference. Therefore, organizations, collectives and social sector movements, must find a new policy at some distance from the State so that this new policy can establish itself as a policy of resistance that questions it constantly and denounces the limitations of the state mechanisms.

We can understand that there can be a total distance from the state, if the state were only an administrative institution, Autonomous Zone types: but if the State is a social process that reflects social conflict, the distance should be shorter.

Thus, it is important to remember the double character of the State. On one hand, it is a monopoly (of violence, for example) that guarantees the private character of capital accumulation (which creates other monopolies). On the other hand, it is a mechanism representing various social classes and sectors—a battlefield—and a distribution of resources and socializing conditions. On one hand it assures the reproduction of the system, and on the other, it has no other option but to open spaces to those who question it. This dialectic is frequently forgotten in its analysis. The state can never be put at the service of general transformation, but it can be used by those who fight for its transformation. Moreover, it is a place where struggles for this transformation reach an effective public dimension. The Bolivian case is an example.

Hence, it is imperative to safeguard the autonomy of the movements, and at the same time create parallel instruments of State intervention.

According to Critcheley, it is necessary to bombard a capitalistic State with "infinite" demands that cannot be satisfied by those in power in order to put an end to it. But history shows that what is truly subversive is bombarding them with strategically selected, *precise* and *finite* demands, that do not admit any excuses.

In the long run and being more optimistic, it is possible to create what some revolutionaries call liberated territories that coerce and transform the State. Socioeconomic organizations can be the foundation for these economic-based political organizations that can count on a "place of their own," are self-governed and function as empty spots on the State official map, even if they are included *de facto* in a province because of their economic ties, organized crime, etc.

Yes. It is not only a question of resisting the State government, but also of appropriating it.[10]

In any case, we must look for the germ of historical change in the social dynamics that break with the inertia of the established. A few examples of the thousand of small cracks that run through the wall of what is given and fatal are: cooperatives and groups of ecological consumption, collective investment alternatives (*crowdfunding*) okupa (squatting) platforms, victims of mortgages, "*slow*" movements, decline, rural and urban-popular resistance organizations, politically aware and mobilized indigenous communities, free distribution of *software* and cultural works through *copyleft* licenses, reception and defense of migrant groups, ethical banking, movements claiming racial or sexual differences, human rights groups that understand them as rights of the poor, Trans-Pacific Partnership treaty (TPP) analysis, barter alternatives, medical alternatives, fight for territories, consumption of local seasonal products, resistance to mining companies and macro-projects and peace with justice. In the quest to weave voices for the common house, the experiences that came together in this colloquium are the first fruits of the society we are building, realities that anticipate the future. All of them are based on the permanent presence of people who suffer and wait. The future reveals the truth of the historical process and the potentiality that opens the way to the good life, to the new life.

It is therefore essential to value and defend the transformation and transcendent value of small collective and domestic actions. They demonstrate that reality, as Ellacuría said, "goes a long way," beyond the common, known paths and channels pre-determined by an imposed and uniform idea of progress. The traditional separation between domestic and political must be overcome. As José Laguna says—a new policy to unite *polis* and *domus* again. Politics is not typical of public institutions and professional politicians. The way to use, to associate and to face work have greater political relevance than the attributed. In fact, they are political events. "Social contract" and "fraternity" must harmonize in discourse and practice. "Common good" is closely linked to "domestic" needs.

According to Lucía Ramon, the new policy must link justice, care and social transformation. The utopias we require must be able to integrate the concern and care for the weakest at the center of their interests.

---

10. I do a broader development of this strategy in Fernández, "La economía social: el acento latinoamericano," 107.

The situation is desperate for the peoples of the world, for the workers, for the indigenous peoples, especially in this moment of global crisis. There seems to be no clear path to move from an alternative popular position to a different one. The dominant ideology is against us, but that gives us a peculiar freedom and the opportunity to experiment. Getting rid of the deterministic model of "objective needs" and the obligatory "stages" of development, and keeping a minimum of anti-determinism is sufficient: not everything is pre-determined in an "objective situation." There is always room for a truly transformative action; waiting patiently for a revolution's "right moment" is not enough. If you just wait, it will never come—It is necessary to begin with "premature" attempts. Remember Mao´s motto, "from defeat to defeat, to final victory." We must simply forget the pre-notion that linear time of evolution is on our side, that History works in our favor.

As Zizek states with sharpness, the English distinction to say "*meta*" can help us say what we want. Anti-capitalism cannot be the immediate "goal" of ESS emancipatory activity, but rather its ultimate "aim": the horizon of all its activity. Marx is present here: although the economic sphere seems "apolitical," it is the secret point of reference and the structural principle of the political struggles. That is why *Capital*, Marx´s major work, was a critique of *political* economy.

The alternative systems of economic production, the desire—like the one that now brings us together—to build a new world in which many worlds fit in, the unity of indigenous peoples and exploited groups, can be fundamental to gradually build a counter-hegemonic globalization in the coming decades. The formula outlined here, to move from the universal idea of equality to imprint a class bias on ESS, to support the organization of poor and marginalized inhabitants, to facilitate politicization, to generate a new non-capitalist culture, to actively await the opportunity for a substantial change from the State´s independent and autonomous position, and to be accompanied by struggles that seek to control the latter can constitute the horizon of change for us to move.

In any case, as Arturo Escobar maintains in his recent work on Latin American Critical Thinking, we must define it as the framework of three major aspects: the thought of the left wing, autonomic thought and the thought of the Earth. For him, these are not separate and prebuilt spheres, but rather overlapping ones, sometimes feeding each other, others in open conflict. I agree with him that today we have to cultivate the three aspects, keeping them in tension and dialogue, abandoning all universalizing ambitions and possession of truth.

Let us then embrace a broad and far-reaching conception of "economy" in which we include objectives such as democratic participation, environmental sustainability, social, racial, ethical and cultural equity, transnational solidarity and also, why not?, the directly anti-systemic action.

BIBLIOGRAPHY

Badiou, Alain. "Fifteen Theses on Contemporary Art." *Lacanian Ink* 23 (2004).
Brown, Wendy. *States of Injury*. Princeton: Princeton University Press, 1995.
De Sousa Santos, Boaventura. *La Democracia al borde del Caos*. México City: Siglo XXI Editores, 2014.
Fernández, David. "La economía social: el acento latinoamericano." In *Miradas sobre la economía social y solidaria en México*. Puebla: Universidad Iberoamericana, 2013.
Francis I, Pope. *Laudato Si': Carta Encíclica sobre el cuidado de la casa común*. México City: Buena Prensa, 2015.
Laguna, José. "Pisar la Luna. Escatología y política." *Cuadernos Cristianisme i Justicia* 195 (September 2015).
Samour, Héctor. *Voluntad de liberación: La filosofía de Ignacio Ellacuría*. Granada: Comares, 2003.
Žižek, Slavoj. *Sobre la Violencia: Seis reflexiones marginales*. Barceolona: Paidós, 2009.
Zubiri, Xabier. *Naturaleza, Historia, Dios*. Madrid: Alianza, 1987.

11

Sustainability
Agreement and opposition:
Possible Cultural Change

Josip Jelenić, SJ

Key words: development, growth, sustainable development, sustainability, values, solidarity, person, good.

INTRODUCTORY CONSIDERATIONS

Only in recent decades has there been talk of *sustainability*, referring, first of all, to economic development and then, with the passing of time, also to integral development, that is, to man in the dimensions which "make" and express him in his fullness and complexity of person. It seems to me that, primarily, sustainability is not an arbitrary process—when and to what degree I want it—left to the momentary desires and moods of the individual but one which requires that constant and permanent commitment which is dictated by human needs. Secondly, this process is imposed as an imperative on human research because the very survival of the whole world depends, and will increasingly depend, on the choices which we make individually and together, given the limits to the resources available to us. In reality, therefore, we are obliged to search for social, economic and environmental sustainability because there is no alternative other than self-destruction. Thirdly, I would like to point out that the demand for sustainability provokes opposing reactions. Those who live in affluence see sustainability as a restriction on their "having" ever more, while those who do not have hope that by means of sustainability they will obtain and share something more for their own needs. Such polarisation on account of limited resources and the desire to have ever more is the cause of conflicts and wars which harm everyone. The complex reality which is the object of this reflection could be expressed in the form of the following hypothesis: it seems that integral sustainable development requires a cultural change. Moreover, I am convinced that, with its social teaching, the church can offer a persuasive and reciprocal contribution and guidelines to our reflection and research.

MEANING AND DIFFERENCE BETWEEN DEVELOPMENT AND GROWTH

Before going on to consider sustainable development, I think it useful and necessary to say a couple of words concerning *development* in general and (economic) *growth*, their respective natures and differences. "According to the common distinction, growth refers to the quantity of goods and services available whereas development also includes qualitative elements of social, cultural and political life."[1] Development, therefore, is a much broader process than the growth which takes place within it. Growth, in fact, shows itself in the increase of material goods which help to improve the standard of the (material) life of man. It is logical, therefore, for an economic system to seek in every way to increase its capacity in this direction. We must not forget that here we are, exclusively, on the economic, material level which, by itself, could lead indirectly to improvement in the other areas of life. That does not mean to say that there is no relationship between growth and development. It seems logical that the increase in material well-being could lead to the happy result of improvement in other areas such as, for example, culture, the social life, the politics, the knowledge and the technical skills of the population etc. In other words, growth would bring both physical capital and human capital. However, that can happen only with a *moderate state of inequality* in the area of a society's population. In the opposite case, growth would enrich only one group and offer them a real opportunity for development while the majority of the population would go backwards both in growth and in development. This logic applies both on the national level (*also inside*) and on the international level.

Another observation about development brings us to the fact that it is not a gift, or the result of someone's whim, but a universal right. In the

1. See Utopie Onlus, "Crescita e Sviluppo" Utopie Onlus, "Crescita e Sviluppo."

Declaration on the Right to Development,[2] it says: "The right to development is an *inalienable human right* by virtue of which every human person and all peoples are entitled to participate in, contribute to, and enjoy economic, social, cultural and political development, in which all human rights and fundamental freedoms can be fully realized, and to benefit from this development." From this text, one can deduce that merely economic development has been superseded. Today, we are fighting for a *human development*, that is, an *integral development*, led by equality, sustainability, participation and productivity.[3]

That said, it is clear that the concept of development has evolved over time. In the process of reflection, the term *development* has itself been the object of growth and maturing from *economic* development to *human* development, to *sustainable* and finally *integral* development (which is true, authentic and sees man at the centre, the good of every man and of the whole man, cf. PP.14). In terms of human survival, wholeness and sustainability impose themselves as the obligatory path for the human race. In the long term, there is no alternative. Thus, the object of the following section is the real possibility of sustainable development amidst agreement, disagreement and opposition.

SUSTAINABILITY: AGREEMENT AND OPPOSITION.

Agreement.

In recent years, one notes the increasing use of the term *sustainability*, or else *sustainable development*, with a richness and importance which increase in step with the progressive knowledge of the limits of the resources at our disposal. Despite this evidence, there is no unanimity when it comes to recognising it effectively and applying it. Moreover, the word itself, *sustainability*, receives its significance only in relation to the areas in which it is applied, that is to economic development, or else social, environmental and cultural development. It seems that these are the areas which offer the best possibilities for application.

Given this, the first question which requires an answer is: to what does the term sustainability refer, or what does it mean? Out of curiosity, in the *Compendium of the Social Doctrine of the church*, we find only once the term "sustainable" under the word "development" and in relation to poverty, demography and the environment. In fact, the text speaks of the

2. General Assembly, *Resolution 41/128*.
3. See n.1.

"development and sustainable use of the environment," where sustainable refers to "integral and sympathetic development" (n. 483). In their activities in chronological order, the international organisations have offered some definitions of sustainability. The *first description* appears in the Brundtland Report of 1987 (later taken up by the International Commission for the *Environment and Development* in Tokyo in 1987) and sets sustainability in relation to sustainable development which it defines as "that development which satisfies the needs of the present generation without compromising the ability of future generations to satisfy their own needs."[4] From these clues, we can deduce that it is something rational, planned, subject to discernment and accepted with full responsibility because the person is capable of autonomous and responsible choices.[5] It is a unique process which must be understood in terms of real life and not something theoretical or, worse, abstract. Moreover, perhaps the simplest and clearest definition is that which describes sustainability as a *balance* between economic, social and environmental development or else between ecology, equity and economics. Thus, the path that leads us to the understanding and realisation of sustainability passes through "the process which integrates the environmental, social and economic dimensions."[6] The question is: of what does this process actually consist?

Returning to the question formulated above, the answer is to be sought within the relation between means and ends, that is, in the rational use of the means to reach the ends in the way that is most in harmony with the good of the person. This rule must be applied to the complex of human thought and action. Thus, sustainability refers first of all to the subjects, to the protagonists of the decisions and actions who have the responsibility for their consequences. In second place, the question recalls attention to the resources available which are always decreasing. Therefore, they are not *unlimited* (Bauman, 2016), and so their use must be rationalised in view of the good of all, both the present generation as well as those of the future. Thirdly, it has to be stated that the importance and the urgency of sustainability increases in step with the fading (to the point of vanishing) of the myth of unlimited resources, that is, of *infinite progress*, which justified egoistic behaviour in the past (SP, 1939, n. 30).

Without entering into the smaller details but remaining on the general level, it seems that there is a world consensus with regard to the need, nay, the urgency of rethinking our way of employing the resources available to

4. *Brundtland Report*, 1987.
5. Cesareo and Vaccarini, *La libertà responsabile* 58–60.
6. *Brundtland Report*, 1987: Concluding Address, 5.

us and of relating to the environment as well as with one another. In confirmation of this, it is enough to read the texts of the International Conferences on the economy, the environment and society, such as, for example, that of 1972, which marks the beginning of the process and what followed. The attitudes and decisions taken in the international conferences on the economy and on the environment reveal, in fact, a certain progress towards a common attitude on the part of the participants: from opposition, there is an increasing movement towards consensus. That does not mean to say that we have arrived at the point of common consensus, but at least, we are moving in this direction, as is clear from the debate on the subject. As a starting point, I indicate the Stockholm *Declaration on the Human Environment* (1972), which identifies the twenty-six principles on the relation between social well-being and the protection of the environmental patrimony.[7] Already the Preamble states that "man is simultaneously creature and creator of his environment which assures him his physical subsistence and offers him the possibility of an intellectual, moral, social and spiritual development"[8]. In the words of the social teaching of the church, this is *integral human development*[9], or *integral ecology*.[10]

Furthermore, I would like to point out two demands which the *Declaration* sets before us and which are as valid today as then. The task which is proposed to us is a permanent one. It is a continuous process which has to be carried forward with an "enthusiastic, but calm disposition of the mind and an intense but ordered effort."[11] The second demand refers to the *state of mind* of the world, similarly relevant today as yesterday, that is, the awareness that we have arrived at the point when we can choose either total destruction or else take care of one another. Thus, this is not theoretical but practical, lived knowledge.

With regard to the principles indicated in the *Declaration*, they deserve our particular attention because they are also close to the social teaching of the church. At the beginning, there is a presentation of the fundamental rights enjoyed by everyone such as liberty, equality, personal dignity and dignified conditions of life, as also the duty and the responsibility to protect them. With various emphases, these elements were to be treated in all the conferences devoted to both the environment and the climate up to the most recent in 2016 at Marrakech (Tunisia). In the *Declaration* of this latest

---

7. *Declaration* of the United Nations on "The Human Environment."
8. *Declaration*, 1972, Preamble, n. 1.
9. PP, 1967, n. 6–42; LCL, 1986, n. 91
10. LS, 2015, 138–46.
11. *Dichiarazione*, 1972, Preamble, n.6

conference, we find the confirmation of the principles and duties of that of 1972. The representatives of the 196 countries, participating in the conference, assume the task and responsibility of an effective promotion of "actions concerning the climate and sustainable development."[12] The signatories of the *Declaration* seek from governments "the highest political *commitment*" and *solidarity* with the "most vulnerable countries" (n.3). Moreover, they seek to "reinforce and sustain the efforts to eradicate *poverty*, and guarantee the security of food" through "commitment and cooperation" among all (n.4). Note 6 expresses a clear orientation towards the good of future generations: "While we are devoting ourselves towards fulfilment and action, we reiterate our resolution to inspire *solidarity*, *hope* and *opportunity* for generations present and future."

Someone could say that the unanimity of the participants expressed in these declarations, both in 1972 and in 2016, is not sincere or else forced in the face of increasing environmental and climactic disasters which also have repercussions on the economic, social, political and cultural levels. In the end, even the fear of possible disasters can be welcome, (even if to a minimum!), if this brings us to full knowledge and responsibility for our own behaviour. This is not being *minimalist*, but doing what is possible which, at a particular moment, becomes the *sustainable*. In other words, we must be realists in what we desire and for what we wish.

We have to do with the sustainability which embraces all the levels of daily life and which, in the climate of the globalised loss of "solidity, becomes increasingly urgent but, at the same time, more demanding and unknown also. "If in the 'solid' phase," thinks Bauman, "the heart of modernity lay in the ability to control/define the future, in the 'liquid' phase, the principal preoccupation is that of *not mortgaging the future* and of avoiding any kind of risk of not being able to enjoy the still secret, unknown, and unknowable opportunities hoped/expected for the future."[13] The real context, therefore, in which we seek to realise the process of sustainability, is that of the fears and *unknowns* which are the true characteristics of "liquid modernity."[14]

That said, I think it useful and necessary to consider the agreement with and the opposition to the process of sustainable development precisely in the context of liquid modernity which, in addition to unknown fears, is marked also by a global consumerism which is gradually reducing us to an anonymous mass of consumers. There are two questions which equally demand answers: who accepts sustainability as the way to integral

---

12. *Declaration* 2016, n.1
13. Bauman, *Modernità liquida*, VIII.
14. Bauman, *Modernità liquida*, X–XI.

development and who does not accept it? The answers are easy and, at the same time, difficult and complex since the actors are we people, our institutions, our governments etc., and so subjective factors are woven together with the objective ones.

After a first reading of the *Declarations* of the conferences on sustainable development on the European and international level, the impression is that all the participants—rich and poor countries—are in agreement with regard to the objectives and means proposed as well as in assuming complete responsibility for their effective realisation.[15] Thus, on the *Declarations* level, all are in agreement. The problems and the opposition begin at the stage of carrying out the duties assumed and the promises made. Bauman attributes one of the causes of opposition to the historical transition (that of the liquid phase) which differs from country to country. "In the different parts of the planet, the transition to the 'liquid phase', . . . takes place at *different* times and with a *different* rhythm . . . [T]he 'late arrivals' tend to condense and abbreviate the paths already followed by the forerunners with results that are often catastrophic and violent" (Bauman, 2011, p. XI). This quoted text refers to the different starting points and the different stages of the *path* followed till now. It is precisely these initial differences and inequalities which generate opposition and agreement in the face of the achievement of a process of sustainable development. In quantitative terms, the have's want more, and the have not's want not only what is necessary but also more. To attain these objectives, methods and means are often employed which harm the environment of the life of all.

To trivialise what we are saying, we can suppose that if all the participants started from the same point and from equal conditions, sustainable

---

15. Chronological list of some events concerning Sustainable Development on the European and international level from 1972 to 2016: 1972, Stockholm: the I UNO *Conference on the Human Environment*; 1980, Nairobi: *World Conservation Strategy: Living Resource Conservation for Sustainable Development*; 1987, Tokyo: *Our Common Future*; 1992, Rio de Janeiro: the II UNO Summit on *Environment and Development*, called Earth Summit; 1992, Brussels: the European Union's *V Plan of Environmental Action* "Towards lasting and sustainable development"; 1994, Aalborg (in Denmark): the *First European Conference on Sustainable Cities*; 1996, Lisbon: *Second European Conference on Sustainable Cities*; 1997, Kyoto: the Conference CP03 of the *United Nations Framework Convention on Climate Change* (UNFCCC); 1998, Aarhus (Denmark): "Aarhus Convention"; 2000, Hannover: Third European Conference on Sustainable Cities; 2001, Gothenburg: the *Third Environmental Conference UE*; 2002, Johannesburg: the *World Summit on Sustainable Development*; 2004, Aalborg: the *IV European Conference on Sustainable Cities*; 2005, Luxembourg: the European Council: *Relaunch of the Lisbon Strategy* (1996); 2006, Brussels: The *European Strategy for Sustainable Development 2006*; 2007, Seville: the *V European Conference on Sustainable Cities*; 2015 Paris. . .; 2016, Marrakech: the *Conference on Climate*;

development (sustainability!) would be easily accepted and followed by all. However, even in this case, the acceptance and application are uncertain because there always remains the disordered and unchecked desire to have more at the expense of others. We are speaking of *greed*, one of the seven capital sins which accompany human thinking and action.[16] Therefore, it is not just a question of quantity but still more of the quality of life. Thus, sustainable development presupposes both quantitative and qualitative changes on the part of people, ones which have repercussions on all the dimensions of daily life. It is necessary to order and direct human plans, choices and behaviour to this end.

For the umpteenth time, I ask myself why, despite the clarity of the objectives and the theoretical determination of the participants to carry out these tasks, is there so much fear and hesitation in the implementation of the obligations taken on? From the behaviour of the participants, as we have already mentioned, it seems that there is a *two-sided fear* standing in the way of serious commitment. The *fear of reciprocal mistrust* among those who have already reached the highest levels of development, determined to continue on the path of well-being and not to share it, and those who are still lying in the swamp of underdevelopment and poverty, material and spiritual. Is it possible to restrain the former and encourage and help the latter? This could seem to be a purely rhetorical question. On the contrary! It is about the reciprocal trust, help and sharing which are so necessary in the modern world which is the victim of individualisms of every kind.

Opposition/Resistance

There is no lack of voices which consider sustainable development within the current economico-political system to be a fallacy, a self-contradictory proposal, something past its sell-by date, in sum, something that cannot be achieved.[17] In fact, sustainable development would have been set up on a base which is called "continuous growth" which, as we have already said, is shown today to be false or even harmful for the simple reason that there are limits to the resources available to us. I shall consider some among the major advocates of this position: Serge Latouche, the major theorist of the idea of *serene degrowth*, and Maurizio Pallante of *happy degrowth*, and, especially, Jean Baudrillard, a true specialist in the taking apart of the *society of growth*. Their common procedure is to lay bare the myth of continuous (economic) growth and, consequently, the impossibility of realising sustainable

16. Cucci, *Il fascino del male* 167–212)
17. Kempf, *Comment les riches détruisent la planète*.

development on such a basis. The shared reasoning of these three authors can be summarised in the following way: the present economico-financial capitalist system follows the logic of working, accumulating capital, investing, gaining (on the individual or group levels), investing anew and gaining ever more. For this end, the capitalist system shows itself to be ideal. However, this logic is incompatible with the principle of the redistribution of goods. Capitalism sees it as an attack on its life and so rejects it. It is simple: it is not suitable for a realisation of an integral development which sees at its centre people, the good of the whole person and of all people.

If one browses through one of Latouche's books—*Altri mondi, altre menti, altrimenti*—one finds numerous examples of failed attempts at promoting sustainable development by means of continuous growth within the sphere of the present capitalist economic system. Before analysing sustainable development, he subjects present development to harsh criticism in general. "The development which actually exists," maintains Latouche, "can be defined as a process which leads to commodifying the relations between people, and between people and nature. The aim is to exploit, put a price on and gain profit from natural and human resources. An aggressive process in its dealings with both nature and people, development is, like the colonisation which precedes it and the globalisation which follows it, an enterprise of dominion and conquest at once economic and military."[18] Therefore, he proposes a liberation from *developmentalism* and an exit from the schemes of *development economics* which have colonised the thinking and action of the whole world. However, he also criticises the so-called *sustainable development*, "an expression which sounds good on first hearing but which in reality is profoundly contradictory, and represents an extreme attempt to cause the survival of development, that is, economic growth, promoting the belief that the well-being of peoples depends on it. The numerous texts of Latouche indicate that the greatest environmental and social problems of our time are due precisely to (forced!) growth and its collateral effects; hence the urgency of strategy for degrowth, centred on moderation, on the awareness of limit, on the "8Rs" (recycling, reusing, etc.) to attempt to respond to the grave emergencies of the present."[19]

In the first instance, the authors of this *sweet degrowth* can be classified as "opposition" to that sustainable development of which we are speaking. Their common idea is that sustainable development is not compatible with the ideology and the logic of the development in force. Different elements are to be indicated which the present system and politics impose as the only

18. Latouche, *Breve trattato sulla decrescita serena*, 133–34.
19. See http://it.wikipedia.org/wiki/Sviluppo_sostenibile.

way to follow. The first common element concerns *forced growth* by means of the *multiplication of new and superfluous needs*. In a cunning way, the productive system presses and leads people according to a consumerist logic. "In fact," claims Latouche, "we are dealing with a society of growth, that is, of a human organisation completely dominated by its economy. To remain in balance, the latter has only one way, the flight to the future, just as a cyclist who ceases from pedalling falls to the ground. When growth is absent, in the consumer society everything comes to a stop."[20]

To the list of *dissenting* voices are added names like Eduardo Viveiros de Castro, the anthropologist, and Déborah Danowski, the philosopher, who propose the return to simple living after the example of the Indians, "masters of survival." The former maintains that "sustainable development" constitutes a "contradiction in terms." It is only a pious desire, "unless 'development' signifies a radical turning point in the way of life which leads precisely to a 'living well' for all" However, the idea of "enduring capitalism" is equally false, a piece of conceptual hypocrisy.[21] Their thought and their proposal—and this goes for all living things on the Earth—is expressed as the imperative to return to living according to this logic: "being" more and "having" less, before it is too late for all. In other words, we must seek to promote a development which is sustainable for all, avoiding the inequalities that we have created. This is a common task both for the physical and the social and human sciences. From the point of view of sustainable development, that means that it includes a vision of development both in the material and spiritual senses. In other words, while we maintain and promote the present economico-financial system, which directs and pushes development exclusively for profit, we cannot achieve integral development.[22]

SUSTAINABLE DEVELOPMENT ACCORDING TO THE SOCIAL TEACHING OF THE CHURCH

It is not excessive to claim that the promotion of sustainable development constitutes one of the objectives of the social teaching of the church. However, if we search the *corpus* of the church's social teaching for the terms "sustainable development" or "sustainability" *expressis verbis*, we find them only once, in the *Compendium*, n. 483, but, in this case too, always in relation to another reality, social, natural, economic or human. Precisely what

20. Latouche, *Incontri di un "obiettore di crescita*," 14.

21. See "Il mondo sta finendo. Facciamoci aiutare degli Indios." Interview with E. Vivieros de Castro in *Il Venerdì*, 8.6.2017, n.1525, p.110)

22. Danowski e de Castro, *Esiste un mondo a venire?*, 32.

is spoken of is the "close link which exists between development . . ., and a sustainable use of the environment." At the same time, however, we find in the social documents of the church other types of development such as, for example, responsible, integral, just and human development Moreover, development is set in strict relation to the dignity of the person, as also to the basic principles of social teaching. The criterion of choice of the social documents cited in what follows consists in considering "what is necessary," in this case with particular attention to *Laudato si'*.

According to Benedict XVI, Paul VI's *Populorum progressio* is the church's point of reference on development because it offers an articulated vision of it which could be compatible with or else able to be identified with sustainable development. In *Caritas in Veritate*, we read: Paul VI "understood the term to indicate the goal of rescuing peoples, first and foremost, from hunger, deprivation, endemic diseases and illiteracy" (CIV, n. 21). All this is possible for sustaining and, at the same time, not destroying the creation because "from the economic point of view this meant their (the peoples') active participation, in equal terms, in the international economic process; from the social point of view, it meant their evolution into educated societies marked by solidarity; from the political point of view, it meant the consolidation of democratic regimes capable of ensuring freedom and peace" (CIV, n. 21). This vision of development includes all the dimensions, not just the economic.

If we look at *Populorum progressio* directly, we find the characteristics and qualities which, taken together, delineate the profile of desired and proposed sustainable development. In the *first place*, we have to place the personalist dimension, that is, the respect for every person in his dignity and integrity. That means that development is not an end in itself but is the instrument of the perfecting of the person in his multidimensional nature (PP, n. 6f). In the *second place*, it is social justice which presses towards a development of each and all in a spirit of sharing and equal participation. This vision is the opposite of the reductionism and economicism which promotes only a single dimension, that is, in the words of *Populorum progressio*, "Development is not reduced to simple economic growth. To be authentic, development must be integral, that is, directed to the advancement of every person and of the whole person."[23] In practice, this is a matter of adjusting the balance between economic development and social progress.[24]

In the *third place*, the process of development like that just described excludes no one: all are invited to participate in a free and responsible

23. PP, n. 14
24. See MM, n. 78.133–177; PT, n. 26b; SRS, n. 27–34.

way. Therefore, Pope Paul VI, calls each and all—Catholics,[25] believing Christians,[26] men of goodwill,[27] statesmen,[28] and thinkers[29]—to collaboration and mutual help. We are speaking of a Christian vision[30] which values industrialisation positively as a sign and factor of development[31] which, therefore, requires urgent, necessary reforms on the national and international levels.[32] Social activity, which spurs the protagonists along the path must be for people and not against them,[33] that is, integral and authentic development must lead to reciprocal solidarity between people and nations.

Forty years on from *Populorum progressio*, it is right to question whether the objectives proposed have been attained. There is no doubt that there have been advances but these have been different from those intended and with results which often turn out to be uncertain if not contrary. The situation today is completely different from that of the times of Paul VI in which, according to *Caritas in Veritate*, "the technical forces in play, the global interrelations, the damaging effects on the real economy of badly managed and largely speculative financial dealing, large-scale migration of peoples . . . , the unregulated exploitation of the earth's resources" make up a mosaic which is not in the least encouraging and lead us today to reflect on the necessary measures.[34] However, according to the Christian spirit, the whole crisis concerning polycentric, sustainable development could become "*an opportunity for discernment in which to shape a new vision for the future*,"[35] something which translates into: having an acceptable "need" and conserving the creation. These are the two essential and identifiable qualities of sustainable development.

As described, the concept of development is close to if not actually identical with that of sustainable development, the object of this reflection, because it is polycentric, that is, not reduced simply to the economic dimension but covers all the areas of human life comprehensively. When development is reduced merely to the economic dimension, it creates and

25. PP, n. 81
26. PP, n. 82
27. PP, n. 83
28. PP, n. 84
29. PP, n. 85
30. PP, n. 6–42.
31. PP, n. 25.
32. PP, n. 32,35.
33. PP, n. 34.
34. CIV, n. 21.
35. CIV, n. 21.

augments the disparities which provoke tension and conflicts. "In poorer areas," we read in CIV, "some groups enjoy a sort of 'super-development' of a wasteful and consumerist kind which forms an unacceptable contrast with the ongoing situations of dehumanising deprivation."[36] These are signs of warped and inhuman development rather than that which is sustainable for the good of all. Moreover, *"progress of an economic and technological kind is insufficient. Development needs above all to be true and integral."*[37] Pope Francis moves in this direction also in *Evangelii gaudium*, stating that "we are not simply talking about ensuring nourishment or a 'dignified sustenance' for all people, but also 'their general welfare and prosperity'. This means *education,* access to *health care,* and above all *employment,* for it is through free, creative, participatory and mutually supportive labour that human beings express and enhance the dignity of their lives. A *just wage* enables them to have adequate access to all the other goods which are destined for our common use."[38] All this forms part of the daily path to the achievement of authentic development.

Today, as we have indicated above, the situation is ever more complex. For example, if we take the State as the protagonist of sustainable development, it "finds itself having to address the limitations to its sovereignty imposed by the new context of international trade and finance which is characterised by increasing mobility both of financial capital and means of production, material and immaterial."[39] To this is increasingly added an inadequate "participation in the *res publica* on the part of the citizens."[40] All this leads to an ever increasing inequality among people which becomes an obstacle to integral development. Our society is divided between a majority of the poor and a shrunken minority of the rich. If we wish to apply the concept of sustainable development to this situation, it is not enough to have plans for aid which are to be considered as "provisional responses." According to Francis, we need radical changes "rejecting the absolute autonomy of markets and financial speculation and attacking the structural causes of inequality" which is "the root of social ills" and, as such, stands in the way of integral development.[41]

In the course of this reflection, we have often mentioned that—authentic and integral—sustainable development is conditioned by the

36. CIV, n. 22.
37. CIV, n. 23.
38. EG, n. 192.
39. CIV, 24b.
40. CIV, n. 24c.
41. EG, n. 202.

application of the personalist criterion. Thus, "the dignity of each person ... and the common good are concerns which ought to shape all economic policies. At times, however, they seem to be a mere addendum imported from without in order to fill out apolitical discourse lacking in perspectives or plans for true and integral development."[42] *Each of us* must be aware of his own responsibility, insists Pope Francis, and so "we can no longer trust in the unseen forces and the invisible hand of the market. Growth in justice requires more than economic growth, while presupposing such growth: it requires decisions, programmes, mechanisms and processes specifically geared to a better distribution of income, the creation of sources of employment, and an integral promotion of the poor which goes beyond a simple welfare mentality."[43] At the end of the day, authentic and integral (sustainable) development requires us all to renounce an "individualist, indifferent and self-centred mentality"[44] which is directly opposed to the dignity of the person and the good of all and each.[45]

According to Pope Francis, there is a relation of reciprocal dependency between integral (sustainable) development and peace among men because "a peace which is not the result of integral development will be doomed; it will always spawn new conflicts and various forms of violence"[46]. The latter are, actually, the result of the opposition to sustainability. In other words, the lack of promotion of sustainable development inevitably leads to violence which is nourished by the rapacity of sum and the desperate misery of others. Such a situation obliges us, both on the micro and macro levels, "to respond consistently to the needs of the times and to the continuous developments in life, social," political, economic and cultural.[47] To be sincere, convincing and lasting, this response must be formulated, analogously, according to four principles laid down by Pope Francis in *Evangelii gaudium*: in promoting sustainable development, we have to accept that time is greater than space which manifests itself as "a constant tension between fullness and limitation."[48] That is to say, giving priority to time (rather) than to space means "being concerned about initiating processes rather than possessing spaces. Time governs spaces," states Francis, "illumines them and makes them links in a constantly expanding chain, with no possibility of return.

42. EG, n. 203.
43. EG, n. 204.
44. EG, n. 208.
45. EG, n. 218.
46. EG, n. 220.
47. CDSC, n. 160.
48. EG, n. 222.

What we need, then, is to give priority to actions which generate new processes in society and engage other persons and groups who can develop them to the point where they bear fruit in significant historical events."[49] Sustainable development is achieved in time, that is, in the reality of the *hic et nunc* and by means of concrete projects.

The *second criterion* recalls our attention to the logic of *unity against conflicts*. The process of development cannot be achieved in a fragmented reality but only in a "united" reality, not in internal divisions but on the basis of the "whole." "In this way," says Francis, "it becomes possible to build communion amid disagreement, but this can only be achieved by those great persons who are willing to go beyond the surface of the conflict and to see others in their deepest dignity."[50] To put it simply, sustainable development can be achieved only in an atmosphere of peace and unity.

The *third criterion* reminds us of the tension between the *ideal and reality*. Applied to development, this criterion brings to light the major discrepancy between "saying" and "acting." No one denies that we need clear ideas about what we want to do and how we do it. However, the ideas are "at the service of communication, understanding and praxis . . . illuminated by reason."[51] As we have seen previously, the participants in the international conferences on climate, the environment and sustainable development contribute and expound many very good ideas in this connection. Most of these ideas remain just that, ideas, without any impact on reality. The ideas remain imprisoned by the interests of the most powerful, by self-interest, individualism, etc. Francis reminds Catholics, Christians and men of good will that "this principle impels us to put the Word into practice, to perform works of justice and charity which make that Word fruitful."[52]

The *fourth criterion*—the whole is greater than the part—refers to the relationship between the "individual" and the "common," between globalisation and localisation. We must reject any opposition between the two realities. We have to promote both simultaneously because the two things together prevent us from falling into the trap of the two extremes, namely, between "an abstract and globalising universalism," on the one hand, and, on the other, a silent and folksy passivism centred on the local which is reduced to admiration without any action.[53] In the light of the demands of these four criteria, sustainable development is presented as a reasonable

---

49. EG, n. 223.
50. EG, n. 228.
51. EG, n. 232.
52. EG, n. 233.
53. See EG, n. 234, 235.

process which requires a constant and responsible commitment on the part of both individual and community.

In addition, I would like to recall two conditions for authentic development that were often repeated by Benedict XVI and that are often ignored particularly in the world of economic affluence. I am talking about *openness to life* and *respect for religious freedom*. "Openness to life," says Benedict XVI, "is at the centre of true development" for, "when a society moves towards the denial or suppression of life, it ends up no longer finding the necessary motivation and energy to strive for man's true good."[54] In fact, to lose personal and social sensitivity towards a new life signifies, as a result, being filled with insensitivity towards other forms of good too. "By cultivating openness to life," states the pope, "wealthy peoples can better understand the needs of poor ones, they can avoid employing huge economic and intellectual resources to satisfy the selfish desires of their own citizens, and instead, they can promote virtuous action within the perspective of production that is morally sound and marked by solidarity, respecting the fundamental right to life of every people and every individual."[55]

The second condition for true development is *respect for religious freedom*. If this is not guaranteed and respected, the whole situation in a society becomes explosive. Instead of being used to promote the good of all, resources are used to root out the seedbeds of conflicts. Unfortunately, today's world is full of religious conflicts which are often simply the cover for conflicts for motives of dominion and wealth. "Violence," states the pope, "puts the brakes on authentic development and impedes the evolution of peoples towards greater socio-economic and spiritual well-being"[56]. He goes on to mention: "the deliberate promotion of religious indifference or practical atheism which contrasts with the need for authentic development" because it withdraws the spiritual and human resources necessary for development.[57]

We are speaking, therefore, of the *obstacles* to true and authentic, the only sustainable development. In Benedict XVI's view, they can be identified both on the material and human levels. For both, the beginning is the erroneous conviction that man is "the sole author of himself, his life and society and can therefore do what he wants and as he wants[58] (CIV, n.34). This presumption, precisely that of the egoist, is the direct fruit of "original sin" which is transmitted to all the levels of personal and public life.

54. CIV, n. 28d.
55. CIV, n.28d.
56. CIV, n.29.
57. CIV, n.29.
58. CIV, n.34.

This human "characteristic" of sin is also reflected in the economic, material sphere which is in direct relation with development. "The conviction . . . that the economy must be autonomous," says the pope, "that it must be shielded from 'influences' of a moral character, has led man to abuse the economic process in a thoroughly destructive way." Moreover, this conviction has disabled the "economic, social and political systems" which have thus "trampled on the freedom of the person and of the social bodies" so that they have become unable to "ensure the justice which they promoted," much less, true and integral development.[59]

LAUDATO SI'

We cannot ignore the proposals of Pope Francis's *Laudato si'* with regard to sustainable development. The entire encyclical is devoted to *integral ecology* which, for its realisation, seeks a change in the present economico-political system. The integral ecology proposed and explained by the pope forms an essential part of authentic development and, increasingly conditions the quality of human life. The Pope's strategy consists in insisting on the changes necessary to reach the end being proposed. In fact, a careful reading of the encyclical makes the reader aware that ecology is only the "cover" of the true cause of the present situation, and that is the radical change of behaviour both of the individual and of the system in force. However, it is not just a question of any change but only of one focused on the "common good and a human development that is sustainable and integral." Thus, it is necessary to reject change "when it causes harm to the world and to the quality of life of much of humanity" (LS, n. 18). The negative change to be avoided manifests itself in concrete form as pollution, rubbish and the culture of waste[60]. It is a change that leads to the destruction of so many natural habitats and vital necessities and to the death of so many people on a global level. To avoid these negative changes, we must never detach development from the common good which "presupposes respect for the human person as such."[61]

The worst thing is that these phenomena (negative changes) are taking place before the eyes of all: before the powerlessness of the poor, the indifference of rulers, the lies of the rich. "Many of those," says Francis, "who possess more resources and economic or political power seem mostly to be concerned with masking the problems or concealing their symptoms."[62]

---

59. CIV, n.34.
60. See. LS, n. 20–22
61. LS, n.157
62. LS, n. 26a.

This irrational behaviour of the rational human being is not easy to grasp or understand. Why do men close their eyes in the face of such clear facts and deny them? Why does man choose destruction instead of a quiet life? Why does he close himself up in self-complacency and not open himself up to the common good? Or perhaps we have not yet learned that the questions of water (n.30), deforestation and global warming are also questions of life and death for so many human beings (n.43).

According to Francis, abandoned to themselves and their own powers, men achieve the deterioration of human life and a social degradation that is many-dimensional (political, economic, cultural) (n.43–47); they lose themselves in the diversity of opinions (n.60–61), something which leads to weak reactions, (n.53–59) because "the alliance between the economy and technology ends up side-lining anything unrelated to its immediate interests." Consequently, "any genuine attempts by groups within society to introduce change is viewed as a nuisance based on romantic illusions or an obstacle to be circumvented."[63] Moreover, sustainable development is not assisted by the situation in which the "economic powers continue to justify the current global system where priority tends to be given to speculation and the pursuit of financial gain which fail to take the context into account, let alone the effects on human dignity and the natural environment."[64] Not only do the economic powers stand in the way of every change; they also influence the political power in carrying out just and effective measures in the direction of sustainable development.[65]

According to Francis, this present situation in the real world is the direct result of the breach in vital relations within and outside us, that is, of sin. The first step which we have to take on the path of sustainable development consists in repairing or reconstituting, (re-establishing) and sustaining "the harmony between the Creator, humanity and creation as a whole."[66] I believe it necessary to restate that the achievement of all three of these elements must always happen "together" and "at the same time." The sustainability of development finds its basis and its justification also in the truth which we all have received from the Creator. Therefore, we cannot behave as absolute proprietors but as stewards of goods received, and so as responsible for our words, decisions and actions[67] (Cfr. LS, n.67).

63. LS, n.54
64. LS, n.56
65. See LS, n. 57–59
66. LS, n.66
67. See LS, n.67.

Again, *harmoniy*, as the natural framework for integral and authentic development, cannot neglect the principle of the common destination of goods which is translated into the universal right to the use of goods, "without excluding or privileging anybody."[68] Therefore, "a type of development," John Paul II maintains, "which did not respect and promote human rights—personal and social, economic and political—would not be really worthy of man."[69] Thus, authentic and integral development promotes the growth of a person in its manifold dimensions. Therefore, when we speak of sustainable development, we understand that *human development*[70] (which expresses the above-mentioned *harmony*.[71]

Moreover, the post-modern context is marked by two situations, namely, dominating technocracy, on the one hand, and man and his actions, on the other. The first refers to the dominant spirit of the technocratic virtual world (which relies on a false omnipotence and on technology) and the science which does not pursue the service of the good of the real person (of all people), but which seeks to dominate him in the sense of directing his thoughts and his actions.[72] Certainly, technology and techno-science have contributed to improving the quality of life of many people.[73] At the same time, however, people and their actions are being subjected to the power of techno-science. Thus, states, "there is a tendency to believe that 'every increase in power means an increase of progress itself, advance in security, usefulness, welfare and vigour, in fullness of values', as if reality, goodness and truth automatically flow from technological and economic power as such."[74] On the contrary, "technological products are not neutral," but change people's style of life and behaviour (cf. LS, n.107). It is necessary, therefore, to make improvements according to sound principles since authentic development is not automatic or the product of technological power but, first and foremost, of the constant and sincere commitment of human beings in the pursuit of the common good.

There are mistaken behaviour and life styles, the product of the dominion of techno-science and technocracy over men, which destroy the environment and stand in the way of a development that is authentic and integral. In connection with the promotion of sustainable development,

---

68. LS, n.93.
69. SRS, n.33a.
70. See PP, n.6–42; LCL, n.91.
71. LS, n.93.
72. LS, n.101ff.
73. LS, n.102,103.
74. LS, n.105.

"our capacity to make decisions, a more genuine freedom and the space for each one's alternative creativity are diminished."[75] Moreover, this promotion cannot be reduced to urgent, partial and intermittent responses, but, rather, must become a continuous and persevering process, despite resistance and opposition. This is the opposite direction to that of modern anthropocentrism which wants to have everything and at once without concern for the consequences which are often contrary to the common good.[76]

The human or integral ecology[77] promoted by Francis forms an integral part of the process of sustainable development. Therefore, analogously, the lack of interest which men show towards nature and the way they destroy it are indirectly contrary to the integral development of which human ecology forms a part.[78] The logic of relativising everything and everyone is begun and followed exclusively for its own sake. Moreover, practical relativism gains the upper hand over personal and communitarian responsibility.[79] Clearly, development can be reached only through the responsible work of each and every one. Thus, *Laudato si'* emphasises the fair and real valuation of the *activities of human labour* so that man is "able to become ... the actor responsible for his material improvement, his moral progress": it is precisely work that "must be the sphere of this manifold development." In today's world, unfortunately, labour is becoming revolutionised and, as such, is ceasing to have its positive function (LS, n.127; 128,129).

Considering the principal object of this reflection, namely, sustainable development, I am convinced that Francis's reflection on integral ecology "which includes ... the human and social dimensions"can contribute to an authentic and integral development. Sustainable development requires an economic, financial social and cultural ecology.[80] The Pope is taking a step forward and seeking an ecology of daily life as itself a condition of development. "To be able to speak of authentic development," says the Encyclical, "it will be necessary to verify that there is an integral improvement in the quality of daily human life."[81]

The *Catechism of the Catholic Church* speaks of *complete development*. This can be identified with sustainable development because it brings the "increase in the sense of God and the knowledge of him," that is, it

---

75. LS, n.108.
76. LS, n.115.
77. LS, n.137ff.
78. LS, n. 117,118.
79. LS, n.122; for the fruits of the culture of relativism, see n.123
80. LS, nn.141–146.
81. LS, n.147.

contributes to the growth of the person in his transcendent and horizontal dimension. In other words: "development multiplies material goods and places them at the service of the person and his freedom." A development of this quality is truly sustainable, that is, it deserves to be sustained because it leads to reducing "deprivation and economic exploitation. It causes an increase in respect for cultural identities and openness to transcendence."[82] Thus, human dimension leads, inevitably, to a just ratio between ends and means, and to respect for the material environment the preservation of which is part of sustainable development.

URGENT NEED FOR A CHANGE IN LIFESTYLE

Having taken this reflection on sustainable development through agreements and opposition, and through the vision of the church's social teaching, we can put forward some proposals with a high degree of possibility which could be considered again at another time. The problem is that the proposals too are "liquid" in the sense that they depend on our immobility and reluctance to change the current economico-financial system which, according to its nature, is in large part irreconcilable with the concept of *authentic sustainable development*. The logic of the present economico-financial paradigm obliges us to take the path of continuous research and unceasing movement, compromises and updatings on a type of development which contents everybody. Given this, we suggest some steps on the path proposed towards sustainable development.

The *first step* towards agreement consists in overcoming the *fear of reciprocal mistrust* because it generates closure and opposition. We have to be really convinced that it is possible to break out of the circle in which we are enclosed and entrapped. In my opinion, the answer is to be sought on the *anthropological* level as well as in terms of social, economic and political relations. Concretely, we are talking about a radical change of habits in every walk of life.

The words of Benedict XVI could be the best invitation to work on the projects which we have suggested during this reflection. The imperative of the present moment is centred on remaking "a deeper reflection on the meaning of the economy and of its goals, as well as a profound and far-sighted revision of the current model of development, so as to correct its dysfunctions and deviations. This is demanded, in any case by the earth's state of ecological health; above all it is required by the cultural and moral crisis of man, the symptoms of which have been evident for some

---

82. CCC, n.2441.

time all over the world."⁸³ Along with the economic system, which has to be rethought and changed, consideration must also be given to the *market* which is often outside man's control. It must be rethought and structured according to *commutative, distributive and social justice*, because only then will it be the motor of true development. Consequently, as an economic institution, the market will be the privileged place since it "permits encounter between persons, inasmuch as they are economic subjects who make use of contracts to regulate their relations, as they exchange goods and services of equivalent value between them, in order to satisfy their needs and desires."⁸⁴ However, the power and the internal movement of the economic institution of the market do not constitute an external framework but "internal forms of solidarity and mutual trust" by means of which there live the authentically human relations which together bring about the common good.⁸⁵

The *second step* towards the promotion of sustainable development is achieved *by a correct approach* towards the *economy* as a whole, that is, valuing it according to its nature as an instrument of human activities. Concretely, this means that we must never confuse the end with the function of the human activity on the material level. Furthermore, "economy and finance, as instruments, can be used badly, when those at the helm are motivated by purely selfish ends."⁸⁶ Thus, the obstacles to an authentic and integral development are not the economy and the market but man who uses them in the wrong way and for ends opposed to his good, or as the Pope says, "it is man's darkened reason which produces" consequences which are harmful for all and which impede sustainable development.

The *third step* consists in *being convinced* that within activities—economic, social, financial, etc.—*are possible "authentically human relationships of friendship, solidarity and reciprocity."* "The economic sphere," affirms Benedict XVI, "is neither ethically neutral, nor inherently inhuman and opposed to society. It is part and parcel of human activity and precisely because it is human, it must be structured and governed in an ethical manner."⁸⁷

The *fourth step* refers to institutions, that is, to the *harmonisation of the activities of the three subjects*—the market, the state, and civil society—in a single system where it is possible to realise an economy of freedom, fraternity and solidarity and, at the same time, without diminishing the

---

83. CIV, n.32d
84. CIV, n.35a
85. CIV, n. 35a, 36b
86. CIV, n.36b
87. CIV, n.36d

material dimension.[88] These are characteristics which, when experienced together, make possible the promotion and sustaining of true development. Moreover, among the subjects mentioned, it is civil society which merits special attention. Recalling *Centesimus annus*,[89] Benedict XVI reminds us that it is precisely civil society which offers "the best sphere for an economy of freedom and fraternity," without, however, downplaying the other two areas. We know, in fact, that the civil order, within civil society, is in need of the redistributive intervention of the State.[90] In other words, we are dealing with a *civilisation of the economy*, understood in the broadest sense)[91]. In practice, this means pursuing a "fully human economy."[92]

The *fifth step* can be formulated as follows: *seeking basically to see and treat the other as oneself*. In addition to recognising the person in the other, something which is certainly the fundamental starting point with regard to the theme being discussed, it is necessary to see him and treat him as *gift* and *help* in the economico-financial context. In other words, this means looking on the poor not as an obstacle to development but as the opportunity for a greater commitment to development, sharing with all and with each. While the rich have the possibility of giving, in the sense of aid to self-help, of sharing the superfluous and practising solidarity towards the poor, the latter, on their part, have to become open and ready for the help offered in the sense of collaborating with that self-sufficiency which is worthy of each person. It is clear that this behaviour of the two groups requires a radical change of habits and of lifestyles. All can contribute together to the good of all and of each thanks, also, to the balance between rights and duties.

The *sixth step* consists in *rethinking globalisation* as an opportunity to diminish inequality, both material and human, among the peoples. The two dimensions of the process of globalisation—socio-economic and "humanity," as "human family"—have to be valued in an equal way. The social doctrine of the church places the emphasis on the dimension of "humanity" "which is becoming increasingly interconnected; it is made up of individuals and peoples to whom this process should offer benefits and development."[93] Moreover, the process of globalisation must take place in step with the universal solidarity which brings both benefits and duties. "Many people today," the document continues, "would claim to owe nothing to anyone,

88. CA, n.29; CIV, n.38.
89. See. n.44ff
90. CIV, n.38;39
91. CIV, n.38
92. CIV, n.39a
93. CIV, n.42a

except to themselves. They are concerned only with their rights, and they often have great difficulty in taking responsibility for their own and other people's integral development. Hence it is important to call for a renewed reflection on how rights presuppose duties, if they are not to become mere licence." Moreover, "an overemphasis on rights leads to a disregard for the poor ['*for duties*', according to the English text]."[94]

The *seventh step*: taking into consideration the *problems related to population growth*. Benedict XVI is convinced that "it is a very important aspect of *authentic development*, since it concerns the inalienable values of life and the family." The situation of the economically advanced countries could be described thus: we have more, but we are fewer! By contrast, "responsible procreation . . . among other things has a positive contribution to make to integral human development."[95] *In fact*, "morally responsible openness to life represents a rich social and economic resource."[96]

The *eighth step: the economy needs ethics*. This offers to economic (and financial) activities principles that are clear and sound, as well as rules of behaviour which help the economic sector to be at the service of the good of people. This is "not any ethics whatsoever, but *an ethics that is people based*"[97] which relies on respect for their dignity and on the recognition of the "transcendent value of natural moral norms."[98] The conviction that the application of ethics to the economic sphere is necessary for all demands that it be accepted by all. It is not enough to be aware of the ethical principles and criteria; it is also necessary to make them a part of daily life, of discerning and deciding, in behaving and in relating to others. It is the only way in which human economic activities can be directed and guided towards the good and not only towards the useful.

The *ninth step*: accepting the fact that the whole world is single family, a single community. If it is to live in peace and harmony, it requires a tolerable inequality which does not offend the dignity of anyone and which assures what is necessary. From the point of view of sustainable development, we have arrived at the point of compulsory international collaboration unless we want self-destruction. Therefore, "international cooperation requires people who can be part of the process of economic and human development through the solidarity of their presence, supervision, training

---

94. CIV, n.43; the whole section is of great importance for our reflection.
95. CIV, n. 44a.
96. CIV, n. 44b.
97. CIV, n. 45a.
98. CIV, n. 45b.

and respect."[99] Therefore, cooperation and sharing become the way to be followed at all levels of personal and communal life in the sense that they become "virtue," that is, a permanent commitment towards the attainment of the objective proposed.

CONCLUDING CONSIDERATIONS

At the end of this reflection on sustainable development, we have certainly not changed the world. However, some facts which we have analysed along the lines of the different conceptions and approaches discussed are revealed with greater clarity. On the one hand, the increasing deterioration of human ecology and of bio-ecology, as an important part of the vision of sustainable development, and, on the other, the growing evils and inequalities between people in various parts of the world force us to get together to negotiate over the destiny of all. Walking together, we must learn to make agreements; to share, to renounce what is not necessary. The core of this request can be summarised in two categorical postulates. The first, then, the one who must act and change is the *individual*, every individual. Sustainable development is possible only if it begins with the person, as the criterion and measure of every action. The second postulate: simultaneously, the *structures*—social, economic, political, cultural and financial—must move and act in harmony with the good of all. In other words, the promoters of authentic, integral development are the individual and society with a view to the common good. Therefore, the possibility consists in walking together in the spirit of subsidiary cooperation in the face of the logic imposed by the current economic system. In any case, it has become clear that, it is impossible to think of achieving sustainable development in terms of the present economico-financial system. However long and difficult, a change is the *conditio sine qua non* for the realisation of the plan proposed.

Perhaps someone might say that we have discovered nothing new: we already know all this. In response, I observe that we are dealing with a work in progress in which each step signifies getting ever closer to the goal. Alongside the multiplication of the obstacles and opposition which are usually caused by the hardness of the human heart, we must increase our attempts to find more agreement on our future destiny. Moreover, every reflection on every question, including this on sustainable development, is carried out on at least two levels, higher and lower (*praxis!*). The first is that of ideal-real theoretical concepts where problems are resolved easily by a clear and convincing logic. However, as soon as one comes back down to reality, the

---

99. CIV, n.47b.

previous clarity vanishes (*vaniquished*) in the face of the complexity of the desires and actions of people in real life. It is here that we must verify the authenticity of our theoretical conceptions. It seems to me that, in our case, we can put forward some concrete steps towards the realisation of the project of sustainable development, and that in the sense of a *continual planning* which aims, step by step, to involve all the participants on the common path.

Furthermore, we have spoken of a necessary change of lifestyle, a cultural change which, in the vocabulary of ethics and morals, signifies conversion of heart: conversion from evil and from indifference to the good in its totality. This, I repeat, is a never-ending process, that is, it requires from each one of us a permanent effort: responsible involvement that is personal and communitarian.

BIBLIOGRAPHY

Baudrillard, Jean. *Il patto di lucidità o intelligenza del male*. Milan: Cortina, 2004.
Bauman, Zygmunt. *Modernità liquida*. Bari: Laterza, 2011.
———. "L'uomo schiacciato dai limiti." *L'Espresso/La Repubblica*, October 6, 2016. Rome, 20–26.
Brundtland Report, 1987. https://www.are.admin.ch/are/it/home/sviluppo-sostenibile/cooperazione-internazionale/l_agenda-2030-per-uno-sviluppo-sostenibile/onu-le-pietre-miliari-dello-sviluppo-sostenibile/1987—rapporto-brundtland.html.
Catechism of the Catholic Church. Vatican City: LEV, 1992.
Cesareo, Vincenzo and Vaccarini, Italo. *La libertà responsabile. Soggettività e mutamento sociale*. Milan: V & P, 2006.
Cucci, Giovanni. *Il fascino del male: I vizi capitali*. Rome: AdP, 2009.
Daly, Herman E. *Beyond Growth: The Economics of Sustainable Development*. Boston: Beacon, 1996.
Danowski, Deborah e Viveiros de Castro, Eduardo. *Esiste un mondo a venire? Saggio sulle paure della fine*. Rome: Nottetempo, 2017.
Declaration of the International Conference on "The Climate." Marrakech, 7–18 November 2016. (DM).
Declaration of the United Nations on "The Human Environment" (1972). Stockholm, 5–16, 6.1972. (D).
Ellena, Aldo. *Enciclopedia sociale: Introduzione ai problemi sociali*. Torino: Paoline, 1959.
Ekonomski, Leksikon. "Rast i razvitak narodnog gospodarstva." Zagreb: Leksikografski Zavod „Miroslav Krleža."1995.
Francis I, Pope. *Evangelii gaudium*. Apostolic Exhortation. Vatican City: LEV, 2013. (EG).
———. *Laudato si'*. Encyclical Letter on care for our common home. Vatican City: LEV, 2015.
General Assembly. *Resolution 41/128*, United Nations, 4 December 1986. http://www.un.org/documents/ga/res/41/a41r128.htm.

International Commission on the *Environment and Development* or *Brundtland Report*. Tokyo, 1987.
John Paul II, Pope. *Sollicitudo rei socialis*. Encyclical Letter on the twentieth anniversary of *Populorum progressio*. Vatican City: LEV, 1987.
Kempf, Hervè. *Comment les riches détruisent la planète*. Paris: La Seuil, 2007.
Latouche, Serge, *Altri mondi, altre menti, altrimenti. Oikonomia vernacolare e società conviviale*. (Introduzione di Pieroni Osvaldo). Soveria Mannelli, Rubbettino, 2004.
———. *Baudrillard o la sovversione attraverso l'ironia*. Milan: Jaca Book, 2016.
———. *Breve trattato sulla decrescita serena e Come sopravvivere allo sviluppo*. Torino: Bollati Boringhieri, 2015.
———. *Incontri di un "obiettore di crescita."* Milan: Jaca Book, 2013.
———. *Mondializzazione e decrescita. L'alternativa africana*. Bari: Dedalo, 2009.
Marchettini, Nadia et al. *La soglia della sostenibilità. Quello che il Pil non dice*. Rome: Donzelli, 2011.
Pallante, Maurizio. *La decrescita felice*. Milan: Feltrinelli, 2011.
Paul VI, Pope. *Populorum progressio*. Encyclical Letter on the development of peoples. Vatican City: LEV, 1967.
Pius XII, Pope. *Summi Pontificatus*. Encyclical Letter on the unity of human society. Vatican City: LEV. n. 30, 1939. (SP)
Pontifical Council for Justice and Peace. *Compendium of the Social Doctrine of the Church*. Vatican City: LEV, 2005. (CDSC)
———. *Dizionario di Dottrina sociale della Chiesa*. Rome: LAS, 2005.
Robèrt, Karl-Henrik. *The Natural Step Framework*. 2002.
Sacred Congregation for the Doctrine of the Faith. *Christian Freedom and Liberation*. Instruction. Vatican City: LEV, 1986. (LCL)
Saviano, Roberto. "Testa lenta-pancia veloce." *L'Espresso/La Repubblica*, 16 April 2017, 21.
Tiezzi, Enzo, and Nadia Marchettini. *Che cos'è lo sviluppo sostenibile? Le basi scientifiche della sostenibilità e i guasti del pensiero unico*, (Prefazione di Leipert Christian) Rome: Donzelli, 2009.
Toso, Mario. *Frontiere della nuova evangelizzazione: la "Centesimus annus." Studi sull'enciclica sociale di Giovanni Paolo II*. Turin: ELLE DI CI, 1991.
UNESCO. *Universal Declaration on Cultural Diversity*. Paris, 2001.
Utopie Onlus. "Crescita e Sviluppo." http://www.utopie.it/sviluppo_umano/crescita_e_sviluppo.htm.

12

Concluding Remarks towards Integral Development

FERNANDO DE LA IGLESIA VIGUIRISTI, SJ

INTRODUCTION

Globalization has come to mean a process by which business organizations and the like develop international spheres of influence and operate on an international scale or seamless world. The *Compendium of Social Doctrine of the Church* reads:

> Our modern era is marked by the complex phenomenon of economic and financial globalization, a process that progressively integrates national economies at the level of the exchange of goods and services and of financial transactions. In this process, an ever growing number of those involved in the economic sector is prompted to adopt a more global perspective concerning the choices that they must make with regard to future growth and profits. The new perspective of global society does not simply consist in the presence of economic and financial bonds between national forces at work in different countries, which have moreover always been present, but in the pervasiveness and the absolutely unprecedented nature of the system of relations that is developing ... This is a multifaceted reality that is difficult to decipher, since it expands at different levels and is in continuous evolution along paths that cannot easily be predicted. (CDSC, 361)

A globalized world proposes and imposes a globalized market economy and cultural relations, not least polity. Today's world is absolutely very diverse from that of our grandparents, or even parents, caused by the economic, political and cultural transformations brought about by globalization. However, in this world we like to call globalized there are still a few rich and a multitude of poor who continue to be exploited and to live in sub-human conditions and misery. Although globalization has not been able to erase the North-South economic divide, it has perhaps contributed to extend that division across every society. The referendum in the United Kingdom regarding its membership in the European Union with its unexpected "No" or Brexit, as well as the unforeseen victory of Donald Trump as president of the United States are two recent events that have accentuated that ubiquitous divide.

Those brief introductory observations should suffice to show that the problem of development subsists, but with a disturbing set of demands, urgencies, and interrogations derived from the unpredictably rapid global changes. Hence, it is opportune to ask whether the *Populorum progressio* (1967) and the *Sollicitudo Rei Socialis* (1987), the first two official documents of the church on development of peoples, are still valid in this new scenario. It would also be interesting to analyse the contributions of the last two papal documents—*Caritas in Veritate* (2009) and *Laudatio si* (2015)—however we shall limit ourselves only to those first two texts and create the historical contexts that led to their production. Hopefully we will be able to answer the question about their validity after all.

I. *POPULORUM PROGRESSIO*

1. Historical Context

Populorum progressio (PP) was born at the end of 60s,[1] years marked by optimism, in the world and in the Catholic Church, which was very expressively portrayed by John XXIII in both *Mater et Magistra* and *Pacem in Terris*.[2] The firm conviction that scientific and technological advances could transform the world drove that optimism. The harnessing of nuclear energy for peaceful purposes, the advances in chemistry that permitted in sophisticated laboratory the production of substances not easily available in nature, the development of cybernetics that propelled the new industrial revolution and development, the progress in agronomy that resulted in green revolution but also in discarding of excessive production, the development of communications and means of transport that shortened travel time between locations and finally a "small step" on the moon at the end of 60s that meant

---

1. Sanz de Diego, "El mensaje central," 13–50.
2. John XXIII, *Mater et magistra*, 46–49 ; John XXIII, *Pacem in Terris*, 39–45.

a "big jump" for humanity, have all reinforced the human optimism in that decade. To all that the economic and social changes must be added.

After the world war and quick reconstruction there comes a time of economic prosperity during which the standard of living and education, particularly in the more developed countries, improved greatly. Social Security eliminated uncertainties about the future for a good part of the population and this facility continue to spread in many countries. Nevertheless, people are today more aware of the social and economic imbalances and injustices in the world thanks to the spread of the mass media of communications.

Between 1945 and 1960 the process of decolonization gave political independence to no less than forty countries, with a total population of 800 million (more than a quarter of the world's population at the time), but not always under conditions that would also ensure them economic independence. In any case, political independence combined with the global economic boom had generated in those peoples who had lived alienated for so long under foreign rules, great expectations for development. National governments were elected democratically by universal suffrage. There was a strong conviction that the democratically elected leaders would render unlimited service towards the welfare of their citizens. In addition, greater opportunity for social advancement as well as for participation of workers and women in their own affairs created an optimism that equality among all human beings could be possible. Furthermore, the active role of international organizations have come to facilitate these processes and optimism.

It is true that in 1961 the Berlin Wall was erected and the world could sigh again after the Cuban missile crisis (1962), but then while the leaders of the superpowers, John F. Kennedy and N. Khrushchev, created a situation of "Cold War," Pope John XXIII encouraged dialogue for deescalation of conflicts.

The optimism shown by the world leaders and their role as social and economic liberators did not convince the youth of the 60s who began expressing their impatience through social revolutions and shouting slogans like "Imagination to power," "be realistic," as in Paris in May 1968. Other counter-establishment movements such as the hippies, the new musical styles, etc. attested to new aspirations for change, but lack of any social commitment on their part made them ineffective. Changes were global indeed, and the communist Chinese cultural revolution for political and economic development and the bloody leftist social movements in Latin America cannot be forgotten.

As we have said, 1967 is almost the end of a phase marked by general optimism in the Society and the church that had followed by the crisis of the World War II. But the signs of hope, optimism and unity in the world begin to disappear, not only by the conflicts between the superpowers and the intensification of the Cold War, but also by the fact that the gap between developed and developing countries continued to increase. This general perception introduced grounds for caution and pessimism which PP did insightfully reflect.

2. Ecclesial Context

There were compelling ecclesial context during which the two papal texts were written. Regarding PP two years had elapsed after the conclusion of the Council of Vatican II and four after writing its famed pastoral constitution *Gaudium et spes* (GS). At this moment of unprecedented renewal and ecclesial hope as well, GS dedicated several paragraphs on development issues. The council fathers, on the one hand aware that the new world economy could resolve many basic human needs and problems and on the other that huge crowds continued to live below the poverty line, proposed that while reforms at the economic social levels were absolutely necessary, they should also be accompanied by a change of mentality and habits (GS, 63).

> Like other areas of social life, the economy of today is marked by man's increasing domination over nature, by closer and more intense relationships between citizens, groups, and countries and their mutual dependence, and by the increased intervention of the state. At the same time progress in the methods of production and in the exchange of goods and services has made the economy an instrument capable of better meeting the intensified needs of the human family . . . Our contemporaries are coming to feel these inequalities with an ever sharper awareness, since they are thoroughly convinced that the ampler technical and economic possibilities which the world of today enjoys can and should correct this unhappy state of affairs. Hence, many reforms in the socioeconomic realm and a change of mentality and attitude are required of all. For this reason the church down through the centuries and in the light of the Gospel has worked out the principles of justice and equity demanded by right reason both for individual and social life and for international life, and she has proclaimed them especially in recent times. This sacred council intends to strengthen these principles according to the circumstances of this age and to set forth certain guidelines, especially with regard to the requirements of economic development.

It is a fact that father Louis Lebret, a Dominican, who knew well the reality of human underdevelopment, poverty, and demographic explosion in large areas of the globe, as well as the unfair trade dealings and international agreements between the rich nations and their former colonies, played a decisive role in preparing the text of PP.[3]

3. Highlights of *Populorum progressio*

1. Development was defined as a transition, for everyone and everybody, from a lesser human condition to a better lifestyle. It is an ideal to be pursue integrally and in solidary.[4] *Populorum progressio* definition of development implies an ethical approach that goes beyond mere production of economic resources and emphasises also an equitable distribution of them. This is also the idea of development proposed by *Gaudium et spes*, but PP expanded further the concept with an analysis of conditions that are less humane, often due to greed an self-love, and those that uplift a person:

   > What are less than human conditions? The material poverty of those who lack the bare necessities of life, and the moral poverty of those who are crushed under the weight of their own self-love; oppressive political structures resulting from the abuse of ownership or the improper exercise of power, from the exploitation of the worker or unjust transactions. What are truly human conditions? The rise from poverty to the acquisition of life's necessities; the elimination of social ills; broadening the horizons of knowledge; acquiring refinement and culture. From there one can go on to acquire a growing awareness of other people's dignity, a taste for the spirit of poverty, (18) an active interest in the common good, and a desire for peace. Then man can acknowledge the highest values and God himself, their author and end. Finally and above all, there is faith—God's gift to men of good will—and our loving unity in Christ, who calls all men to share God's life as sons of the living God, the Father of all men. (PP 21)

2. The Relationship between development and Christian humanism was also discussed in PP. It stated that development is not only a human ethical question but it has also to do with the Christian vision of the

---

3. De la Iglesia, "Louis Lebret," 313–25.
4. PP 20.

human person. This is what constitutes the true Christian humanism which does not see any dichotomy between the human and Christian aspirations, but rather perceives Christian life as the most profound human achievement. Borrowing some thoughts from Fr. De Lubac, Paul VI refers to this Christian humanism as:[5]

> The ultimate goal is a full-bodied humanism (PP 42). Does this not mean the fulfillment of the whole man and of every man? A narrow humanism, closed in on itself and not open to the values of the spirit and to God who is their source, could achieve apparent success, for man can set about organizing terrestrial realities without God. But "closed off from God, they will end up being directed against man. A humanism closed off from other realities becomes inhuman. (PP45)

True humanism points towards God and acknowledges the task to which we are called, the task that offers us real meaning in life. Man cannot be the ultimate measure unto himself. Man becomes truly man only by going beyond himself, when "Man infinitely surpasses man," as Blaise Pascal famously said.

3. Progress is, in its source and its essence, a vocation and "In the design of God, every man is called to a development, because every life is a vocation."[6]
4. The doctrine of ownership of property and its consequences has also been highlighted by PP. With an explicit biblical inspiration often misinterpreted by human greed, the encyclical places property in the context of the universal destiny of the goods of the earth:

> In the very first pages of Scripture we read these words: "Fill the earth and subdue it." (Gn 1. 28) This teaches us that the whole of creation is for man, that he has been charged to give it meaning by his intelligent activity, to complete and perfect it by his own efforts and to his own advantage. (PP 22)

This means that the right to property is not an unconditional and absolute right of anyone.

Everyone knows that the Fathers of the church laid down the duty of the rich toward the poor in no uncertain terms. As St.

---

5. De Lubac, *Le drame de l'humanisme athée*, 10.
6. PP 32.

Ambrose put it: "You are not making a gift of what is yours to the poor man, but you are giving him back what is his. You have been appropriating things that are meant to be for the common use of everyone. The earth belongs to everyone, not to the rich." (PP 23)

No one has the licence to appropriate surplus goods solely for his own personal pleasure when others lack the bare necessities of life. In short, as the Fathers of the Church and other eminent theologians tell us, the right of private property may never be exercised to the detriment of the common good. When "private gain and basic community needs conflict with one another," it is for the public authorities "to seek a solution to these questions, with the active involvement of individual citizens and social groups."[7]

5. The need for deeper social and economic reforms to prevent the recourse of revolutionary violence is another highlight in PP. This is one of the points that had the most mediatic discussions and criticism. The Pope was accused of favouring revolutionary movements so prevalent in the Third World in the 60s. But what Paul VI affirmed was that a revolution, which was always a bad solution, could be ethically justified if the injustices were serious and persistent. And to prevent resolution of conflicts through violent revolutions he insisted so vehemently on the urgency of addressing profound reforms and human needs. (PP 30–31).

6. PP denounced capitalism in its liberal version of the past and disproved liberalism as the main driving force in world market economy.[8] Paul VI criticized excessive unshared profits as the essential driving engine of economic progress, unethical competition, and private property of means of wealth production as absolute individual right. This model, which he called "liberalism without restraint" leading to dictatorship, had already been denounced by Pius XI (PP 26). Evidently, the liberal capitalist model was excluded for being unethical.

Paul VI was critical of the market economy as the best means for allocation of resources to all. However, the market players do not want to work under conditions of equality or on level ground. Certainly, the world markets follow the rule to their own advantage and the developing countries constantly bear the brunt of the economic onslaught of the multinationals that impose unethical conditions for maximum

---

7. PP 23.
8. De la Iglesia, "Cinquenta anni della dalla 'Populorum progressio.'"

profit. If there is no equality in the market, there will never be equity in its operations. (PP 58)

In *Rerum Novarum* this principle was laid down with regard to a just wage for the individual worker. Now it should be applied with equal force to contracts made between nations. Trade relations can no longer be based solely on the principle of free and unchecked competition, for very often such approach creates a dictatorship of economy. Free trade can be called just only when it conforms to the demands of social justice. Paul VI wrote:

> As a matter of fact, the highly developed nations have already come to realize this. At times they take appropriate measures to restore balance to their own economy, a balance which is frequently upset by competition when left to itself. Thus it happens that these nations often support their agriculture at the price of sacrifices imposed on economically more favored sectors. Similarly, to maintain the commercial relations which are developing among themselves, especially within a common market, the financial, fiscal and social policy of these nations tries to restore comparable opportunities to competing industries which are not equally prospering. One Standard for All. (PP 60)

7. The document being discussed recommended a mixed system of economic organization.[9] The Social Doctrine of the church had earlier disapproved both the pure liberal model as well as the pure collectivist approach for the developed or western world, now PP extended that idea to the developing countries, confirming thus what was stated in the previous section. PP emphasized that neither the single private initiative nor the simple game of competition are enough for an authentic development.(7) The way out is when public authority sets clear objectives, establish practical means and encourage everyone to do the best, not by replacing individual initiatives but rather but coordinating and guiding them to the optimum levels. (PP 37)

8. The idea of respect for, and defence of, local autonomous cultures facing slow extinction as well as the materialistic and market onslaught finds mention in PP. Economic development for the pursuit of only material prosperity poses a threat not only to more integral models of development but also to people's cultures and life's meanings. Economically poor nations can be very rich in cultural wisdom hence

---

9. De la Iglesia, "Cinquenta anni della dalla 'Populorum progressio.'"

they must not be tempted to surrender themselves to market-oriented culture that threatens their best customs and traditions (PP 40–41).

9. Rich nations have the duty of assist the poor countries and share their knowledge. Although always bilateral in nature, this duty must transcend economic and commercial spheres if an integral development is to be achieved. What is being talked about now is unilateral transfers (aid)—a duty that arises from the fact that "the superfluous of the rich countries must serve the poor countries." (PP 49) More concretely, Paul VI proposed the creation of a world fund assisted in part by monies that would otherwise be spent on military armament. This fund could not only aid development but also serve to overcome international rivalries and initiate paths for other exchanges and conversation (PP 51).

10. A more attentive attitude towards strangers. If until now there has been talk about economic mechanisms (unilateral in the assistance, bilateral in trade), now a more human dimension is touched in the North-South relations. The host nations that are normally the developed ones need to have an open outlook towards foreign students and emigrants that arrive there, (PP 67–69) particularly the visiting technicians and experts from international organizations, and entrepreneurs (PP 70–72).

11. Development became synonymous with peace in the document. Although this idea in one of the final paragraphs, (PP 76), it has beautifully synthesized PP. It resonates very much with the last chapter of *Gaudium et spes* and with the intervention of Paul VI at the General Assembly of the United Nations in 1965. It is worth recalling the words of the encyclical:

> Combating misery and fighting against injustice is promoting, along with the greater well-being, the human and spiritual progress of all, and, consequently, the common good of humanity. Peace is not reduced to an absence of war, fruit of the always precarious balance of forces. Peace is built day by day, in the establishment of an order dear to God, which entails a more perfect justice among men (PP 76).

12. This is a world of interrelated authority. This idea already formulated in *Pacem in terris* by John XXIII appeared here again. After stating what both the developing and the developed countries have to do, a new perspective is presented—that of collaboration among all the

institutions as means "to constitute a universally recognized legal order" (PP 78). In this so-interdependent world, the actions of the sovereign States and their governments are no longer enough, rather a moral order is required to impose itself as well as to ensure the general interest of humanity amidst world diversity, or, as John XXIII put it, for the universal common good.

II. SOLLICITUDO REI SOCIALIS

1. Historical Context

As already shown, the 60s was a decade of rapid growth and changes both in world production and international trade. The context began to change rapidly when the Bretton Woods system was abandoned and the first oil price jump took place. After the war between Israel and Egypt in 1973, the OPEC quadrupled its price. This meant a great disturbance to the productive apparatus of the industrialized world prepared to operate with cheap energy.[10]

In 1979 and 1980 the world experienced again a sharp rise in the price of crude oil. Concurrently, there were significant changes of government and in political life. Mrs. Margaret Thatcher came to power in the United Kingdom in 1979, Ronald Reagan was elected president of the United States in 1980, François Mitterrand president of France in 1981, and in 1982 the Social Democrat Chancellor, Hemult Smitdt, was replaced by the Christian Democrat Helmult Kohl in the Federal Republic of Germany. The changes in these countries, with the exception of France, was marked economic liberalism.

To add to that portrait, the international financial system allocated ample financial resources to developing countries in the 1970s. The funds that the oil exporting countries placed in the western financial system were channelled to the emerging economies in the developing world since the industrialized countries were in deep recession. Thus, by 1979 the developing countries had accumulated a debt of 533,000 billion dollars that generated a service of debt-interest plus amortizations—of 82,000 million which accounted for 14 percent of the exports of these countries altogether. In the case of countries in Latin America this percentage amounted to almost 40 percent. After the second hike in oil prices in the early 80s, the recession in the Western economies caused by contractionary monetary policies set a very bad precedent for the developing countries. The industrialized countries reduced imports from developing economies and the price of raw materials and basic products slumped significantly. In addition, interest

10. Tugores, *Economía internacional*, 340–46.

rates rose on a global scale which led to an increase in the external debt burden that had been incurred at floating interest rates. Mexico's declaration in 1982 of not being able to meet the payments accrued from external debt marked the beginning of the debt crisis.

What to say about the Second World 70 years after the October Revolution? When Russia became a communist country in 1917, many expected that the central planning would facilitate the emergence of a robust system of economic activity that would surpass the limitations of the market economy, and that it would achieve a just distribution of wealth and income. In fact, central planning was able to transform Russia from an essentially agrarian economy into a great industrial superpower. Still in the early sixties Khrushchev's prediction that the Soviet Union would soon overtake the United States was not taken for a joke, but a real possibility. But in the 70s and 80s the Soviet Union was increasingly unable to meet its own expectations and in the early nineties a real economic crisis triggered the fall of communism.[11]

The increasing complexity of the economic system and the nature of required innovations to service it, made the central planning in Russia a very poor substitute for private market economy. As the output growth slowed down, those responsible for the Soviet economic policy felt an increasing need to introduce economic reform. The 80s witnessed a succession of reforms that introduced incentives for companies to be more efficient, but within the framework of central planning. At the end of 80s, Mikhael Gorbachev, then the prime minister, came to the conclusion that it was necessary to introduce more far-reaching reforms and tried to carry out a slow transition to a market economy. But it was too late. The fall of communism and the introduction of private market economy were to set in sooner than anticipated. The Soviet model showed that an economic system driven by dictatorship was at the most able to mobilize resources to accelerate economic growth, but at the cost of great human sacrifice, loss of human lives and political repression. Furthermore, in the modern world of open borders and high quality of goods and services, absolute state control over economy suffered from lack of incentives to do better as well as market creativity for competition. But whatever the virtues of a centrally planned economy, the repressive political system was unacceptable to the peoples in the Soviet Union and in Eastern Europe, which led to the overthrow of dictatorships there in 1989, two years before the release of SRS document.[12] As we see, the referred concerns at the end of sixties have nothing to do with the dominant pessimism twenty years later when John Paul II published SRS.

11. Blancherd, *Macroeconomia*, 506–7.
12. Samuelson and Nordhaus, *Economia*, 545.

The oil crises in 1973–74 and in 1979 had revolutionized the world economy and gave rise to a new international division of labour. This proved a great opportunity for some of the Third World countries especially in Asia. But the crisis also brought the revival of liberal ideologies and the application of such principles to economy, which led many populist and paternalistic regimes and governments, many of them in Latin America with dictatorial character, to follow the principles of liberal economic thought.
In the third world more begins a separation between those countries (almost all Asian) that exploit their opportunities and embark on a path of development and others (Latin America and sub-Saharan Africa) where drastic policies of adjustment, created tension and violence and lack of growth. All this happened in the midst of a far reaching cry in the West for minimum interfere of the state in economy, a slogan made popular between 1980 and 1988 by a declaration of the president of the United States, Ronald Reagan, who stated that "the state is not the solution, the state is the problem." On the other hand, liberalization favours the transnationalization of economy or in today's terminology "globalization," with great repercussion especially for the most backward and vulnerable peoples. The great crisis in the communist was only two years away!

A period of twenty years would not seem enough for such pronounced changes, but there are facts.[13]

2. Ecclesial Context

It is well known that one of the characteristics of the pontificate of John Paul II was, without doubt, the importance it gave to the Social Doctrine of the church (SDC), both quantitatively and qualitatively. In addition to his encyclicals, the *Catechism of the Catholic Church* (2005), which included for the first time a SDC treatise, together with the 7th Commandment, as well as the *Compendium of the Social Doctrine of the Church* (2004) are examples of the social concern of the church.[14]

The newly elected Pope then had direct experience, unlike the previous Popes, of what capitalism and Marxism could offer. John Paul II had been a professor of Social Ethics and was interested in the SDC at the academic level. He was very close to those who wanted to change the communist model in their homeland like Lech Walesa and the Solidarnosc Union. All this offered him clear and original ideas about several points regarding the DSI. This was

---

13. Camacho, "¿Qué merece la pena," 10.
14. Sanz de Diego, "El mensaje central," 13–50.

shown in some of his interventions in the preparation of *Gaudium et Spes* and in an interview that he gave months before being elected Pope.

The revitalization of the SDC carried out since Vatican II, the sharp pro-poor social and economic analysis proposed by Liberation Theology, the distancing of a large number of Catholics from the church following the Magisterium's *Humanae Vitae*, but on the other hand the respect that Paul VI showed towards the conscience of the believer immersed in very concrete situation, are compelling events in the ecclesial context of SRS. Moreover, secularism and the crisis of Marxism in Europe that led to the fall of the Berlin Wall in 1989 or two years later in 1989, influenced considerably Karol Wojtyla.

In such a charged situation, John Paul II took the initiative to uphold the DSC, and clarify, at the same time, his response of concerns towards Liberation Theology (LT). However, the Pope did not use again the word "doctrine" in respect for the Council's and Paul VI's reluctance to use that term; rather he gave it a strong theological character, putting it in the context of the great theological concepts and underlined that it was an essential part of the message of the church and of the New Evangelization. This explains why many commentators have related the social gospel to the recovery made by John Paul II. The publication of SRS exactly twenty years after the PP was an occasion for John Paul II and the church to commemorate and recall the latter.

Until then almost all the social documents had been issued to commemorate the epoch making *Rerum Novarum* (RN). John Paul II did so with *Laborem exercens* in 1981 (ninety years of RN) and again with *Centesimus Annus* in 1991 (hundred years of RN). However, it is not without reason why PP has been well received. It spoke about contemporary times with greater vigour. Just as the encyclical RN of Leo XIII helped to understand the social thought of the church as well as relations between the worker and owner of means of production, PP reflected the Social Teaching of the church vis-à-vis the global market economy in the postmodern society.

3. Highlights of *Sollicitudo Rei Socialis*

i. Inclusive Concept of Development

Following up from what Paul VI wrote, SRS attempted to broaden the basic concept of development. It argues that authentic human development is not automatic or unlimited (SRS 27). Moreover, the concept does not refer only to mere accumulation of material goods which creates a materialistic consumer mentality and an illusion that to have more is the same as to be more. To have is not evil, but the lack of priorities is (SRS 28). Development is measured and directed by the vocation of man, the image of God. (SRS 29) Development has begun from the time of creation or beginning of history but it is retarded or constantly threatened by sin (SRS 30). However, the faith in Christ the Redeemer enlightens and guides us to understand the authentic and inclusive meaning of development. That is why the church has a word that say and a praxis to perform (SRS 31). The obligation to participate in the development of peoples is not individual—it is a vocation of each and everyone (SRS 32). We cannot talk about a humane development if it does not respect human rights: fundamental equality, solidarity and freedom, and commitment to truth and goodness (SRS 33).

Furthermore, human beings need also to respect the order of nature and of the cosmos. In this regard, the Pope advances three considerations: 1) The nature of each being and its connection with others must be taken into account; 2) it is necessary to be aware of scarcity of natural resources; 3) and it is an obligation of all to take care of quality of life itself (SRS 34).

It is obvious that authentic development cannot be reduced to economic and technological progress, rather it must cover all spheres of human life: political, educational and cultural, ecological and theological, as well health care. The direction of development outlined in the PP for integral and solidary development continues to be reaffirmed in SRS.

In its final part, SRS returns to the idea of development, noting some structural reforms that must be addressed and accompany it: the international trading system, the global monetary and financial system, the exchange of technologies as well as the revision of the structure of international organizations (SRS 43–44). Paul VI had already drawn our attention to the importance of structural reforms for authentic development.

ii. Structures of Sin: Concept and Concretions

The concept of structures of sin comes from the ethical-theological judgment that if the world is divided into two distinct and unbridgeable blocks—the rich and the poor—it is because of man's self-love. The concept of structures of sin refers to norms of behaviour or self-internalized criteria for action that we apply them almost mechanically in our dealings with others. In other words it is charged by the desire to gain power, which then becomes the only criterion of one's conduct (SRS 37a). The dominant structures of sin are not external to us; they are values imparted authoritatively by our educational system and civilizational organizations.[15]

---

15. Camacho, "¿Qué merece la pena."

iii. Solidarity as the Key to a New Value System

Reeled under this dominant value system tainted by structural sin, John Paul II proposes 'solidarity' as an alternative to it. The definition he offers of solidarity is closely related to interdependence. Interdependence is a fashionable word in the current world affairs, in economic agreements, cultural exchanges, political and religious conversations, and must be assumed as a moral category. Thus once understood in that way, it carries moral consequence, a moral and social attitude to foster solidarity. This attitude is not just a passing feeling but a commitment towards the common good—the good of each and of all. All must truly be responsible for all (SRS 38t).

The definition of solidarity (feeling that everyone is truly responsible for all) contrasts with the value system based on the desire for profit and power, which are the rules of a competitive game, where one seeks always to be a winner no matter what. In addition, the encyclical highlights how solidarity is enriched when it is placed in Christian perspective (SRS 40).

iv. Preferential Option (or Love) for the Poor

Here John Paul II does not really intend to discuss the subject per se, which has aroused so much interest in post-Vatican II theology as he himself recognizes, but to approach it from an international perspective. Although originally the preferential option for the poor refers to life of every Christian, it can also be treated as a social and economic category which in fact is how the world sees it. However SRS wants all to understand that the goods of this world are originally destined for all (SRS 42).

v. SRS Is a Pessimistic Diagnosis of the Situation

It may be for some but for others it is a realistic assessment, but more importantly it does not forget the responsibility of the rich countries towards the peripheral ones. The diagnosis of the situation made by John Paul II in SRS is much more negative than that in PP, something that can be explained in terms of what happened in twenty years preceding it. It is a diagnosis that gets even darker when it said that the Third World has already lost hope (SRS 12a). Delay is not only economic, but also cultural, political and human (SRS 15f). The hope of attaining economic development had reached the nadir by then. The causes were varied: negligence on the part of the developing countries, lack of responsibility of the developed countries and unfair economic mechanisms in place.

In the enumeration of different manifestations of this very pessimistic audit there is a passage that unequivocally alludes to the collectivist countries, a concern that John Paul II carried very much in his heart throughout his pontificate. Without there being an explicit mention to these countries which the Pope had visited, in the aforementioned passage the denial of the right of economic initiative and of the true sovereignty of the nations is denounced, as well as the pretension of a ruling party to become the only one guide of society (SRS 15b–d).

vi. Human Beings Related to Nature

This issue is approached from the central theme of the document that is "development." Because development must also integrate the idea of nature, which is intrinsically related to humanity in that unique system, or the larger cosmos. Two more considerations are added: the limitation of natural resources and the dangers of a certain type of development for the quality of life in the industrialized regions (SRS 34). Going into a more detailed analyses would take us beyond the scope of this paper, but a suggestive and fruitful connection is established and some aspects of interest are pointed out.

III. CONSEQUENCE: THE CONCEPT OF HUMAN DEVELOPMENT

After all this, it is worth to ask ourselves how economics understand development and how the declarations of the international organization envisages it.[16] In 1990, Simon Kuznets, Nobel Prize for Economics, wrote that economic development is the sustained increase over time of the capacity to provide economic goods increasingly diversified to the population. This explanation is based on technological development and requires institutional and ideological changes. Five years later we find the following statement of the United Nations: "The purpose of development is to create an ideal environment for people to enjoy a long, healthy and creative life. This truth, as simple, it is frequently forgotten in the search for material and financial wealth."[17]

From it comes a definition of human development as a continuous improvement of conditions that allow the population to live a long life in good health and be creatively peaceful. From this conception is derived the Index of

---

16. De la Iglesia, "Una nota sobre."
17. United Nations Development Program, *Human Development Report*.

Human Development (HDI), which is an indicator of human development by countries, prepared by the United Nations Development Program (UNDP).

It was proposed for the first time by the Human Development Report of the 1990 for the United Nations Development Program. His director, Mahbul ul Haq, formulated and helped to calculate and translate into figures such concept for all countries. Therefore, the HDI is a synthetic indicator of the average achievements obtained in the three areas considered as fundamental to assess the level of development, namely to have a long and healthy life, acquire knowledge, and enjoy a decent standard of living. The HDI is the average geometry of the normalized indices of each of the three dimensions of development. The dimension of health is evaluated according to life expectancy at birth, and that of education is measured by the average years of schooling of adults of 25 years or more and for the expected years of schooling of children of school age. The standard of living is measured according to GNP per capita.

Despite a considerable advance in the necessary task of understanding and measure the different elements involved in human development, it is, however, not yet a very appropriate measure for a new inclusive vision of development as human capacity building. Amartya Sen[18] another laureate with the Nobel Prize for Economy has refurbished this concept further. This renowned economist and philosopher understands that development should be valued in relation to whether it allows both choices to be exercised as alternatives—for example, between work and consumption—so that one has the possibility to choose from the binary, only the is the person really free. As he himself recognizes this approach is very individualistic and cannot be easily reconciled well with the social and institutional concept of development. Social justice, security in social relationships, and even the guarantee of continuity in the standard of living, demand both individual freedom and initiative as well as collective action. It is necessary to complete the HDI with indicators of social justice, availability of public goods, and cooperation and collective action. Hence, the necessity of including the inequalities index, economic conditions in the society in question, gender inequality opportunity, and life of marginal groups that suffer deprivation.

We must mention two results of the econometric studies. First is that there is a positive relationship between per capita income and the HDI. The higher income levels are associated with higher values in the HDI, there is a positive correlation, as it is said in the language of econometrics, but it is not linear, it is not one to one. The second is that it has been observed or better measured that improvements in human development sustain economic

---

18. Sen, *Development as Freedom*, 14.

development to the point that not a few experts consider human development a component, a critical input of economic development.

The social dimension of development requires recognition that a society must eliminate or at least drastically reduce absolute poverty. Without this social achievement or if parts of its population have to look at each moment of their lives for means to survive, that civilization cannot be considered developed. Since 2015, the World Bank defined that one lives below poverty line if he does not have an income of $ 1.90 per day. The obvious question that arises here is how this threshold has been established. For this, the first task addressed was to estimate the income that cannot meet the minimum needs of nutrition, clothing, and shelter. It is obvious that in rich countries this threshold tends to be higher than in poor countries. A line is thus drawn, poverty line, which may be different for people living in the same poor countries. To measure poverty in the world on the basis of the poorest countries, we must perform two conversions. The first by means of the exchange rate to a common currency, and then the consideration of the same international prices. Calculation of the figures based on the purchasing power parity takes time and not a little effort. It is good to know the ambitious project of the "Penn World Tables." In fact the World Bank estimated that the poverty line in the six poorest countries in the World was, in 1990, at $ 1 per person per day. In 2005 reviewed the calculations from the fifteen levels of the poorest countries, fixing it at $ 1.25. Since October 2015, the demarcation has been established at $ 1.90. It should be clear that there are many important non-monetary indicators that reflect the multiple dimensions of poverty. We refer to education, health, health services, water, electricity, etc. All these indicators are decisively complementary elements to coordinate actions to improve the life of the poor. Needless to emphasize that to reach this level it is not easy. There can be only little human development if the living conditions of the entire population are not improved, and here it is necessary to emphasize that the fight against poverty cannot be reduced only to increasing the Gross Domestic Product. What is also needed are redistributive policies in favour of the poor and specific attention to policies aimed at universalizing social services, social security, health and education. Economic growth in the first stages of development can increase inequality, but redistributive policies can offset such imbalances. The cases of China, India and Brazil are cases in point. With stronger policies and more efficient redistributive measures the results could be better. Similar conclusions are arrived at by studies conducted by reputed international organizations. This dispels the idea that assisting the poor in one's own country or worldwide compromises economic development and human achievement.

It is imperative to recognize that integral development as we read in the Social Doctrine of the Church is an indisputable example of all that we have been discussing. We do think it is right to recognize that the integral development of the Social Doctrine of the church is an indisputable precedent of all this. Moreover: we do think to have shown the validity and rigor of the analysis of both encyclicals the PP and the SRS.

BIBLIOGRAPHY

Blancherd, Olivier. *Macroeconomia*. Madrid: Prentice Hall, 1997.
Camacho, Idelfonso. "¿Qué merece la pena recordar de las dos encíclicas sobre el desarrollo de los pueblos? A 40 años de Populorum progressio y 20 de Sollicitudo rei sociales." In *Derecho al desarrollo hoy sobre la base de los documentos de la DSI*. Madrid: Instituto social León XII, 2007.
de la Iglesia, Fernando. "Cinquenta anni della dalla 'Populorum progressio .'" In *La Civiltà Cattolica* 4001 (2017) 468–80.
———. "Louis Lebret, mentore della 'Populorum progressio.'" *La Civiltà Cattolica* 3987–3988 (2016) 313–25.
———. "Una nota sobre el desarrollo en el 50 aniversario de la Populorum progressio," *Gregorianum* 98/3 (2017) 613–40.
de Lubac, H., SJ. *Le drame de l'humanisme athée*. 3rd ed. Paris: Spes, 1945. Translated by Edith M Riley. London: Sheed & Ward, 1949.
John XXIII. *Mater et Magistra*. 1961.
———. *Pacem in Terris*. 1963.
Samuelson, Paul, and William Nordhaus. *Economia*, Madrid: McGraw-Hill, 1999.
Sanz de Diego, Rafael Mª. "El mensaje central de Populorum Progressio y de Sollicitudo Rei Socialis." In *Vers el desenvolupament solidari de la humanitat Als quaranta anys de la Populorum Progressio*, 13–50. Barcelona: Facultat de Teologia de Catalunya, 2008.
Sen, Amartya. *Development as Freedom*. New York: Knopf, 1999.
Tugores, Juan. *Economía internacional*. Madrid: McGraw-Hill, 2005.
United Nations Development Program. *Human Develpment Report*. New York, 1995.

www.ingramcontent.com/pod-product-compliance
Lightning Source LLC
Chambersburg PA
CBHW051641230426
43669CB00013B/2392